BEST of the BEST from ARKANSAS

Selected Recipes from Arkansas' FAVORITE COOKBOOKS

EDITED BY
Gwen McKee
AND
Barbara Moseley

Illustrated by Tupper England

QUAIL RIDGE PRESS
Preserving America's Food Heritage

Library of Congress Cataloging-in-Publication Data

Best of the Best from Arkansas: selected recipes from Arkansas' favorite cookbooks / edited by Gwen McKee and Barbara Moseley; illustrated by Tupper Davidson.

p. cm.
Includes bibliographical references and index.
ISBN 0-937552-43-7
1. Cookery. I. McKee, Gwen. II. Moseley, Barbara.
TX714.B443 1992
641.5--dc20 92-12155
CIP

ISBN 0-937552-43-7
Printed in Canda
Cover photo Falling Waterfall Recreation Area, Ozark National Forest, by A. C. Haralson.
Cover and chapter opening photos courtesy of Arkansas Department of Parks and Tourism.

First printing, June 1992 • Second, June 1994 • Third, September 1998 • Fourth, October 2000
Fifth, January 2005

QUAIL RIDGE PRESS
P. O. Box 123 • Brandon, MS 39043 • 1-800-343-1583
Email: info@quailridge.com • www.quailridge.com

Contents

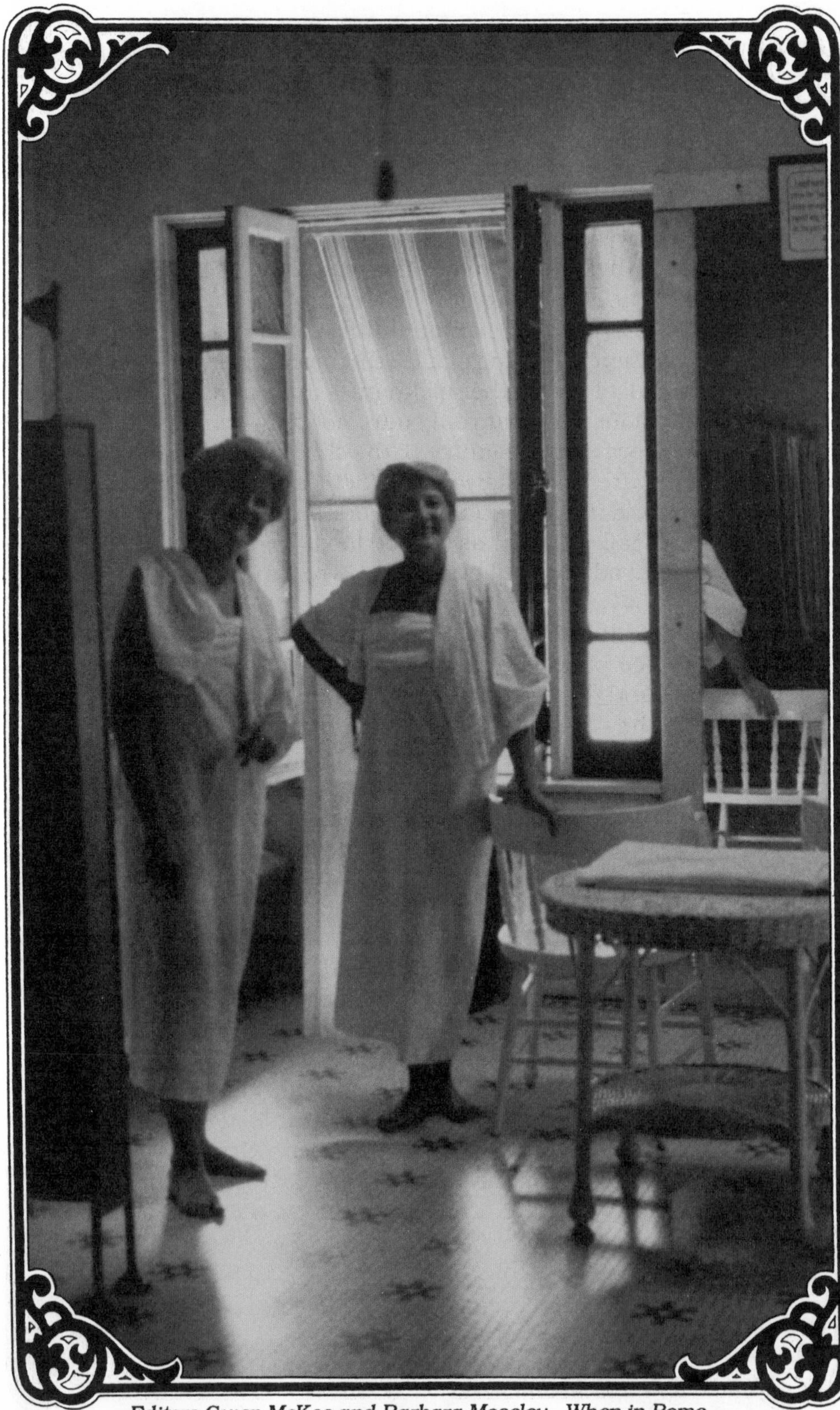

Editors Gwen McKee and Barbara Moseley. When in Rome... or Hot Springs....

Preface

Arkansas was once called "The Wonder State," then "The Bear State," then "The Land of Opportunity." It is presently known as "The Natural State." We didn't see any bears, but judging from its lush green mountains, sparkling lakes, mystical caves, thermal springs, and other exciting discoveries at every turn, all of these other nicknames aptly apply. We traveled throughout this beautiful state, not only on major highways, but down quiet country paths that opened onto wonderfully picturesque getaways. Whether it was a lakeside cabin or an old mill or a quaint inn, our search for good cookbooks never failed to lead us to good food. Perhaps we should make a slight adjustment and call it, "The Naturally *Delicious* State."

We learned that the chief crop in Arkansas is rice. In fact, Arkansas rice production has led the nation for more than ten years. And the Arkansas broiler industry has been number one in the nation for many years, too. There's an abundance of honey and sorghum, walnuts and pecans, fish and ducks. . .add to that the regional crops of superior grapes, huge watermelons, sweet strawberries, juicy peaches, and pink tomatoes (to name just a few), and it is easy to see how such a variety of recipes have been created around these abundant crops.

Much of Arkansas' taste leans toward down-home-style cookin'. . .recipes like "Stovepipe Bread," "Sadie's Deep Dish Chicken Pot Pie," "Fried Green Tomatoes," and "Coon Cake." But "elegant" recipes are equally as abundant. . ."Oven-Poached Rainbow Trout with Cucumber Dill Cloud," "Chocolate Decadence," "Praline Parfait". . . . And there is evidence of more healthful cooking, like "Whole Wheat Buttermilk Muffins," "No-Yolk Mayonnaise," and "Strawberry Granite." From "Popeye's Pie" to "Mammy's Strawberry Shortcake," from quite simple to simply elegant, there is indeed no shortage of delicious variety.

The fifty-four cookbooks that contributed to this outstanding collection are all special to us. Besides wonderful recipes, many expound on the history and culture of the people of Arkansas. The time we spent corresponding with the authors, editors, committee chairpersons, and publishers was very enjoyable. It enabled us to also learn about the people behind the recipes—and no wonder their cooking is so delicious! We are grateful to all the contributors for their cooperation in making this book possible. We invite you to order their individual books directly from them (see catalog section in the back of the book). And please forgive us if we inadvertently overlooked any book that might have been included.

We are particularly grateful to Irene Wassell and Marlene Satter, and the many other newspaper food editors and home economists all across the state who helped us get the word out in gathering cookbooks. Many of our "Best Club" members in Arkansas (these are cookbook collectors who have ordered each volume in our "Best of the Best" series) helped us with our research by suggesting their favorite cookbooks. The book and gift store managers helped us, too, with their knowledgeable information about the cookbooks they sell. To all these people we are deeply appreciative.

Tupper Davidson is our "Best" artist, and "Best" she is—thanks, Tup. We also thank the Arkansas Department of Parks & Tourism for the photographs and assistance they provided.

We particularly thank all the folks who helped us along the way. Our work is not all clipboard note taking, thank goodness, and we enjoyed friendly encounters everywhere we went—mingling with the downtown lunch crowd, experiencing a Hot Springs thermal bath, stopping at a roadside stand for some sweet, juicy peaches, encountering some enthusiastic Razorbacks on a beautiful campus,and generally just chatting with the local people wherever we went. All of this enabled us to absorb the diverse culture and cuisine of Arkansas. It is our hope that we have perhaps been able to set the table—we proudly and enthusiastically invite you to partake.

Gwen McKee and Barbara Moseley

Contributing Cookbooks

Arkansas Celebration Cookbook
Arkansas Favorites
Around the Bend
Asbury United Methodist Church Cook Book
Betty "Winks" at Cooking
Betty is Still "Winking" at Cooking
The Bonneville House Presents
Camper's Guide to Outdoor Cooking
Celebration, A Taste of Arkansas
Clabber Creek Farm Cookbook
Classroom Classics
Cookin' Along the Cotton Belt
Cookin' in the Spa
Cooking For Good Measure
Cooking to Your Heart's Content
Cooking With Ms. Watermelon
Crossett Cook Book
The Dairy Hollow House Cookbook
Dixie Cookbook IV
Dixie Cook Book V
Dutch Oven Cooking
Eat To Your Heart's Content!
Eat To Your Heart's Content, Too!
Eating Healthy in the Fast Lane
Enjoying the Art of Southern Hospitality
Evening Shade Cookbook
The Farmer's Daughters

Contributing Cookbooks

Favorite Recipes from Associated Women for Harding
Feasts of Eden
A Great Taste of Arkansas
A Heritage of Good Tastes
High Cotton Cookin'
Home for the Holidays and Other Special Occasions
In Good Taste
A Kaleidoscope of Creative Healthy Cooking
Kids Cuisine
Nibbles Cooks Cajun
Nibbles Fa La La
Nibbles Ooo La La
Perfectly Delicious
The Pink Lady...in the Kitchen
Prairie Harvest
Pulaski Heights Baptist Church Cookbook
The Sicilian-American Cookbook
Southern Accent
Southern Flavors' Little Chocolate Book
Southwest Cookin'
Sunday Go To Eatin' Cook Book
Take It To Heart
Thirty Years at the Mansion
A Very Special Treat!
Victorian Sampler
War Eagle Mill Wholegrain and Honey Cookbook
The Wonderful World of Honey

Appetizers

The Territorial Restoration. Little Rock.

Holiday Cider

1 medium orange
1 1/2 teaspoons whole cloves
1 gallon apple cider or juice
3/4 cup cinnamon candies (red)
2 (3-inch) cinnamon sticks

Pour cider and candy into Dutch oven or large pot and place over medium heat. Cook slowly until candy is dissolved and mixture is well heated. Pour cider mixture into heat-proof punch bowl and add cloves, orange wedges and cinnamon. Makes 1 gallon.

Southwest Cookin'

Cranberry Punch

3/4 cup brown sugar, packed
1 cup water
1/2 teaspoon cinnamon
1/4 teaspoon nutmeg
1/4 teaspoon ginger
1/2 teaspoon allspice
1/4 teaspoon salt
3/4 teaspoon cloves
2 cans cranberry sauce
1 quart pineapple juice
3 cups water

Bring sugar, water, spices to boil; add cranberry sauce, 3 cups water, and mix until smooth. Add pineapple juice; simmer 5 minutes. Serve hot. Makes 2 1/2 quarts.

High Cotton Cookin'

Hot Perked Party Punch

9 cups unsweetened pineapple juice
9 cups cranberry juice cocktail
4 1/2 cups water
1 cup brown sugar
4 cinnamon sticks, broken
4 1/2 teaspoons whole cloves
1/4 teaspoon salt

Combine pineapple juice, cranberry cocktail, water, and sugar in a 30-cup coffee maker. Place all other ingredients in basket. Perk a regular cycle. Serve piping hot.

Prairie Harvest

Coffee Punch

1/2 of 2-ounce jar instant coffee (more, if desired stronger)
1 cup sugar
2 cups hot water
4 quarts milk
1 gallon carton vanilla ice cream
1 gallon carton chocolate ice cream

Blend first three ingredients and cool. Soften ice cream slightly before adding to mixture. Serves 45.

Southern Accent

Punch

1 (46-ounce) can pineapple juice
1 (6-ounce) package raspberry Jello
3 cups sugar
1 quart hot water
2 quarts ginger ale
1 quart lemon-lime drink (example: 7-UP, Sprite)

Combine Jello and hot water; stir until dissolved. Add sugar and pineapple juice. Chill or freeze. Add ginger ale and lemon-lime drink to serve.

If frozen, set out and thaw until slushy before adding ginger ale and lemon-lime. Serves 35.

Cooking For Good Measure

Smoothie

1 cup ice
1 cup skim milk
1 (3-ounce) scoop low-fat vanilla frozen yogurt (1 gr per 100 calories)
1/2 cup frozen strawberries
1/2 banana

Combine all ingredients in blender for approximately 30 seconds. Serves 6.

Amount per serving: Calories 268; Grams of fat 1.9; Cholesterol trace; Sodium 44mg; % of Fat 6%

Eat To Your Heart's Content!

Slush

1 (6-ounce) can orange juice, frozen
1 (6-ounce) can lemonade, frozen
3 (6-ounce) cans water
1 (6-ounce) can bourbon

Blend together and put in big plastic container and put in freezer.

Makes a good slushy drink for bridge club drinkers.

The Bonneville House Presents

Hurricane Punch

1 large can Hawaiian Punch
1 (12-ounce) can frozen orange juice
1 (6-ounce) can frozen lemonade
3/4 cup sugar
4 ounces rum per glass
Cherries
Orange slices

In large bowl mix punch, orange juice, lemonade and sugar. Fill (16-ounce) glasses with crushed ice and add 4 ounces rum per glass. Fill glasses with punch. Garnish with cherries and orange slices.

Nibbles Cooks Cajun

Champagne Punch

3 cups sugar
2 cups lemon juice (not frozen)
1 can pineapple chunks and juice
1 1/2 quarts chilled sparkling water
1 quart chilled sauterne wine
1 quart bag whole frozen strawberries
2 bottles chilled champagne

Mix well and chill first 3 ingredients. Just before serving, add remaining ingredients. Float an ice ring in serving bowl to keep chilled. Serves 30.

A Heritage of Good Tastes

Apricot Eggnog

1 (16-ounce) can apricot halves, drained
1 (12-ounce) can apricot nectar
1/2 cup pineapple juice
4 eggs, separated
1/2 cup sugar
1 cup milk
2 teaspoons vanilla extract
1/4 teaspoon allspice
1 cup whipping cream, whipped
Nutmeg for garnish

Process apricots, nectar, and pineapple juice in blender until smooth. Set aside.

Beat egg yolks and sugar in a large mixing bowl until thick and pale. Gradually add apricot mixture and milk in a slow steady stream, beating well. Beat in vanilla and allspice. Chill overnight.

An hour before serving, pour apricot mixture into a punch bowl. Beat egg whites until stiff peaks form. Lightly fold in whites and whipped cream (mixture will be lumpy). Refrigerate until serving time. Sprinkle each serving with nutmeg. Makes 10 cups.

Home for the Holidays

Egg Nog

6 eggs
3/4 cup sugar
1/2 teaspoon nutmeg
8-10 tablespoons good bourbon
2 cups whipping cream
1/2 teaspoon cinnamon
Whipped cream for garnish

Separate eggs. Beat egg yolks and add sugar 1 tablespoon at a time until dissolved. Add bourbon, a little at a time, beating constantly. Beat egg whites until very frothy. Whip cream. Add egg yolk mixture to cream. Add egg whites last. Stir in nutmeg and cinnamon. Serve with whipped cream on top and sprinkled with nutmeg.

Nibbles Fa La La

Spinach Dip

1 (16-ounce) carton (2%) low-fat cottage cheese
2 tablespoons skim milk
3 tablespoons lemon juice
1 (8-ounce) can water chestnuts, drained, chopped fine
1 package Knorr Vegetable Soup Mix
4 ounces onions, chopped fine
1 (10-ounce) package frozen spinach, thawed and well drained

Blend cottage cheese, milk and lemon juice in blender until smooth. Add remaining ingredients and stir well. Serve with raw vegetables. Yield: 3 cups (24 servings).

Per Serving (2 tablespoons): Calories 35; Cholesterol Tr; Fat Tr; Sodium 235mg; ADA Exchange Value: 1/4 cup = 1 meat

Take It To Heart

Bean Dip
(Microwave)

Tools: colander, measuring spoons, electric blender or food processor, rubber scraper.

1 (21-ounce) can pinto beans, rinsed and drained
6 tablespoons frozen, chopped onion
2 garlic cloves, peeled
1 teaspoon chili powder
1 teaspoon cumin
1/4 teaspoon cayenne red pepper
2 whole green chilies

Put all ingredients and a small amount of water in food processor. Process to desired consistency. Yields 2 cups (1/3 cup per serving).

Kids Cuisine

Granny's Attic, a touch-and-see gallery, is a special room in the Old State House where children can relive "the olden days."

Water Chestnut Dip

1 (8-ounce) can water chestnuts, drained
1 (8-ounce) carton sour cream
1 (8-ounce) package cream cheese
1 cup mayonnaise
1 clove garlic, minced
1/4 cup fresh parsley
2 tablespoons onion, minced
1 teaspoon soy sauce
1/2 teaspoon ground ginger

Combine all ingredients in food processor and process about 1 minute. Chill.

Serve with fresh vegetables. Yield: 3 cups.

Betty is Still "Winking" at Cooking

Broccoli Dip

1 (10-ounce) package frozen chopped broccoli
3/4 teaspoon salt
1 cup water
2 tablespoons butter
1 onion, chopped
1 can cream of mushroom soup
1 (6-ounce) roll garlic cheese
1 teaspoon monosodium glutamate
1 teaspoon Worcestershire sauce
1/4 teaspoon Tabasco sauce
1 (4-ounce) can mushrooms, drained
1 cup slivered almonds

Cook broccoli with 1/2 teaspoon salt in water; drain and set aside. Sauté onion in butter; add mushroom soup, cheese, monosodium glutamate, Worcestershire sauce, 1/4 teaspoon salt, and Tabasco sauce. Cook on medium heat until cheese melts. Add cooked broccoli and cook 1 minute longer, stirring occasionally to blend. Add mushrooms, stems and all, and almonds.

Serve hot as dip with chips or crackers. Yield: 4 cups or more.

Favorite Recipes from Associated Women for Harding

Dairy Dip with Parmesan Potato Wedges

Crunchy, flavorful potatoes with a smooth rich dip.

2 cups cottage cheese
1/2 cup blue cheese, crumbled
1/2 cup sour cream
2 tablespoons lemon juice
1 teaspoon Worcestershire sauce
2 tablespoons green onions, sliced

Blend all ingredients until almost smooth. Chill. Serve as a dip with Parmesan Potato Wedges. Makes 3 cups.

PARMESAN POTATO WEDGES:

2 cups puffed rice cereal, crushed
1/4 cup Parmesan cheese, grated
1 teaspoon salt
1 teaspoon paprika
6 baking potatoes
3 tablespoons butter or margarine, melted

Mix crushed puffed rice, Parmesan cheese, salt, and paprika. Scrub, dry, and cut potatoes into wedges. Dip each wedge into melted butter, then roll in rice coating. Place wedges on a buttered 15x10x1-inch pan and bake at 425° for 15 minutes. Makes 8 servings.

Home for the Holidays

Dilly Garden Dip

1 1/2 cups lowfat cottage cheese
1 tablespoon lemon juice
2 tablespoon shredded carrot
1 tablespoon sliced green onions
1 tablespoon chopped fresh parsley
1/2 teaspoon fresh dill or 1/2 teaspoon dill weed
Dash of pepper
1 tablespoon Beau Monde Seasoning

In a blender combine cottage cheese and lemon juice. Blend for 3-5 minutes at medium speed. Stir in remaining ingredients and refrigerate overnight. Serve with crackers or veggies. Makes 1 1/2 cups or 24 (1-tablespoon) servings.

Amount per serving: Calories 12.2; Grams of fat .51; Cholesterol 47mg; Sodium 0mg; % of Fat 38%

Eat To Your Heart's Content!

Dill Weed Dip

2/3 cup mayonnaise
2/3 cup sour cream
1 tablespoon grated onion
1 teaspoon Beau Monde Seasoning
1 teaspoon dill weed
1 teaspoon parsley flakes

Mix ingredients and refrigerate overnight.

Liza suggests serving this dip in the center of hollowed-out pumpernickel bread. Great with vegetables!

Thirty Years at the Mansion

Sooie Cheese Dip

1/2 pound pork sausage
1/2 pound ground round beef
1 can Cheddar cheese soup
1 (8-ounce) jar taco sauce
1 (4-ounce) jar mushrooms
1 pound process American cheese, cubed

Brown sausage and beef. Drain well. Add remaining ingredients, stirring often. Heat until cheese melts.

Serve hot with your choice of chips or French bread cubes. Serves 12.

Cookin' in the Spa

Cold Cheese Dip

1 pint mayonnaise
1 (8-ounce) carton sour cream
3 tablespoons Parmesan cheese
1 tablespoon onion flakes
1 1/2 cups grated Cheddar cheese
1 1/2 cups grated mozzarella cheese
Garlic powder to taste

Combine all ingredients. Serve with pretzel rods or corn chips. Also good as a baked potato topping.

Classroom Classics

Chipped Beef Dip

2 (8-ounce) packages cream cheese
1 (8-ounce) carton sour cream
1 teaspoon milk
1 banana pepper or 1 bell pepper, minced
1/2 cup onion, finely chopped
2 (2 1/2-ounce) packages smoked beef
1/2 jalapeño pepper, finely chopped

Cut beef in fine strips, then chop. Mix all ingredients together and pour in large pie plate. Bake at 350° for 45 minutes. Chopped nuts can be sprinkled on top. Serve hot. Best when served with nacho cheese tortilla chips.

The Farmer's Daughters

Cheese and Bacon Spread

1 pound Hoffman's Super Sharp Soft Cheddar Cheese
16 slices crisp bacon, crumbled
1 teaspoon salt
12 green onions, chopped (include tops)
1 cup slivered almonds, toasted
2 cups mayonnaise

Grate cheese. Mix all ingredients in order given. Serve on Ritz Crackers or Sesame Melba Rounds. Keeps for days. Also good cooked in scrambled eggs.

Southern Accent

Artichoke Spread

1 (14-ounce) can artichokes
1 cup Hellmann's Mayonnaise
1 cup Parmesan cheese, grated
Dash of garlic
Paprika

Drain and chop artichokes finely. Add mayonnaise, cheese, and garlic. Pour into an oven-proof dish and sprinkle top with paprika. Bake at 350° until bubbly and slightly brown on top. Serve with crackers.

In Good Taste

Pepper Jelly

1 cup ground bell pepper
2 tablespoons ground hot peppers
1 1/2 cups cider vinegar
6 1/2 cups sugar
1 (6-ounce) bottle liquid fruit pectin
Green food coloring

Mix everything except fruit pectin in saucepan and bring to a boil. Let boil for 5 minutes, remove from heat and add fruit pectin, stirring until mixture starts to jell. Pour into sterile jelly jars and seal. (This is good spooned over a brick of cream cheese and served with ginger snaps).

The Farmer's Daughters

Cheese Fondue

1 clove garlic
2 cups dry white wine
1 pound Swiss cheese or 1/2 pound Swiss and 1/2 pound Cheddar, grated or finely cut
1 tablespoon cornstarch
Pinch of nutmeg
Dash hot pepper sauce
1 large loaf French or Italian bread with hard crust, cut into bite-size pieces, each of which must have at least one side of crust

Rub an enameled metal casserole with garlic. Pour in wine and set over low heat. Heat until air bubbles rise to the surface and then add cheese mixed with cornstarch, stirring constantly until the cheese is melted. Season with nutmeg and pepper sauce.

Place casserole on the table on a hot plate or over an alcohol burner to keep it faintly bubbling. Guests spear pieces of bread on fondue forks and dip them into the hot cheese.

Serves 6.

The Pink Lady...in the Kitchen

Boursin Cheese

8 ounces sweet butter, room temperature
2 (8-ounce) bars cream cheese, room temperature
1 clove garlic, chopped
1/2 teaspoon each: basil, chives, dill, marjoram, thyme and pepper

Mix sweet butter and cream cheese together. Add remaining ingredients, mixing well. It's best to use fresh herbs. Will keep for a couple of weeks in refrigerator. Serve with crackers and fruit.

Cookin' in the Spa

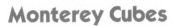

Monterey Cubes

8 eggs
1/2 cup flour
1 teaspoon baking powder
3/4 teaspoon salt
12 ounces shredded Monterey Jack cheese
12 ounces cottage cheese
2 (4-ounce) cans mild green chilies, chopped and drained

In large bowl, beat eggs until light, 4 or 5 minutes. Stir flour, baking powder and salt. Add to eggs and mix well. Fold in cheeses and chilies. Turn into 9x13-inch baking dish and bake at 325° for 40 minutes. Cut into one-inch cubes and serve warm. Makes 4 dozen.

Pulaski Heights Baptist Church Cookbook

Spinach Cheese Squares

4 tablespoons butter
3 eggs
1 cup flour
1 cup milk
1 teaspoon salt
1 teaspoon baking powder
1 medium onion, grated
1 pound sharp cheese, grated
2 packages chopped, frozen spinach, thawed and well drained

Preheat oven to 350°. Melt butter in 9x13x2-inch pan in oven; remove. In mixing bowl, beat eggs, flour, milk, salt and baking powder; mix well. Add grated cheese, onion and drained spinach. (If you run the spinach through a food processor, it makes a better texture.) Pour into pan; bake for 35 minutes. Cool thoroughly; cut in squares. This freezes well.

The Bonneville House Presents

Ville Marre, the Victorian home on the TV series, *Designing Women*, is in the Quapaw Quarter, a historic area of Little Rock. The home is open for tours on Sunday afternoon.

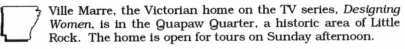

Vegetable Bars

2 packages crescent-shaped rolls
2 (8-ounce) packages cream cheese
3/4 cup mayonnaise
1 (1-ounce) package ranch-style dressing (original)
Black olives, chopped
Sharp Cheddar cheese
Choose your favorite vegetables: carrots, mushrooms, broccoli, cauliflower, red onion, green onion, radishes, bell pepper, zucchini

Lay out rolls on jelly roll pan. Bake at 350° for 8-10 minutes. Cool. Combine cream cheese, mayonnaise and ranch dressing. Spread cream cheese mixture over crescent crust. Chop vegetables into small pieces. Press chopped vegetables and black olives into cream cheese mixture. Top with shredded sharp Cheddar cheese. Refrigerate at least 4 hours or overnight. Cut into bars to serve. Yield: 48.

Cookin' in the Spa

Mexican Rollups

2 (8-ounce) packages cream cheese, softened
16 ounces sour cream
1 small bottle picante sauce (medium)
1 (18-ounce) package flour tortillas
1 small bottle picante sauce (mild, medium, or hot)

In large bowl, mix cream cheese, sour cream, and medium picante sauce well. Spread mixture on flour tortillas generously. Roll up tortillas and put them in a glass rectangular pan. Put in freezer for at least 1 hour.

Take out and cut into bite-sized pieces. Arrange on plate with other bottle picante sauce in a bowl in the middle for dipping. Yield: 40.

Cookin' in the Spa

Mushrooms Diablo

Hot, sweet, spicy, dark, and malevolent-looking, these mushrooms always thrill our guests. Judge Tom Glaze finished off a whole batch of them at a dinner, leaving his wife Phyllis only one teeny tiny portion. Of course he did later on write me a letter, on his official letterhead and all, thanking me and saying, "If there's ever anything I can do for you..." A letter like that from a judge could be very handy in the future!

These do very well as part of a lineup at a cocktail buffet, placed in a chafing dish after their savory sauce has been reduced.

1/3 cup butter
1 large onion, cut into very thin crescents
1 each: red and green bell pepper, finely slivered
1 pound mushrooms, wiped with a damp paper towel, if dirty, and quartered
2/3 cup red wine vinegar
2 tablespoons each Dijon mustard and Pickapepper Sauce (if available; if not, substitute a teaspoon of Tamari Soy Sauce and several dashes of Tabasco)
3 tablespoons brown sugar
Freshly ground black pepper and salt to taste
3 tablespoons golden raisins

Sauté onion in butter; add peppers and mushrooms and continue to sauté over low heat, while you whisk together in a bowl, the vinegar, Dijon mustard, Picapepper sauce, brown sugar, and salt and pepper to taste. When mushrooms have softened, raise the heat and pour over them the red wine mixture, adding the raisins. Keep the heat medium high and, stirring often, let cook, uncovered, until the sauce has reduced greatly. Serve hot or at room temperature.

Warning: People will be congregating in your kitchen as you cook this, because its aromas are totally tantalizing. Serves 4-6 as appetizer or 2-3 as entrée.

The Dairy Hollow House Cookbook

Champignons Marine
(Marinated)

1 pound mushrooms (medium)
1/2 cup olive oil
1/2 cup red wine
1 teaspoon crushed oregano
1/2 teaspoon crushed basil
1 teaspoon capers
2 cloves crushed garlic
2 teaspoons seasoned salt
1 teaspoon parsley

Mix everything but mushrooms together. Add mushrooms. Chill at least 24 hours. Serve with toothpicks. Serves 8-10.

Nibbles Ooo La La

Escargots Bourguignonne

1 cup white wine
1 tablespoon chopped shallots
2 tablespoons chopped parsley
2 cloves garlic, crushed
1 cup butter
4 dozen canned snails
4 dozen mushroom caps, cleaned and de-stemmed

Boil wine and shallots; reduce to half. Strain, keeping shallots. In skillet, melt butter; add shallots, parsley, garlic. Cook until bubbly. Add mushrooms for 2 minutes. Remove mushrooms and place in baking dish. Add snails to sauce. Cook 2 minutes. Place 1 snail in each mushroom cap. Add 1 teaspoon butter mixture on top of each snail. Bake at 400° for 10 minutes.

Serve as an appetizer. Serves 8-12.

Nibbles Ooo La La

One of America's top thoroughbred race tracks is Oaklawn Park. From late January through mid-April, the action is fast and so are the horses. The Arkansas Derby has become a major prep-race for the Kentucky Derby.

Crabmeat Mold

I've been making this for more than a decade. No one ever seems to get tired of it. I like it best made with good, fresh crabmeat, but it's also tasty made with frozen snow crab (which has the advantages of not having to be picked over to remove shell), and with the less expensive imitation crab, available at most seafood counters and in some freezer cases. The original recipe used cream cheese and mayonnaise. I've changed it to the lower-fat Neufchâtel cheese.

1 1/2 cups crabmeat (canned, fresh or frozen)
1/2 can cream of mushroom soup
8 ounces Neufchâtel cheese
1 envelope plain gelatin
2 tablespoons cold water
2 tablespoons minced onion
1/2 cup light salad dressing
1/2 cup chopped celery

Pick over the crabmeat, if necessary, to get rid of the shell bits. In a small saucepan put the soup and cheese, stirring over medium heat until they are mixed.

Soften the gelatin in 2 tablespoons cold water. Mix the gelatin, onion, dressing, celery, and crabmeat into the soup and cheese mixture. Pour into an oiled mold. Chill until set, at least 4 hours.

To serve, unmold on a bed of endive lettuce and serve with crackers. Makes about 3 1/2 cups of spread.

Enjoying the Art of Southern Hospitality

Asparagus Spears Rolled in Ham

18 canned asparagus spears
3/4 cup salad oil
1/4 cup wine vinegar
Salt
Freshly ground black pepper
1/2 teaspoon dried basil
9 slices thin ham

Marinate asparagus in oil, vinegar, salt, pepper, and basil for 2 hours. Drain thoroughly. Cut ham in half crosswise and wrap around asparagus spear, securing with a wooden pick. Yield: 6 servings.

Around the Bend

Sweet and Sour Meatballs

MEATBALLS:

1 pound ground beef
1 egg, beaten
1/4 cup onion, finely chopped
1 1/4 cups bread crumbs
1 teaspoon pepper
1 tablespoon parsley flakes

Mix first 7 ingredients together and form into bite-size meatballs. Brown in large skillet. Drain and put in baking dish.

SAUCE:

1 (16-ounce) jar apricot preserves
3/4 cup hot barbecue sauce

Mix apricot preserves and barbecue sauce and pour over meatballs. Bake at 350°, uncovered, for 30 minutes. Serve hot in chafing dish.

Cookin' Along the Cotton Belt

Frosted Ham Ball

1/2 pound cooked ham, finely ground
1/3 cup white raisins
1 tablespoon grated onion
1/4 teaspoon curry powder
1/4 cup mayonnaise
1 (3-ounce) package cream cheese
1 tablespoon milk
Chopped parsley

Mix ham, raisins, onion, curry powder and mayonnaise. Chill. Shape into ball. Whip cream cheese with milk. Frost Ham Ball. Roll in parsley. Chill. Serve with crackers.

Nibbles Fa La La

Party Pizza

1 pound sausage
1 pound processed American cheese
1/4 can tomatoes and green chilies
1 small onion, chopped
1/2 teaspoon oregano
Party rye bread

Brown sausage and onion. Melt cheese, add tomatoes and green chilies and oregano. Add to meat. Put about a teaspoonful on small pieces of party rye bread and heat in oven until it bubbles and browns a little, about 15 minutes at 350°. Serves 16.

Cookin' in the Spa

Pauline's Rotel

1 gallon tomatoes, peeled
3/4 cup white vinegar
1/4 cup sugar
2 tablespoons salt
2 onions, chopped
2 bell peppers, chopped
8-12 hot peppers, chopped

Mix in large pan: tomatoes, vinegar, sugar and salt. Add chopped onion and peppers. Cook at least an hour or until desired thickness.

Cooking For Good Measure

Cornmeal Cheese Crisps

1/2 cup yellow cornmeal
1 3/4 cups flour
1/2 teaspoon soda
1 teaspoon sugar
1/2 teaspoon salt
Pepper to taste
1 stick margarine
1 1/2 cups shredded sharp Cheddar cheese
2 tablespoons vinegar
1/2 cup ice water

Mix all dry ingredients together. Use pastry blender to cut margarine into mixture. Use fork and stir in shredded cheese, vinegar, and water. Mix till you have a soft dough. Divide the dough into 3 pieces so it will be easier to work with. On a floured surface, roll the dough paper thin. Cut into abstract pieces and place on a greased cookie sheet. Bake at 375° about 10 minutes or until they're brown and crisp. Makes about 40.

Clabber Creek Farm Cook Book

Cucumber Sandwiches I

1 large cucumber
1 (8-ounce) package cream cheese, softened
1/2 cup mayonnaise
1 tablespoon fresh lemon juice
3 small green onions and tops, finely chopped
Tabasco Sauce, to taste
Garlic salt, to taste
Seasoned pepper, to taste

Peel, seed and coarsely grate cucumber. Wring out excess cucumber juice in clean cup towel. Cream cheese with mayonnaise and lemon juice. Add cucumber, onions, and seasonings to taste. Serve on party rye slices. Also good for dips. Keep refrigerated.

Prairie Harvest

Hot Pepper Pecans

1 cup pecans
2 tablespoons melted butter
Salt
1 teaspoon soy sauce
Dash hot sauce

Spread melted butter over pecans in single layer in baking pan. Bake at 300° about 30 minutes stirring often. Remove from oven, salt lightly. Mix about 1 teaspoon soy sauce with a dash of hot sauce. Stir in pecans, spread on paper towel to dry. This recipe is a specialty of my sister Brenda.

Clabber Creek Farm Cook Book

Eureka Springs, named for the 63 springs found there, is a charming village etched into the mountainside. It has been called "Little Switzerland of America," "The Stairstep Town," and "The Town That Water Built." A real getaway from the hustle and bustle—there are no traffic lights. "Eureka" means "I have found it."

Bread and Breakfast

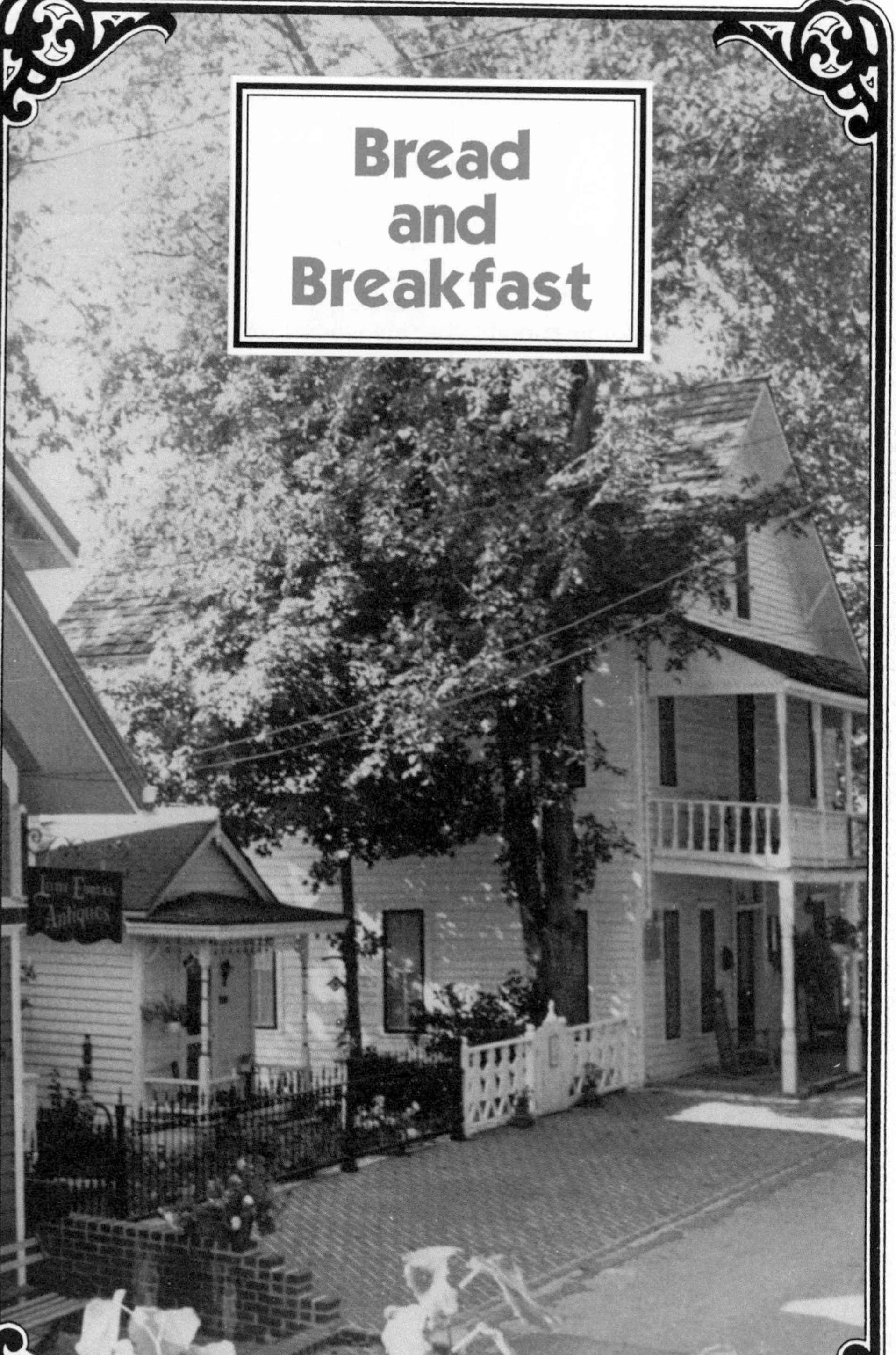

An artists' and writers' colony, Eureka Springs is famous for its exceptional collection of Victorian structures.

Cloud Biscuits

2 1/4 cups self-rising flour
1 tablespoon sugar
1/2 cup butter-flavored shortening
1 egg, beaten
2/3 cup milk

Combine flour and sugar. Cut in shortening until mixture resembles coarse meal. Combine egg and milk; add to flour mixture. Stir until moistened. Turn dough onto floured board. Cut with 2 1/2-inch cutter. Brush top with melted butter. Bake at 325° for 10-12 minutes.

The Pink Lady...in the Kitchen

Buttermilk Biscuits

2 cups self-rising flour
Pinch of soda
3 tablespoons oil
3/4 cup buttermilk

Mix all this together. Dough should be soft and sticky. Scrape out on a floured board. Now get your hands covered in flour and knead all that mess around and over till you have a dough that is not sticky. Pat out till it's about a half-inch thick. (That is more or less, just depends on how thick you like biscuits.)

Cut the biscuits out with a biscuit cutter. Now you can buy a nice biscuit cutter or use an old cookie cutter, or a water glass. I use a little canned milk can that has had one end melted off so it leaves a nice slick cuttin' surface, and some holes punched in the other end to let the air out. After you cut the biscuits out, get a glass pie pan or a cake pan or a cookie sheet or whatever. Don't make much difference as long as the oil won't run off the edges, cause I want you to pour enough oil in the pan to cover the bottom, and then take them biscuits and sop the top in oil, turn it over on its bottom and set it down.

Cook em about 20 minutes in a oven that is close to 375°. Now keep watchin' em cause when they get the shade of brown you like, they'll be done.

Ever recipe you have ever read will tell you to serve biscuits wrapped in a napkin or such and then put in a basket. Tell you a little secret. Reach in that oven, take the pan out and put 1 biscuit on everybody's plate and stick the rest back in the oven. Course you know to turn that sucker off! When everybody has lapped up that biscuit, go get em another one.

Biscuits is good with anything, anytime, but if you want a real treat, set that bucket of molasses and the peanut butter jar on the table. Let each one mix up about half & half of syrup & peanut butter. Talk about good! After you have made these biscuits a time or two, you'll sure chunk rocks at canned biscuits.

Sunday Go To Eatin' Cook Book

Yeast Rolls

2 cups warm water
2 packages active dry yeast
1 tablespoon salt
1/2 cup sugar
2 eggs, beaten
6 tablespoons oil or 1/2 cup margarine, melted
5 1/2 cups sifted all-purpose flour

Mix all ingredients in a large mixing bowl in order given. Mix thoroughly. Let rise until double in bulk in a warm place, bowl covered. Punch down and cool in refrigerator until needed. Make out into rolls at least 2 hours before using. Grease fingers with oil, pinch off a piece of dough about the size of a walnut, and place 2 of these in each hole of a greased muffin tin. Let rise 2 hours. Bake in a 400° oven for 12 minutes or until brown. Makes 3 dozen rolls.

Favorite Recipes from Associated Women for Harding

Quick Rolls

1 cup milk
3 tablespoons shortening
1 package yeast
2 cups flour
3 teaspoons sugar
1 teaspoon salt

Heat milk and shortening to lukewarm. Add yeast to the mixture. Add flour, sugar and salt and beat well. Place on floured doughboard. Roll and cut. Let rise for 1 hour and bake in 400° oven till lightly browned (about 15-20 minutes).

A Heritage of Good Tastes

One of many grist mills in Arkansas, The Old Mill in North Little Rock, featured in an opening scene of "Gone With the Wind," is a favorite place for photographers and romantics as well.

Homemade Sourdough Yeast or Wild Yeast Starter

Today, dry packaged yeast does make bread making easy, but if you don't have store-bought yeast and have the desire to make your own yeast, the following recipe works well.

1 cup whole wheat flour **1 cup warm water**

Scald a 1-quart wide-mouth glass jar, a 2-cup measuring cup, and a mixing spoon.

Stir flour into water until well mixed; spoon into quart jar. Cover jar with 3 layers of clean cheese cloth and secure with a rubber band. Set jar of mix at room temperature for 2-4 days until it has a yeasty smell and small bubbles form . The yeast is now ready to use. Always save back at least 1 cup of starter to keep your yeast going, cap lightly and refrigerate. To freshen starter, just add more flour and water.

Yield: 1 1/2 cups yeast starter.

Arkansas Celebration Cookbook

Stovepipe Bread

3 1/2 cups flour (all-purpose or whole wheat)
1 package active dry yeast
1/2 cup milk
1/2 cup water
1/2 cup salad oil
1/4 cup sugar
1 teaspoon salt
2 eggs
Butter

Place 1 1/2 cups flour into large bowl of mixer. Add yeast and blend at low speed 1/2 minute. Combine milk, water, oil, sugar, and salt in small saucepan, and heat just until warm. Add to dry ingredients in mixer bowl and beat at low speed until smooth.

Add eggs and beat at medium speed until blended. Scrape beaters, remove bowl from mixer, and stir in remaining flour with wooden spoon. This will make a soft dough or stiff batter. Spoon into 2 well-buttered 1-pound coffee cans. Cover with buttered plastic lids and let stand in warm place, draft free.

When dough has risen almost to top of cans, remove lids. Bake in 375° preheated oven for 30-35 minutes, or until brown. Cool about 10 minutes in cans before removing to rack.

Perfectly Delicious

Fancy Bread Sticks

1/2 cup butter
1/2 teaspoon dill seed
1 1/2 teaspoons parsley flakes
1 tablespoon onion flakes
2 tablespoons Parmesan cheese
1 can Pillsbury Crescent Dinner Rolls

Melt butter in pan. Stir in herbs and cheese. Let stand 30 minutes. Shape each crescent triangle into a roll and twist, forming a bread stick. Brush with herbed butter. Bake at 425° for 12-15 minutes.

In Good Taste

Mini-French Loaves

Yes! Homemade bread in less than an hour.

2 cups whole wheat flour
1 tablespoon (or 1 package) baker's yeast
1/8 teaspoon salt (optional)
1 teaspoon honey
1 cup warm water

In a mixing bowl combine flour, yeast and salt. In a separate bowl combine honey and water thoroughly, and add to the flour mixture. Stir well to combine all ingredients. Cover and place in a warm place to rise for approximately 10 minutes. Preheat oven to 350°.

Punch dough down and shape into 4 small loaves. Place on a lightly oiled cookie sheet and bake 20-30 minutes. Crust should be light golden brown. Serve warm. Yields 4 small loaves.

Eating Healthy in the Fast Lane

Italian French Bread

1 loaf French bread, split lengthwise
1 stick margarine, softened
1/2 cup real mayonnaise (Hellman's)
4 or 5 green onions, finely chopped
1 small can of black olives, sliced
4 - 5 ounces shredded mozzarella cheese

Divide ingredients in half and layer on each half of the bread in the order given above. Close bread together and wrap in foil and place in refrigerator overnight. When ready to bake, unwrap and discard foil. Open up the 2 halves and place on a Pam-sprayed cookie sheet and bake at 350° for 15-20 minutes uncovered. Slice and serve immediately.

This is wonderful with spaghetti, lasagna, or any Italian dish. Also goes great with grilled steak or grilled chicken. Yield: 6-8 servings.

Betty is Still "Winking" at Cooking

Honey Egg Twist

2 packages yeast
6 tablespoons honey
3/4 cup lukewarm water
3/4 cup milk
1/2 stick butter
1 tablespoon salt
1/4 cup shortening
3 eggs
About 6 cups flour
Egg wash (1 egg white plus 1 tablespoon water)

Mix yeast, honey and lukewarm water, stirring to dissolve. Warm milk to about 110° and add butter, salt and shortening, stirring to dissolve. Add to yeast mixture with beaten eggs and about 2 cups of flour. Stir well. Add remaining flour to make a stiff dough. Knead about 8 minutes. Let rise until double. Shape as desired and let rise again. Brush with egg wash and sprinkle with sesame or poppy seed. Bake at 325° for about 30 minutes. Makes 2 twists or 3 loaves.

High Cotton Cookin'

Whole Wheat Quickbread

Preparation time a little over an hour—great toasted.

2 1/2 cups whole wheat flour
1 teaspoon baking powder
1 teaspoon soda
1 teaspoon salt
1 1/2 cups buttermilk
1/4 cup sorghum or honey
1 egg, slightly beaten
2 tablespoons oil

Mix together dry ingredients. Stir together liquid ingredients; blend into dry. Spoon into a buttered loaf pan. Let stand, covered, in a warm place for 20 minutes. Bake in a preheated 375° oven for 40-50 minutes.

Arkansas Celebration Cookbook

Sunflower Seed Bread

1 1/2 cups water
1 cup quick oats
1/2 cup margarine
3 tablespoons honey
1 teaspoon salt
1 cup whole wheat flour
3 cups all-purpose flour
1 package dry yeast
1 egg, beaten
2 egg whites, beaten
2/3 cup shelled sunflower seeds

Place water, half the oats, margarine, honey and salt in a saucepan. Heat until margarine is melted. Cool to lukewarm. Mix together the flours and yeast. Combine liquid ingredients with the one beaten egg, and add dry ingredients. Beat well until it's mixed well and there are no lumps.

Cover bowl and let rise in a warm place for about 45 minutes. Stir down and spread evenly in a greased 9x13-inch pan. Brush batter with egg whites and sprinkle with remaining oats and sunflower seeds. Cover and let rise until almost doubled. Bake at 400° for 30 minutes. Cool and cut in squares. I like to slice it thin and put deviled ham-peanut butter spread on it.

Clabber Creek Farm Cook Book

War Eagle Southern Spoon Bread

Light and delicate!

1 cup white corn meal
1 1/2 teaspoons salt
4 tablespoons margarine
1 1/3 cups boiling water
3 eggs
1 tablespoon baking powder
1 1/3 cups hot milk
2 teaspoons honey

Grease 2-quart casserole. Mix corn meal and salt; blend well. Add margarine; pour in boiling water, stirring constantly. Allow to cool.

Beat eggs with baking powder until very light and fluffy; add to corn meal mixture. Stir in milk and honey; mix thoroughly. Pour into casserole. Place casserole in shallow pan of hot water; bake in preheated 350° oven for 35-40 minutes.

War Eagle Mill Wholegrain and Honey Cookbook

Bacon Spoon Bread

3/4 cup cornmeal
1 1/2 cups cold water
2 cups sharp Cheddar cheese, shredded
1/4 cup soft butter or margarine
2 cloves garlic, crushed
1/2 teaspoon salt
1 cup milk
4 well beaten egg yolks
1/2 pound bacon, crisp-cooked and drained
4 stiffly beaten egg whites

Combine cornmeal and water; cook, stirring constantly, until the consistency of mush. Remove from heat; add cheese, butter, garlic and salt. Stir to melt cheese. Gradually add milk. Stir in egg yolks. Crumble bacon, reserving some for garnish if desired, and add to cornmeal mixture. Fold in egg whites. Pour into greased 2-quart soufflé dish or casserole. Bake in slow 325° oven about 65 minutes or until done.

Spoon into warm dishes; top with butter and serve with spoon. Serves 6.

Bacon Spoon Bread is a hearty main dish soufflé that makes a simple supper with a salad and fruit. It is also good for a breakfast party.

Feasts of Eden

Company's Comin' Cornbread

Dedicated to the Arkansas Sesquicentennial of 1986.

2 tablespoons shortening
1 cup buttermilk or sweet milk
2 eggs
2 tablespoons honey
1/2 cup chopped onions
1 small jar pimentos, drained
1 (17-ounce) jar whole kernel corn, drained
1 (4-ounce) can chopped green chile peppers or about 1/2 cup pickled peppers, chopped
1 cup yellow cornmeal
1 cup white flour
1 teaspoon salt
1 teaspoon baking soda
1 cup grated cheese

Place a 10- or 12-inch cast-iron (or heavy weight) skillet in oven with the 2 tablespoons shortening while preheating oven to 350°. Stir together liquid ingredients and combine with dry, reserving the cheese to fold in as the last step. When oven is preheated and skillet sizzling hot, pour mixture in and bake for 1 hour.

Arkansas Celebration Cookbook

Cornmeal was the pioneers' "flour," as corn was easier than other grains to make into meal. It could be milled by hand in a mortar and pestle made of wood or stone.

Mexican Corn Bread

1/2 onion, diced
2 ounces green chilies, diced
1 cup flour
1 cup corn meal
4 teaspoons baking powder
1 (15-ounce) can creamed corn
2/3 cup skim milk, or non-fat buttermilk
1/2 cup shredded Lite Line Cheddar Cheese
4 egg whites

Dice onion and green chilies. Add all ingredients in mixing bowl and stir. Place in muffin cups or square cake pan that has been sprayed with cooking spray. Bake at 350° until center is firm, approximately 25 minutes. Serves 12.

Note: Do not overcook! When cooking without oil, baked goods will tend to dry out quickly. Check continually when baking, since every oven tends to require different baking times.

Amount per serving: Calories 156; Grams of fat 1.28; Cholesterol 0mg; Sodium 331mg; % of Fat 7%

Eat To Your Heart's Content!

Spicy Corn Bread Muffins

1 1/2 cups yellow cornmeal
1 teaspoon baking soda
1 teaspoon sugar
1/2 teaspoon salt
2 egg whites
1/4 cup picante sauce
1/4 cup vegetable oil
1 (8-ounce) carton plain non-fat yogurt
Vegetable cooking spray

Combine first 4 ingredients in a large bowl. Make a well in center of mixture. Combine egg whites and next 3 ingredients; add to dry ingredients, stirring just until moistened. Spoon into muffin pans coated with cooking spray, filling two-thirds full.

Bake at 425° for 18-30 minutes. Remove from pans. Yield: 1 dozen.

The Pink Lady...in the Kitchen

Whole Wheat Buttermilk Muffins

A quick, easy-to-prepare and very tasty muffin that can be served with any meal, or add a little more sweetening for a dessert muffin or to serve at tea time.

2 1/2 cups whole wheat flour
1 teaspoon salt
1 teaspoon baking soda
2 teaspoons baking powder
2 1/2 cups buttermilk
1 tablespoon honey
2 tablespoons oil
1 egg, slightly beaten

Mix all ingredients, stirring just enough to blend. Spoon into well greased muffin tins. Bake in a preheated 450° oven or 15-20 minutes. Makes 15-16 muffins.

Variations:

Fruit Muffins—add 1 tablespoon honey and 1/2 cup huckleberries, blueberries, chopped apples, dried apricot bits, raisins, or diced pineapple.

Nut Muffins—add 1/2 cup chopped nutmeats.

War Eagle Mill Wholegrain and Honey Cookbook

Peach Muffins

1 1/2 cups flour
3/4 teaspoon salt
1/2 teaspoon baking soda
1 cup sugar
2 eggs, well beaten
1/2 teaspoon vanilla
1/8 teaspoon almond extract
1/4 cup chopped almonds, optional
1/2 cup salad oil
1 1/4 cups coarsely chopped fresh, or drained canned peaches

In mixing bowl combine dry ingredients; make a well in center of mix. Add eggs and oil, stirring only until dry mix is moistened. Stir in remaining ingredients. Spoon 1/3 cup batter into greased muffin tins; bake at 350° for 20-25 minutes, or until muffins test done.

Variation: Peach Bread—spoon batter into a greased and floured 5x9-inch loaf pan; bake at 350° for 1 hour, or until bread tests done.

Celebration

Blueberry Lemon Muffins

1 3/4 cups flour
1/4 cup sugar
2 1/2 teaspoons baking powder
3/4 teaspoon salt
1 well-beaten egg
3/4 cup milk
1/3 cup cooking oil
3/4 - 1 cup blueberries
2 tablespoons sugar
1 teaspoon grated lemon peel

Stir together thoroughly, first 4 ingredients; make well in center. Combine egg, milk and oil; add all at once to dry mixture. Stir just until moistened. Combine blueberries and sugar; fold into batter along with lemon peel. Fill well greased muffin pans two-thirds full. Bake at 400° for 20-25 minutes.

While muffins are warm, dip tops in melted butter, then sugar. Makes 12 muffins.

Arkansas Favorites Cookbook

Blueberry Oatmeal Muffins

3/4 cup unsweetened, frozen blueberries
1 cup quick-cooking oats
1 cup buttermilk
1 cup flour
1/4 cup sugar
1 tablespoon baking powder
1/4 teaspoon salt
1/8 teaspoon cinnamon
1/4 cup egg substitute
1/4 cup polyunsaturated oil

Thaw, rinse and drain blueberries. Combine oats and buttermilk; let stand for 5 minutes. Combine flour, sugar, baking powder, salt and cinnamon in large bowl. Make well in center. Combine oat mixture, egg substitute and oil, stir well. Add to center of dry ingredients and stir just until moistened. Gently stir in blueberries.

Spray muffin pan with vegetable spray. Fill cups two-thirds full. Bake in preheated 425° oven for 20 minutes or until browned. Yield: 16 muffins.

Per Serving (1 muffin): Calories 100; Cholesterol Tr; Fat 4gm; Sodium 150mg

Take It To Heart

Bite-Size Applesauce Muffins

1/2 cup butter or margarine
1/2 cup sugar
2 eggs
3/4 cup applesauce
1 3/4 cups all-purpose flour
1 tablespoon baking powder
1/2 teaspoon salt
1/4 cup butter or margarine, melted
1/4 cup sugar
1/8 teaspoon ground cinnamon

Cream 1/2 cup butter; gradually add 1/2 cup sugar, beating until light and fluffy. Add eggs, one at a time, beating well after each addition. Stir in applesauce. Combine flour, baking powder, and salt; add to creamed mixture and stir just until moistened. Spoon batter into lightly greased miniature muffin pans. Fill to two-thirds full. Bake at 425° for 15 minutes or until done.

Remove from pan immediately and dip muffin tops in melted butter. Combine 1/4 cup sugar and cinnamon. Sprinkle sugar mixture over each muffin. Yields about 3 1/2 dozen.

The Bonneville House Presents

Apple Muffins

2 cups flour
3/4 teaspoon salt
4 teaspoons baking powder
1/4 cup sugar
3/4 teaspoon cinnamon
1/4 teaspoon nutmeg
1 beaten egg
1 cup milk
1/3 cup melted shortening
3/4 cup chopped raw apples

Sift dry ingredients. Add combined egg, milk and shortening. Stir until moistened. Add apples. Fill greased muffin pans two-thirds full. Bake in 400° oven for 25 minutes.

Crossett Cook Book

Hill Country Coffee Cake

(Cooked in Dutch oven)

2 1/4 cups flour
1/2 teaspoon salt
1 tablespoon cinnamon
1 cup brown sugar
3/4 cup sugar
3/4 cup cooking oil
1 teaspoon soda
1 teaspoon baking powder
1 egg, beaten
1 cup buttermilk

Mix ingredients well and place in an oiled baking pan in [Dutch] oven. Bake 30 minutes, test for doneness.

Serves 8.

Variations: 1) Sprinkle 1/2 cup chopped pecans on top after butter is in baking pan.

2) Pour mixture of confectioner's sugar and milk on top after cooking and removing from oven.

3) Add 1 teaspoon lemon flavoring to batter.

4) Sprinkle brown sugar on top after batter is in baking pan.

Camper's Guide to Outdoor Cooking

Apple Pancake

You can whip up this pancake in no time with a blender or food processor. The first time I made it everyone in my family stood around the kitchen sampling and making suggestions for toppings. We had votes for maple syrup, whipped cream, cold applesauce, and light molasses. I chose vanilla ice cream. Then we tried it in soup bowls with cold milk poured over it. My sainted magnolias, but it's good all those ways!

2-3 apples
1/4 cup butter
Ground cinnamon
2 eggs, beaten
1 1/3 cups milk
3 tablespoons granulated sugar
1/2 teaspoon vanilla extract
2 cups self-rising flour
Ground nutmeg (optional)

Preheat oven to 450°. Peel, core, and slice the apples. Melt the butter in a 10- or 12-inch iron skillet, swirling it around so the sides are completely coated. Cover the bottom of the pan with the apples. Sprinkle them heavily with cinnamon.

In the blender or food processor, blend the eggs, milk, sugar, and vanilla. Add the flour and blend again until the mixture is smooth. Pour the batter over the apples. Grate a small amount of nutmeg over the batter if you wish.

Bake 15-20 minutes, until the batter is cooked through and the pancake begins to come away from the sides of the pan. Turn the pancake out onto a serving plate carefully, using a spatula to coax all the apples loose from the bottom of the pan if necessary. Serve hot with any topping that appeals to you. May be baked ahead and reheated in the microwave oven. Makes 6 servings.

Enjoying the Art of Southern Hospitality

Malvern is the brick capital of the world. "Brickfest" is held there in July.

Black-Cherry Almond Coffeecake

1 cup whole wheat flour
1 cup white flour
1/2 cup sugar
1 tablespoon baking powder
1/2 teaspoon salt
1/4 teaspoon nutmeg
1 cup pitted fresh black cherries or 1 (16-ounce) can, drained, patted dry with paper towel
2 eggs
3/4 cup milk
1/2 cup butter, melted
1/2 cup slivered almonds
1 tablespoon sugar

In large bowl, mix flours, sugar, baking powder, salt, and nutmeg. Add cherries; toss to coat. In small bowl, beat eggs with fork; stir in milk and butter. Add to flour mixture; stir just until blended. Fill greased 9-inch square pan. Sprinkle top with almonds and sugar.

Bake in preheated 400° oven until toothpick inserted in center comes out clean, 30 minutes.

Arkansas Celebration Cookbook

Sour Cream Coffee Cake

1 cup sugar
1/2 cup butter or oleo
2 cups flour, sifted
1/4 teaspoon nutmeg
1/2 teaspoon cinnamon
1 (8-ounce) carton sour cream
1 teaspoon soda

Combine sugar, butter and flour; crumble like pie dough. Set aside half of this mixture for topping. To other half add nutmeg, cinnamon and sour cream to which soda has been added. Mix well. Pour into a greased 8x8-inch pan. Sprinkle reserved crumb mixture on top. Bake at 350° for 45 minutes. Yields 1 coffee cake.

Southern Accent

Wiffle Waffles

Tools: waffle baker, liquid and dry measuring cups, measuring spoons, large mixing bowl, medium mixing bowl, stirring spoon, 2 forks, no-stick cooking spray.

1 cup whole wheat flour
3/4 cup all-purpose flour
1 tablespoon baking powder
1/4 teaspoon nutmeg
1 ripe medium banana, mashed
1 egg, beaten
1 3/4 cups skim milk
2 tablespoons oil
3/4 cup finely chopped pecans (optional)

1) Place flour, baking powder and nutmeg in a large mixing bowl. Stir together. Put mashed banana, egg, milk and oil in a medium mixing bowl and stir with a fork until combined.
2) Preheat waffle baker sprayed with no-stick cooking spray. Add banana mixture to flour mixture all at once. Stir until mixture is combined but still slightly lumpy.
3) Pour 1/4 cup of batter onto each waffle grid. Sprinkle about 1 tablespoon nuts over each grid, if desired. Close lid.
4) Do not open during baking. Bake until steam stops escaping from sides. Use a fork to lift waffle off grid.
5) Repeat with remaining batter. Yields 14 squares (1 square per serving).

Kids Cuisine

Batesville, the second oldest city in Arkansas (Fort Smith is the oldest), hosts four annual festivals: Ozark Scottish Festival, Chicken Fest, White River Water Carnival, and an air festival.

War Eagle Whole Wheat Waffles

1 1/2 cups whole wheat flour
2 teaspoons baking powder
1/2 teaspoon salt
1/2 teaspoon baking soda
1 3/4 cups buttermilk
1/4 cup oil
1 egg
1 tablespoon honey or sorghum

In medium-size bowl, stir together dry ingredients. Beat together buttermilk, oil, egg, and honey. Stir into dry ingredients; mix well. Spoon onto lightly greased, hot waffle iron. Makes 4 waffles. Double the ingredients for 8 waffles.

Variations:

Raisin Waffles—fold 1/2 cup raisins into batter.

Blueberry Waffles—lightly crush 1/2 cup blueberries; drizzle on 2 tablespoons honey. Stir blueberry mixture into batter. Top cooked waffles with a few whole blueberries and whipped cream. Pass the syrup.

Sweet Milk Waffles—substitute 1 3/4 cups sweet milk for the buttermilk and delete the baking soda.

War Eagle Mill Wholegrain and Honey Cookbook

Spicy Pineapple Zucchini Bread

3 eggs
1 cup oil
2 cups sugar
2 teaspoons vanilla
3 cups flour (or 1/2 cup wheat germ and 2 1/2 cups flour)
1 teaspoon salt
2 teaspoon soda
1/2 teaspoon baking powder
1 1/2 teaspoons cinnamon
3/4 teaspoon nutmeg
2 cups grated zucchini (skin and all, about 2 medium)
1 cup well drained crushed pineapple
1 cup walnuts
1 cup raisins (optional)

Beat eggs, oil and sugar until thick and foamy, add vanilla, wheat germ, flour and salt, soda and baking powder, cinnamon and nutmeg. Mix until smooth. Stir in by hand the zucchini, pineapple, and walnuts and raisins. Divide into 2 large loaf pans—greased and floured. Bake at 350° about 1 hour or until toothpick comes out clean. Let cool 10 minutes, then turn out on wire rack.

Betty "Winks" at Cooking

Brunch Casserole

1 1/2 cups egg substitute
6 ounces lean Canadian bacon, diced
2 cups skim milk
1/2 teaspoon salt
1 teaspoon dry mustard
2 slices wheat bread, cubed
1/2 cup part-skim mozzarella cheese, grated
1/2 cup low-fat Weight Watchers Cheddar Cheese, grated

Beat egg substitute. Add Canadian bacon, milk, salt and dry mustard. Stir in bread and cheese. Spray 8x12-inch dish with vegetable spray and pour mixture into dish. Bake at 350° for 50 minutes. Yield: 15 servings.

Per Serving: Calories 90; Cholesterol 10mg; Fat 3gm; Sodium 500mg; ADA Exchange Value: 1 meat

Take It To Heart

Bread Soufflé

4 slices white bread
Butter
1/2 pound hoop cheese
1/2 teaspoon salt
1 teaspoon dry mustard
4 eggs
2 1/2 cups milk
3 jalapeño peppers, chopped, peeled and seeds removed
Seasoned salt

Cut off crusts of bread and butter each slice. Grate cheese and mix salt and mustard. Beat the eggs and add milk. Butter soufflé dish and place 2 slices of bread on bottom. Top with half of cheese mixture, half the peppers and sprinkle with seasoned salt. Repeat. Pour egg and milk mixture over all.

Prepare this dish 6 hours ahead of time or let it stand in refrigerator overnight. Bake at 300° for 1 1/2 hours. Yield: 5-6 servings.

In Good Taste

Cream Cheese Soufflé

4 eggs, separated
1/4 teaspoon salt
1 teaspoon flour
1 cup sour cream
6 ounces cream cheese
1/4 cup honey

Beat yolks of eggs until thick and creamy. Add salt and flour. Combine sour cream and cream cheese; blend until smooth. Add to egg yolks, beat with electric beater until smooth, adding honey gradually. Beat egg whites until stiff but not dry, and fold in yolk mixture. Pour into ungreased 1 1/2-quart soufflé dish. Place in pan of water and bake in preheated 300° oven 1 hour. Serves 4-6.

This unusual soufflé has been served with dinner every Saturday night since the Red Apple opened. Many people have requested the recipe and it has appeared in the Arkansas Gazette several times.

Feasts of Eden

Baked Eggs

[For cooking at a campfire]

1 egg per person

Crack and pour an egg in an oiled dessert mold, foil cupcake pan or constructed foil holder. This constructed foil holder can be made of a piece of heavy aluminum foil pressed around a 10-12-ounce can, then removed to serve as your egg holder. You may want to put cupcake papers in the mold or foil pan, then remove the egg in cupcake paper when done.

Place egg containers in the [Dutch] oven and bake for about 10 minutes to the consistency preferred.

You may wish to enhance the eggs by adding one of these ingredients before baking:

Crumbled, crisp bacon
Grated cheese
Italian seasoning
Dill weed
Salt, pepper

Eggs can be prepared for individual preferences.

Dutch Oven Cooking

Karen's Breakfast Scramble

This is one of the easiest and tastiest buffet dishes I know of. Make a little more than you think you'll need, because people always come back for more. For each diner, allow:

Butter
1 medium-sized red boiled potato, skin on, sliced
1/2 medium onion, sliced
1/4 cup chopped cooked ham or corned beef
1 egg, beaten
1/4 cup cottage cheese
2 tablespoons dry Pepperidge Farm Poultry Stuffing
Salt and pepper
Sliced tomatoes or oranges

In a heavy skillet melt enough butter to cover the bottom of the pan generously. Over medium heat, sauté the potato and onion until the onion begins to soften. Stir in the cooked

CONTINUED

meat. When all these ingredients are hot, pour in the beaten egg and cook until the egg is barely set. Remove from the heat. The egg will continue to cook for several minutes. Stir in the cottage cheese and dry stuffing, and salt and pepper to taste. Move the scrambled eggs to a warm platter and season to taste. Garnish with tomatoes, or oranges if tomatoes are out of season. For buffet service, use an electric warming tray.

To prepare ahead, have all ingredients ready and refrigerated so that all you have to do is scramble them together to serve. Makes 1 serving. Multiply ingredients for each additional diner.

Enjoying the Art of Southern Hospitality

Baked Grits

4 cups water
1 teaspoon salt
1 cup grits
3 eggs, separated
2 tablespoons all-purpose flour
2 tablespoons butter
1 1/2 cups milk
9 drops of Tabasco sauce
1/2 teaspoon seasoned salt
1 cup grated Cheddar cheese
1/2 cup garlic cheese

Heat water to boiling. Add salt and grits and cook as directed on package. Beat egg yolks and add slowly to the hot cooked grits, stirring until well blended. Blend flour into melted butter and stir in milk. Cook over low heat, stirring constantly to make a thin white sauce. Add Tabasco sauce, seasoned salt and cheeses (reserving 1/4 cup cheese for topping) to white sauce; stir until cheese is dissolved and add to grits mixture. Beat egg whites until stiff; fold into the grits; pour into a 13x9-inch buttered casserole. Sprinkle with the reserved cheese. Bake in 350° oven for 45 minutes or until set and lightly browned on top. Yields 12 servings.

Favorite Recipes from Associated Women for Harding

Egg and Cheese Specialty

10 slices day-old bread
1/2 cup grated Cheddar cheese
6 or 7 eggs
2 2/3 cups milk (or part cream)
1/4 teaspoon cornstarch
1/4 - 1/2 cup cooking sherry
1/4 teaspoon almond extract
3-4 tablespoons butter, melted
1/2 cup slivered almonds

Trim bread and cube. Layer bread and cheese in a 2-quart casserole. Beat eggs, milk, cornstarch, sherry and almond flavoring together in blender. Pour over bread and cheese; pour melted butter over this. Refrigerate overnight or at least 8 hours before baking. When ready to bake, sprinkle almonds on top of casserole. Cook 1 hour at 325° or until brown on top. Serves 12.

A Man's Variation: Add chipped beef, cubed ham or crisp bacon. Leave out almond flavoring and almonds when adding meat, and top with more grated cheese.

Southern Accent

World's Best Pimento Cheese

We had never liked pimento cheese until we ate it at Papa Robin's, a now-defunct restaurant in Jasper, Arkansas. Our re-creation of their marvelous pimento cheese:

4 tablespoons mayonnaise
1 (3-ounce) package cream cheese, softened
3 cloves garlic
Handful fresh parsley
Several vigorous shots of Pickapepper and Tabasco sauces
1 cup pecans
1 small jar diced pimentos and all juice
12 ounces extra sharp Cheddar cheese

Purée till smooth in processor the mayonnaise, cream cheese, garlic, parsley and sauces. Turn into a bowl. Now, in food processor, process just till coarsely chopped, 1 cup pecans; add pecans and pimentos, with juice, to mayonnaise mixture. Now grate in food processor 12 ounces extra sharp Cheddar cheese. Turn into bowl with remaining ingredients. Stir well to combine. Let stand, refrigerated, at least 1 hour. Even better the next day.

The Dairy Hollow House Cookbook

Shrimp Sandwiches

1 large (or 3 small) packages cream cheese
1 flat can shrimp, drained and chopped fine
Juice of 1 large lemon
1 chopped garlic button
Salt and pepper
Juice of 1 onion, or a little grated onion
1 tablespoon Worcestershire
1 teaspoon mustard
Thin-sliced bread

Cream the cheese. Marinate shrimp (deveined) in lemon juice and add to cheese. Add the mustard, garlic, Worcestershire, salt and pepper. Butter thin-sliced bread on both sides, and spread a good layer of the shrimp mixture on the bread, making open faced sandwiches. Bake in a slow oven until the sandwiches are lightly browned and are hot through.

Perfectly Delicious

Turkey Cranberry Sandwiches

6 ounces smoked turkey breast, thinly sliced
4 slices low fat cheese (Swiss, mozzarella, Cheddar)
8 tomato slices
4 lettuce leaves
8 slices whole-wheat bread

DRESSING:
1/2 cup whole berry cranberry sauce
1 tablespoon Kraft Free Nonfat Miracle Whip
1/3 cup diced celery
1 tablespoon lemon juice

Mix together dressing ingredients and set aside. Assemble sandwiches dividing turkey and cheese evenly among the 4 sandwiches. Spread bread with dressing and serve.

Amount per serving: Calories 361; Grams of fat 10.7; Cholesterol 20mg; Sodium 746mg; % of Fat 28%

Eat To Your Heart's Content, Too!

Lentil Walnut Burgers

This delightful meatless cheeseburger is a popular item on the daily menu of the Station restaurant in Fayetteville, Arkansas. The owners were kind enough to let me share the recipe, presented here with a few "low-cholesterol" substitutions.

1/2 pound lentils
1/2 cup walnuts
2 cups bread crumbs
4 egg whites
1 cup chopped onions
1/4 cup ketchup
1/4 teaspoon ground cloves
1/2 teaspoon salt
1/2 teaspoon pepper
4 slices or 1/2 cup shredded imitation mozzarella cheese
Cooking spray
1 tablespoon olive oil

Cook lentils until tender. Drain and cool. Chop lightly roasted walnuts. Lightly toast bread crumbs. Mix all ingredients and mash into a slightly lumpy paste. Portion into 3-ounce patties and cook in a sprayed skillet to which you have added 1 tablespoon olive oil. (Some people prefer crisp patties.) Top each patty with cheese and serve on bun with traditional garnish. Serves 4.

Cooking to Your Heart's Content

No-Yolk Mayonnaise

2 large egg whites
1 teaspoon Dijon mustard
1/8 teaspoon sugar
1/4 teaspoon salt
1/4 teaspoon pepper
3/4 cup corn oil
1 tablespoon fresh lemon juice
1 teaspoon white wine vinegar

In blender, blend egg whites, mustard, sugar, salt, and pepper at slow speed for 1 minute. With motor running, add oil in a thin stream, and then turn motor off. Add lemon juice and vinegar. Blend mixture until it is combined. Makes about 1 cup.

Cooking to Your Heart's Content

Simple Watermelon Rind Preserves

2 quarts watermelon rind
1/2 teaspoon salt
6 cups sugar
3 cups water

Cut all the green and all the pink from watermelon with thick rind. Cut rind in half-inch cubes, add water just to cover, add the salt, and boil until the rind is clear and tender.

Drain well. Make a syrup of sugar and 3 cups of water, part of which may be the juice of a lemon. Boil until thick, then add the rind and boil until the rind is transparent and the syrup is thick. Fill jars and seal.

Cooking with Ms. Watermelon

Hope, Arkansas, is known around the world as "Home of the World's Largest Watermelons." Visitors to the annual festival in August can see the incredible 150 to 200-pound watermelons on display by the dozens! The weight record is 260 pounds.

Soups

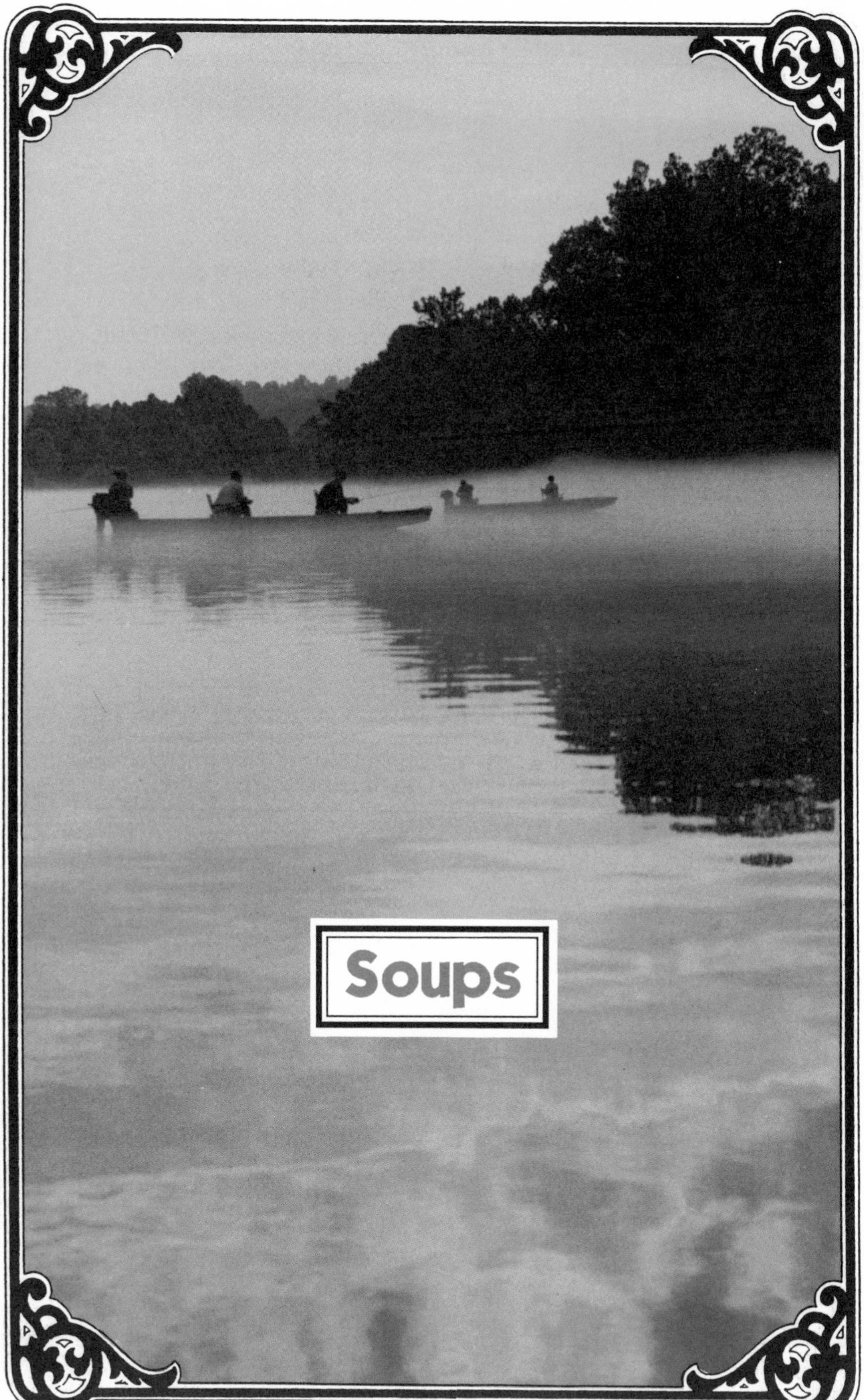

Early morning fog on one of Arkansas' crystal clear mountain lakes.

Herbed Corn Chowder

1 medium onion, diced
1 medium green pepper, diced
2 (1-pound) cans of creamed corn
2 cans potato soup
2 cans skim milk
1 tablespoon fresh parsley
1 tablespoon fresh chives
1 tablespoon fresh dill or thyme

Sauté onion and green pepper in skillet sprayed with cooking spray. Add corn, potato soup and milk and stir until smooth.

While chowder is warming, add chopped parsley, chopped chives, and either the dill or thyme. Serves 6.

Amount per serving: Calories 120; Grams of fat 2; Cholesterol 0mg; Sodium 575mg; % of Fat 15

Eat To Your Heart's Content!

Country Potato Soup

3 cups raw potatoes, diced
1/2 cup diced celery
1/2 cup onion, diced
2 chicken bouillon cubes
1 1/2 cups water
2 cups milk
1 (8-ounce) carton sour cream
2 tablespoons flour
1 teaspoon chives (optional)
Bacon, crumbled

Cook potatoes, celery, onion, and bouillon cubes in water about 20 minutes in large saucepan. Add 1 cup milk and heat. In medium bowl mix sour cream, flour, chives and 1 cup milk. Slowly add to heated mixture. Cook, stirring until thickened. Serve hot, topped with crumbled bacon and fresh bread.

Pulaski Heights Baptist Church Cookbook

Indian Corn Stew

2 tablespoons vegetable oil
1 medium onion, chopped
3 cloves garlic, minced
3-4 skinless, boneless chicken breasts, cut in bite-size pieces
1 (4-ounce) can diced mild green chiles
1 (16-ounce) can tomatoes, chopped, with liquid
1 cup of water
1 (16-ounce) package frozen corn, or 2 cups fresh grated corn
1/4 teaspoon salt (optional)
1/2 teaspoon cumin
1 teaspoon chili powder
2 medium ripe tomatoes, diced
1 bell pepper, diced

In a Dutch oven or large soup pot, over medium-high heat, sauté in oil the onion and garlic until onion is transparent. Add the chicken and brown, stirring frequently for about 5 minutes.

Add green chiles, canned tomatoes, water, corn and spices. Simmer 5 minutes. Add chopped tomatoes, bell pepper and simmer 20 minutes. Yields 6-8 servings.

Serve with warm buttered tortillas.

STEAMING CORN TORTILLAS:
1 dozen corn tortillas

Wet a clean dish towel and ring out excess water until cloth is damp. Remove tortillas from their package and place them on the damp towel on a baking sheet. Fold the towel over the tortillas and tuck in all sides.

Place in the preheated 350° oven for 10 minutes.

Eating Healthy in the Fast Lane

Cheese Soup

1 cup carrots, finely chopped
1 cup celery, finely chopped
1 cup green onions, chopped
Enough water to cover
1 medium white onion, sliced
1/4 cup margarine
1/4 cup flour
2 cups milk
1 can Swanson's Chicken Broth
1 (8-ounce) jar Cheese Whiz
Pepper to taste
1/4 teaspoon cayenne pepper
1 rounded teaspoon prepared mustard

Boil carrots, celery and green onions just covered in water for 5 minutes. Sauté white onion in margarine, then add flour. Stir in milk and chicken broth, and bring to a boil. Add remaining ingredients. Keep warm over low heat.

Makes a lot and keeps well—uum good! Serve with Keebler's green onion bite-size crackers.

Betty "Winks" at Cooking

Cream Soup Mix

1 cup powdered lowfat milk
3/4 cup cornstarch
1/4 cup instant chicken bouillon cubes
2 tablespoons dried onion flakes
1 teaspoon basil
1 teaspoon thyme
1/2 teaspoon pepper

Mix all ingredients together. Store in an air-tight container until ready to use. For the equivalent of 1 can of cream soup, substitute 1/3 cup dry mix and 1 1/4 cups cold water. Cook in a saucepan until thick.

Dry mix yields the equivalent of 9 cups of canned soup.

Amount per serving: Calories 285; Grams of fat 1.0; Cholesterol 5mg; Sodium 905mg; % of Fat 3%

Eat To Your Heart's Content, Too!

Ozark Bean Soup

1 package Ozark (mixed) beans (2 cups)
1 (48-ounce) can V-8 juice
1 onion, sliced
1 cup each: carrots and celery, sliced
1 green pepper, diced
3 cups water
1/4 cup garlic, crushed
1 tablespoon basil, thyme, and oregano
2 tablespoons Worcestershire sauce
1/4 pound Italian sausage

Combine all of the above ingredients in a large pot and cook for several hours until beans are tender. Serve with Mexican Corn Bread for a great low-fat meal. Serves 8-10.

Amount per serving: Calories 109; Grams of fat 2.85; Cholesterol 7.25mg; Sodium 259mg; % of Fat 24%

Eat To Your Heart's Content!

Capitol Hill Bean Soup

1 pound dried navy beans
1 pound (about) ham bone
3 cups chopped onions
3 cups chopped celery
1/4 cup chopped fresh parsley
1 clove garlic, minced
1/2 cup mashed potatoes
2 teaspoons salt
Pepper to taste

Sort and wash beans. Cover with water and soak overnight. (If you have forgotten to put beans on to soak, you can: cover beans with water and heat to a rolling boil; cover and let sit for an hour or so; drain and then begin to cook.) Drain and cover with water; add soup bone or chopped ham.

Bring to a boil and add onion, celery, parsley and garlic. Cook until done. Add the mashed potatoes and seasonings; cook slowly for a while longer. Twelve to 15 servings.

Note: I usually use turkey ham cut in small cubes.

Asbury United Methodist Church Cook Book

Meatless Split Pea Soup

1 (1-pound) package green split peas
2 quarts chicken broth
2 cups diced onions
2 tablespoons garlic, crushed
1/2 teaspoon oregano
1/4 teaspoon thyme
1/2 teaspoon pepper
1 bay leaf
2 cups carrots, diced
1 1/2 cups celery, chopped
Mrs. Dash to taste

Wash and sort peas. In a 5-quart Dutch oven combine peas, chicken broth (fat skimmed off), onions, garlic, oregano, thyme, pepper, and bay leaf. Bring to a boil. Reduce heat; simmer 1 1/2 hours. Stir in carrots and celery. Simmer another 1 1/2 hours or until soup reaches desired thickness. Pick out bay leaf. Put all ingredients through a blender to cream. Serves 6. Tip: To thicken soup stir in instant mashed potato flakes to desired thickness.

Amount per serving: Calories 165; Grams of fat 4.6; Cholesterol 0mg; Sodium 104mg; % of Fat 25%

Eat To Your Heart's Content, Too!

Cauliflower Soup

4 cups water
3 cubes chicken bouillon
1 head cauliflower, broken into flowerets
1 carrot, sliced
3 tablespoons butter
3 tablespoons flour
1/2 teaspoon salt
1/2 teaspoon pepper
1 egg yolk
1 pint half-and-half

Bring first 4 ingredients to boil, then simmer until vegetables are tender, about 20 minutes. Melt butter and mix in flour and spices, stirring constantly, about 1 minute. Add slowly to first mixture. Cook over low heat 5 minutes. Beat egg yolk in half-and-half. Add to mixture. Take off heat and serve. Real Good!

A Heritage of Good Tastes

Lentil Stew

This hearty stew is so colorful and special that we serve it every Christmas Eve.

2 tablespoons olive oil
3 red bell peppers, cut in 1/4 inch crescent shapes
2 cloves garlic, minced
1 large onion, chopped coarse
1 medium potato, cut in large chunks
1 large carrot, cut in 1/4-inch rounds
1 stalk celery, sliced chunky
1 (14 1/2-ounce) can whole tomatoes
1 3/4 cups brown lentils, rinsed and drained
4 cups water
1 teaspoon dried basil
1 teaspoon dried thyme
2 tablespoons red wine vinegar

In a 4-quart soup pot over medium high flame, heat oil and add all ingredients (except red wine vinegar) in the order listed.

Bring to boil over high heat. Cover and reduce to simmer. Simmer 40 minutes or until lentils are tender. Stir occasionally to prevent sticking. Just before serving, stir in vinegar. Yields 6-8 servings.

Variation: Add preservative-free turkey Italian sausage, sliced in 1/4-inch rounds.

Eating Healthy in the Fast Lane

Chicken Soup

1 whole chicken
4 yellow onions
1 bulb garlic
5 stalks celery, chopped
1 bottle dry white wine
2 cups diced carrots
2 cups diced zucchini
1 pound thin pasta
2 cups diced celery
1 pound sliced mushrooms

Cover first four ingredients with water and the bottle of wine. Simmer for 60 minutes. Strain broth and dice or shred chicken. Add rest of ingredients to strained broth, simmer 30 minutes. Add chicken; warm and serve. Serves 8.

The Bonneville House Presents

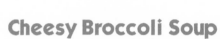

Cheesy Broccoli Soup

(Microwave)

1/2 of a 10-ounce package frozen chopped broccoli
1/2 cup thinly sliced carrot
1/2 cup water
1 teaspoon instant chicken bouillon granules
1 cup milk
1/2 cup shredded American cheese (2 ounces)
1/2 cup chopped cooked chicken or finely chopped fully cooked ham
1/8 teaspoon pepper
1/4 cup water
2 tablespoons all-purpose flour

In a 1-quart casserole, combine the frozen chopped broccoli, thinly sliced carrot, the 1/2 cup water, and instant chicken bouillon granules. Micro-cook, covered on 100% power for 5-7 minutes or until the vegetables are tender, stirring once.

To the vegetables in the 1-quart casserole, stir in the milk, shredded American cheese, chopped chicken or finely chopped ham, and pepper. In a small bowl stir together the 1/4 cup water and flour; stir into the vegetable/cheese mixture in the casserole. Micro-cook, uncovered, on 100% power about 5 minutes or until the mixture is thickened and bubbly, stirring every minute. Micro-cook, uncovered, on 100% power for 30 seconds more. Makes 2 servings.

Around the Bend

Ham and Cannellini Soup

2 (19-ounce) cans Cannellini (white beans), drained
1 1/2 cups chicken broth
1/2 cup chopped celery
2 ounces (1/2 cup) fully cooked smoked ham, chopped
Black pepper, to taste
1/4 cup red onion, chopped

In food processor or blender, purée 1 can of beans with 3/4 cup chicken broth. Scrape into a medium-sized saucepan. Stir in remaining beans and broth, celery and ham. Bring to a boil over medium heat. Cover and simmer 15 minutes. Season with pepper. Ladle into bowls. Sprinkle with chopped onion. Makes 5 cups or 4 servings.

A Heritage of Good Tastes

Mr. Zat's Faculty Favorite

1 pound lean ground beef
1 small onion, chopped
1/2 cup chopped bell pepper
1 (16-ounce) can tomatoes
1 (16-ounce) can okra and tomatoes
1 (16-ounce) can Veg-All
1 (16-ounce) can whole kernel corn
1 (16-ounce) can Chinese vegetables
1 (10-ounce) can Rotel

Brown together ground beef, onion and pepper. Drain excess fat. Do not drain liquid from any of the remaining ingredients. Add remaining ingredients to meat mixture; put into Dutch oven or large pot. Simmer at least 1 hour. This soup improves with age.

High Cotton Cookin'

Bayou Bartholomew in southeast Arkansas is the world's largest bayou.

Crab and Mushroom Soup

The easiest way to make this outstandingly good soup is in a metal double boiler with a top that can be set directly on the burner. A food processor is helpful for chopping the celery and parsley fine and slicing the mushrooms. Do not put the onion in a food processor because it makes the flavor strong and bitter.

3 tablespoons butter
2 cups finely chopped celery
1/2 cup finely chopped parsley
1 small onion, minced by hand
3 tablespoons flour
1 cup chicken stock
1 cup sliced mushrooms
1 cup crabmeat
1/4 cup Sauterne cooking wine
2 cups milk

Melt the butter in the top of the double boiler over direct heat. Stir in the celery, parsley, and onion. Cook and stir over medium heat until the vegetables are soft and translucent but not brown.

Stir in the flour and cook a few minutes more until the flour begins to be golden. Whisk in the chicken stock, beating until all lumps are gone from the flour. Set the mixture over hot water in the double boiler and steam for about one hour, until the celery is tender.

Stir in the mushrooms, crabmeat, and wine. The recipe may be prepared ahead to this point.

At serving time, add the milk and reheat the soup until it is piping hot. Do not let it cook further once the milk has been added. Makes 6-8 servings.

Enjoying the Art of Southern Hospitality

Bisque Crevettes

(Shrimp Bisque)

1/2 cup butter
1/2 cup chopped green onion
2 tablespoons parsley
2 tablespoons flour
1 cup milk
1 teaspoon salt
1/2 teaspoon white pepper
1/8 teaspoon cayenne
1 1/2 cups half-and-half
2 cups boiled shrimp, cut in pieces
2 tablespoons vermouth

Sauté onions and parsley in 4 tablespoons butter. In skillet, melt the remaining butter and flour. Mix like a roux. Add milk and cook until thickened. Add salt, pepper, and cayenne. Add onions and parsley and half-and-half. Bring to boil, stirring constantly. Reduce heat. Add shrimp and simmer 5 minutes. Add vermouth. Serves 4.

Nibbles Ooo La La

Chilled Cherry Soup

1 cup sugar
1 cinnamon stick
3 cups cold water
2 (16-ounce) cans pitted tart cherries
1 tablespoon cornstarch
1/2 cup heavy cream
3/4 cup dry red wine
1/2 cup dairy sour cream

In a 2-quart saucepan, combine sugar, cinnamon stick and water. Bring to a boil and add cherries. Partially cover and simmer over low heat for 10 minutes. Remove cinnamon stick. Add enough of the hot liquid to the cornstarch to make a paste. Blend paste into hot cherry mixture. Stir over medium-high heat until boiling. Reduce heat and simmer about 2 minutes until clear and thick. Refrigerate until chilled.

To serve, add heavy cream, wine and sour cream. Stir until smooth, leaving cherries whole; or if desired, purée in blender until smooth. Makes approximately 6 servings.

Variation: For Chilled Plum Soup, substitute equal amount of purple plums for cherries and add 3 tablespoons brandy and 2 tablespoons lemon juice.

Victorian Sampler

Arkansas Post, the first permanent settlement in the lower Mississippi Valley, was the capital of Arkansas Territory from 1819 until 1821, when the capital was moved to the new town of Little Rock. Except in 1863-65 when the Confederate state government was at Washington in Hempstead County, Little Rock has been the capital ever since.

Salads

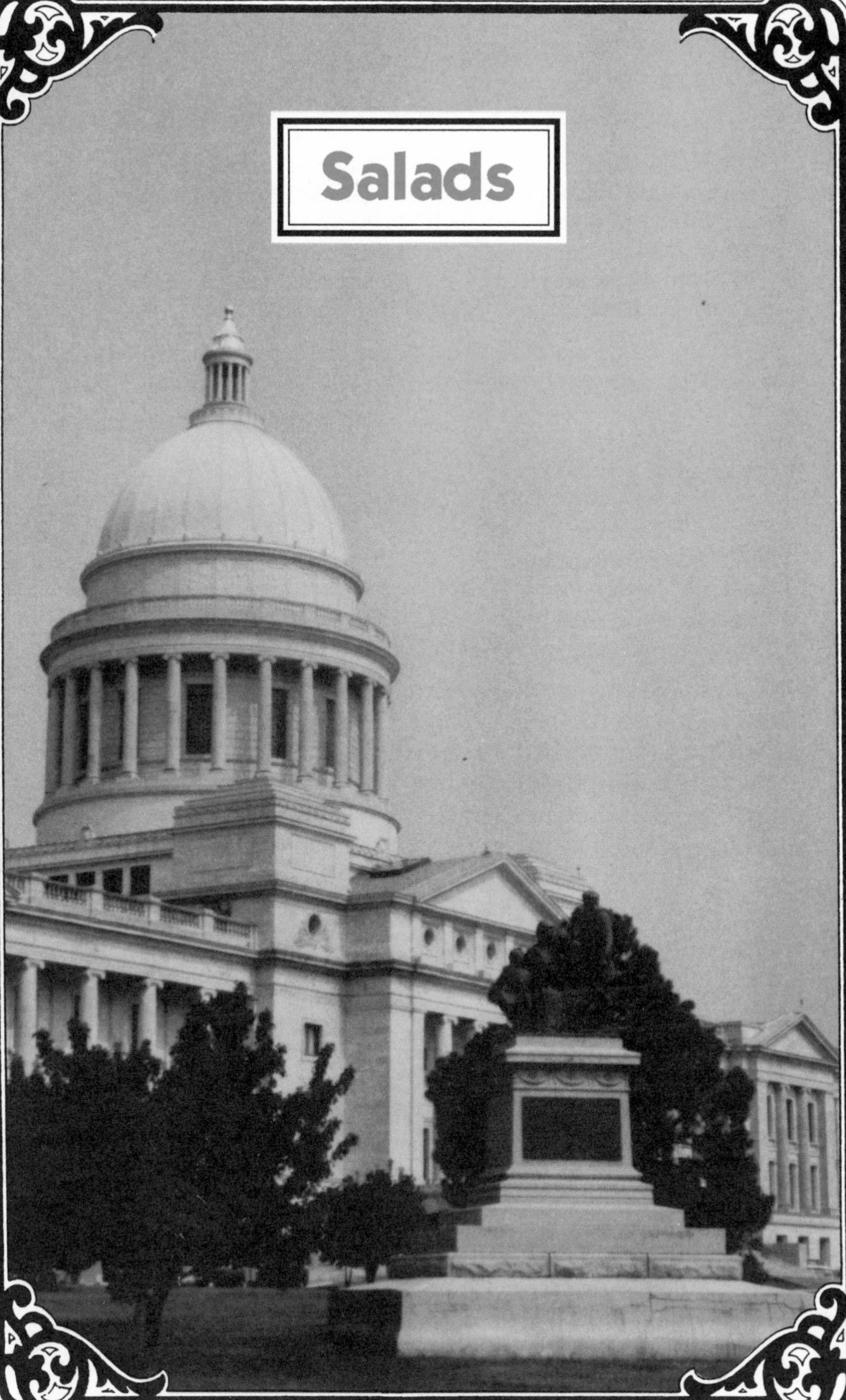

The Arkansas State Capitol in Little Rock.

Mom's Cranberry Salad

3 bananas, cubed
2 tablespoons lemon juice
1 can jelled cranberry sauce, cubed
1 (15-ounce) can crushed pineapple, drained
1 (9-ounce) carton frozen whipped topping, thawed
1/2 cup sugar
1 cup nuts, chopped
2 drops red food coloring (optional)

Stir cubed bananas in lemon juice to keep from turning dark. Fold all ingredients together gently. Freeze in 9x13-inch pan.

The Farmer's Daughters

Spiced Peach-Mandarin Salad

1 package lemon Jello
1 package orange Jello
1 can Mandarin oranges, drained
1 (16-ounce) can spiced peaches, drained, pitted, and mashed

Prepare Jellos according to directions, using the juice from both fruits for the required liquid, plus water to make the correct amount. Add the mashed peaches and Mandarin oranges when partially thickened, and pour into oiled molds or into long pan. Chill until firm, unmold on salad greens or cut into squares and serve on lettuce.

Perfectly Delicious

Watergate Salad

1 (8-ounce) container Cool Whip
1 small package pistachio instant pudding mix
1/3 cup cherries, chopped
1 large can crushed pineapple
1/2 cup pecans, chopped
1/2 cup miniature marshmallows

Mix Cool Whip and pudding together. Add remaining ingredients. Chill.

Southwest Cookin'

Fresh Fruit Salad a la Watermelon

1 3/4 cups sugar
2 1/2 cups water
1/2 cup fresh lemon juice (2-3 lemons)
1 teaspoon almond extract
2 1/2 cups watermelon, (keep juice)
Fresh fruit
1/4 cup fresh orange juice (one orange)
1/2 teaspoon Kirsch (optional)

Bring the sugar and water to a boil, and boil for 5 minutes. Set aside to cool. Squeeze lemons for juice. Add lemon juice, almond extract, watermelon cubes, and any watermelon juice. Put into blender and mix. Put in 2-quart ring mold, stir twice, and then freeze.

Unmold; fill center with other fresh fruit—strawberries, cantaloupe, pineapple, honeydew, peaches, pears, kiwi, oranges, etc. Moisten salad with orange juice and Kirsch.

Serves 8-10.

A Great Taste of Arkansas

Raspberry Salad I

Delicious!

1 package black raspberry Jello, dissolved in 1 cup hot water
1 small (3-ounce) package Philadelphia Cream Cheese, mashed
1 small can crushed pineapple, without juice
1 can fruit cocktail, juice and all
Some chopped nuts and miniature marshmallows
1 pint whipping cream

Add cream cheese to warm Jello. Add remaining ingredients except whipping cream. Refrigerate until it starts congealing, and then add 1 pint cream, whipped. Let it congeal in refrigerator.

This makes a beautiful lavender-colored salad.

Perfectly Delicious

Avocado Mousse

1 (1/4-ounce) envelope unflavored gelatin
1/2 cup cold water
1/2 cup boiling water
4 avocados, mashed
1 tablespoon lemon juice
1/2 teaspoon onion juice
1 teaspoon salt
1/2 cup cream, whipped
1/2 cup mayonnaise

Soak gelatin in cold water; dissolve in boiling water. Let cool.

Mash avocado and add lemon juice, onion juice, and salt. Whip cream stiff and fold in mayonnaise. Add dissolved gelatin. Combine with avocado mixture. Pour into individual molds and chill. Yield: 6 servings.

In Good Taste

Waldorf Salad

4 green apples, cut in cubes
4 red apples, cut in cubes
1/4 cup white raisins
1/2 cup English walnuts
1/4 cup maraschino cherries, chopped
1/4 cup diced celery
1 tablespoon lemon juice
1/8 cup mayonnaise
1 tablespoon powdered sugar
1/2 cup whipping cream, whipped
Lettuce leaves

Combine chopped apples (the peeling is left on), raisins, walnuts, cherries and celery. Toss with lemon juice. Add mayonnaise; mix powdered sugar into the whipped cream. Fold into apple mixture. Serve on leaves of lettuce.

Nibbles Fa La La

Should you see someone waving a large white cloth over the porch railing at Dairy Hollow House in Eureka Springs, it is not a surrender signal, but merely their method of spinning lettuce in a pillow case. It works beautifully.

Smokey's Eastport Salad

DRESSING:

1/3 cup salad oil
Juice of 1 lemon
Freshly ground pepper
1/2 teaspoon oregano or thyme

Mix ingredients and chill well. Pour dressing over greens and toss just before serving.

2 tablespoons salad oil
1 clove garlic, crushed
2 tomatoes, cut in wedges
1 large head Romaine lettuce
4 green onions, chopped
1/4 cup Romano cheese, grated
1/2 pound fried bacon, crumbled

Put salad oil in large wooden bowl. Add crushed garlic and stir well. Add tomatoes and stir. Do not stir again until serving time. Break lettuce into bowl. Add onions, cheese, and bacon. Cover tightly and refrigerate 1-2 hours.

Serves 6.

Cookin' in the Spa

Carrot Raisin Salad

3 cups grated raw carrots (about 5 or 6)
1 cup seedless raisins
1 tablespoon honey
6 tablespoons mayonnaise
1/4 cup milk
1 tablespoon fresh lemon juice
1/4 teaspoon salt
1/4 teaspoon nutmeg

Toss carrots lightly with raisins. Blend remaining ingredients and stir into carrot mixture. Chill at least 30 minutes before serving. Makes 6-8 servings.

The Wonderful World of Honey

Caesar Salad

1 clove garlic
6 anchovy filets
2 eggs, coddled* 1 to 1 1/2 minutes
1/2 cup olive oil (fresh press or virgin, be sure to use very delicate oil)
Juice of 1 large lemon
2-3 heads young romaine lettuce, washed, dried and torn
1/2 cup freshly grated Parmesan cheese
Fresh ground pepper to taste
2 cups croutons (if purchased, get plain)

Crush the garlic in a wooden bowl with the back of a wooden spoon and rub around the bowl, keeping the garlic in one piece. Stir in anchovy filets and rub around bowl. Remove remaining garlic, but leave anchovy pieces in the bowl. Add the eggs and beat well. Add the oil and lemon juice, beating the entire time. Add the lettuce, and Parmesan cheese; toss. Add the croutons, toss again and serve. Grind pepper to taste over each serving. Serves 8-10.

*Cook in water just below the boiling point.

The Bonneville House Presents

Better-Than-"Store-Bought"-Croutons

Bread slices
Butter
Parmesan cheese
Seasoned salt
Italian seasoning

Butter slices of bread. Sprinkle Parmesan cheese over bread, then seasoned salt, then Italian seasoning. Freeze slightly. (This makes cutting easier.) Cut into cubes. Preheat oven to 350°. Turn oven off. Put bread cubes in a pan, 1 layer thick; put in oven; allow to remain overnight. Place in airtight container. Keeps indefinitely. So good on top of a tossed salad, floating on soup, or crushed into crumbs for a special topping.

High Cotton Cookin'

Marinated Vegetable Salad

1 (16-ounce) can English peas
1 (16-ounce) can French green beans
1 (12-ounce) can shoe-peg corn
1 small can or jar of pimentos
1/2 to 1 cup celery, chopped
1/2 to 1 cup onions, chopped
1/2 cup green pepper, chopped
1 cup sugar
Pepper to taste
1/2 teaspoon salt
1/2 cup vegetable oil
3/4 cup vinegar

Drain all vegetables and put in a large bowl. Mix sugar, pepper, salt, oil and vinegar. Bring to boil. Pour over the vegetables while hot. Let set at least 24 hours in a tightly sealed bowl. Better several days old. Will keep in refrigerator a long time; stir once in a while.

Southwest Cookin'

Fresh Spinach Salad

1/2 pound fresh spinach
1 small head lettuce
3 green onions, chopped
3 hard-boiled eggs, sliced
1 cup frozen peas (uncooked)
1/2 cup chopped celery
1 cup grated Cheddar cheese
1/2 pound bacon, crumbled

RANCH DRESSING:
1 cup Hellman's Mayonnaise
1 cup sour cream
1 package Hidden Valley Ranch Dressing

Tear spinach and lettuce in bite-size pieces. Layer all in order given except bacon. Seal with dressing and let set several hours. Add crumbled bacon, toss and serve.

Victorian Sampler

Sensational Spinach Salad

1 pound spinach, torn into pieces
1 cup sliced mushrooms
1/2 cup pitted ripe olives
1/2 cup coarsely chopped walnuts
1/3 cup bacon bits
3/4 cup Wish-Bone Creamy Italian Dressing
3 hard-cooked eggs, sliced
1/2 cup seasoned croutons

In large bowl, combine spinach, mushrooms, olives, walnuts and bacon. Just before serving, toss with creamy Italian dressing; top with eggs and croutons. Makes about 6 servings.

Around the Bend

Mark Twain, who piloted steamboats past Helena, wrote in *Life on the Mississippi*: "Helena occupies one of the prettiest situations on the river."

Greek Salad

1 head lettuce
3 tomatoes
1 onion, thinly sliced
1 green pepper, chopped
1 cup black olives, halved
1 cucumber, sliced
1/2 cup olive oil
1/4 cup red wine vinegar
1/2 teaspoon oregano
Salt and pepper
Feta cheese, crumbled

Combine all vegetables and chill. When ready to serve, beat oil and vinegar until smooth. Pour over salad. Add oregano, salt and pepper. Then add crumbled cheese. Toss. Serve at once. Serves 8.

Arkansas Favorites Cookbook

Broccoli Rice Salad

3 stalks broccoli
1 small head cauliflower
3 cups cooked rice
Endive, leaf lettuce, romaine, or other salad greens

Rinse broccoli; with sharp knife, cut off flowerets; pare stalks thinly and slice inner stalk into thin slices. Separate cauliflower into small flowerets; slice thinly. Separate and wash salad greens; pull leaf sections from stalks and stems in bite-size pieces. Combine all ingredients; chill. Serve with dressing.

BLENDER DRESSING:

1 cup vinegar
2 cups oil
1 cup catsup
1 cup sugar
1 onion, chopped
2 bell peppers, chopped
1 tablespoon salt
1 teaspoon black pepper
1 teaspoon garlic powder

Combine all dressing ingredients in blender; process until smooth. Refrigerate. Yield: 1 quart.

Celebration

Brown Rice Salad

2 1/2 cups water
6 ounces long grain brown rice
1/2 cup Kraft Free Mayonnaise
1/2 cup plain nonfat yogurt
1/2 cup green onions, sliced with tops
1/4 cup parsley, chopped
Mrs. Dash and pepper
1 cup cucumbers, diced
1 cup tomatoes, peeled and diced
1/2 cup celery, chopped
1/2 cup frozen peas, thawed

Bring water to boil in a 3-quart pan. Add rice and return to boil. Reduce heat, cover, and simmer until rice is tender (about 30 minutes). Let stand at room temperature, uncovered, until cool.

Fluff rice with a fork; then stir in mayonnaise, yogurt, green onions, and parsley. Season to taste with Mrs. Dash and pepper. Transfer mixture to a salad bowl. Layer cucumbers, tomatoes, celery, and peas over rice. Mix lightly just before serving. Serves 6.

Amount per serving: Calories 85; Fat .13gr; Cholesterol .4mg; Sodium 94mg; % of Fat 1%

Eat To Your Heart's Content, Too!

Tuna-Macaroni Salad

1 (7-ounce) package macaroni rings
2 or 3 (6 1/2-ounce) cans tuna
1 onion, chopped
1 small jar pimento, chopped
2 dill pickles, chopped
1/8 teaspoon dry mustard
1 tablespoon dehydrated parsley flakes
1 (10-ounce) can green sweet peas
Mayonnaise
2 eggs, hard-boiled and chopped
Paprika

Cook macaroni rings according to package directions. Drain and pour into large mixing bowl. Add all other ingredients through the green peas. Mix carefully. Use enough mayonnaise and pickle juice to mix well. Salt and pepper to taste. Garnish with boiled egg slices and paprika.

The Farmer's Daughters

Tomato Salad

6 medium-to-large tomatoes
2 large bell peppers
1 large onion
2 tablespoons sugar
Salt and pepper
2 tablespoons vinegar

Dice vegetables. Mix together and sprinkle with sugar, salt and pepper. Add vinegar and stir. This will make it's own juice from the vinegar. Let set several hours and stir at intervals before serving.

The Farmer's Daughters

There are 47 thermal springs which flow from the lower west slope of Hot Springs Mountain. They produce about 900 thousand gallons each day. The 143°F water is believed to be heated by hot rocks some 4,000 feet below ground level. There are several display springs where visitors can feel, taste, and jug this delicious water.

Broiled Chicken Salad

2 cups diced cooked chicken
Salt and pepper to taste
1 cup diced celery
1/4 cup French dressing
1/2 cup salad dressing
1/3 cup sour cream
1/4 cup toasted slivered almonds
2 cups crushed potato chips
1 cup grated Cheddar cheese

Salt and pepper the cooked chicken lightly. (Almost all the other ingredients are already salted!) Marinate with the celery in the French dressing 1 hour. Combine salad dressing and sour cream. Add to almonds and place salad in a large shallow broiler-proof pan. Mix together potato chips and cheese and cover the top of salad with the mixture. Put under broiler only till cheese melts (you don't want to heat the salad). Serves 4.

Clabber Creek Farm Cook Book

Chinese Chicken Salad

1 medium head lettuce, torn into bite-size pieces
2 chopped green onions or purple onion rings are sometimes used
2 tablespoons toasted almonds
2 tablespoons toasted sesame seeds
4 or 5 broiled chicken breasts, taken off the bones in small pieces
Won ton skins, cut into thin strips and fried until golden brown

DRESSING:
2 teaspoons salt
1 teaspoon black pepper
4 tablespoons sugar
2 teaspoons Accent
1/2 cup salad oil
6 tablespoons salad wine vinegar

Mix all salad ingredients together, adding the dressing just before serving.

Asbury United Methodist Church Cook Book

Cold Chicken Curry

4 quarts boiling water
1 tablespoon salt
1 (16-ounce) package regular white rice
1 cup raw cauliflower
1 (8-ounce) bottle creamy style French dressing
1 cup mayonnaise
1 teaspoon curry powder
1 tablespoon salt
1/2 teaspoon pepper
1/2 cup milk
6-7 cups chicken, cooked and cut into chunks
1 cup thin bell pepper rings
2 cups celery, chopped
1 cup red onions, thinly sliced

Day before serving: bring water to a boil and add salt; then add rice. Cook, covered, over low heat until rice feels tender. Drain. Cool, cover, and refrigerate.

Early on serving day: toss rice with cauliflower and French dressing. Cover and refrigerate at least 2 hours. In large pan, combine mayonnaise, curry powder, salt, and pepper. Slowly stir in milk. Add chicken, toss, and refrigerate, covered, at least 2 hours.

Just before serving: combine in a large bowl, rice mixture with chicken mixture. Add bell pepper rings, celery, and onion. Yield: 20 servings.

Suggested condiments: coconut, canned onion rings, peanuts, chutney, hard-boiled eggs, mandarin orange sections, bacon bits, and pineapple cubes.

In Good Taste

Chicken Nut Salad

1 1/2 cups cooked chicken
2 tablespoons pine nuts, chopped
2 tablespoons pecans, chopped
3 tender stalks celery, cut in 3-inch julienne pieces
1/2 medium sweet red onion, sliced thin
3/4 cup black olives, sliced

DRESSING:
1 1/4 tablespoons lemon juice
1/4 cup extra virgin olive oil
1/2 teaspoon black pepper
3/4 teaspoon salt
1/2 - 1 teaspoon garlic powder or to taste
1/4 - 1/2 teaspoon flaked red pepper or to taste

Place all ingredients except dressing in a mixing bowl and toss. Add salad dressing and toss again. Chill 2 hours. Arrange lettuce leaves on salad plates. Garnish with chopped parsley. Yields 6 servings.

The Sicilian-American Cookbook

Mexican Olé Salad

2 cups shredded lettuce
1 (15-ounce) can kidney beans, drained
2 medium tomatoes, chopped and drained
1 tablespoon chopped green chilies
1/2 cup sliced ripe olives
1 large avocado, mashed
1/2 cup sour cream
2 tablespoons Italian salad dressing
1 teaspoon minced onion
1/4 teaspoon salt
3/4 teaspoon chili powder
1/2 cup shredded Cheddar cheese
1/2 cup coarsely crushed corn chips

Combine lettuce, beans, tomatoes, chilies, and olives in salad bowl. Blend avocado and sour cream; add Italian dressing, onion, salt, and chili powder. Mix well and chill. Toss salad with avocado mixture. Top with cheese and crushed corn chips. Garnish with ripe olives. Serves 8.

Arkansas Favorites Cookbook

Cold Steak Salad

This is one of Hillary Clinton's very favorite meals.

2 pounds boneless sirloin, cut into 1/2-inch cubes
1/2 cup butter
3/4 pound mushrooms, sliced
1 (9-ounce) package frozen artichoke hearts, cooked and cooled
1 cup finely diced celery
1 pint small cherry tomatoes
2 tablespoons chopped chives
2 tablespoons chopped parsley
2 cups Italian salad dressing
2 teaspoons Dijon mustard

In large skillet over high heat, sauté meat in butter, a few cubes at a time until browned on all sides. Transfer to a large bowl and cool.

Quickly sauté mushrooms in remaining butter and add to meat. Add artichoke hearts, celery, tomatoes, chives and parsley. Mix lightly.

Mix dressing with mustard. Pour over salad, toss, cover and marinate overnight.

ITALIAN SALAD DRESSING:

2 1/4 cups oil
3/4 cup wine vinegar
6 shallots, finely chopped
1/3 cup chopped parsley
1/3 cup fresh dill weed
Salt and freshly ground black pepper to taste
1/3 teaspoon Tabasco Sauce

Combine all ingredients in a glass jar and shake. Yields 3 cups.

Thirty Years at the Mansion

The "little rock," the stone outcropping which gives the city its unusual name, is featured in Riverfront Park, site of a river walk, fountains, playgrounds, and an amphitheater.

Honey-Mustard Dressing

1 cup mayonnaise
4 tablespoons prepared mustard
4 tablespoons vinegar
4 tablespoons honey
3 sprigs parsley, chopped
1/4 medium onion, finely chopped
Pinch of salt
1/2 teaspoon sugar
1 cup vegetable oil

Combine all ingredients, except oil. Add oil slowly, beating it in constantly. Refrigerate in covered jar. Keeps well for several weeks.

Victorian Sampler

Honey-Orange Dressing

1/4 cup mayonnaise or salad dressing
2 tablespoons honey
2 tablespoons orange juice
2 teaspoons lemon juice
2 teaspoons grated orange rind
1/2 cup heavy cream, whipped

Combine first 5 ingredients. Fold in whipped cream. Wonderful for fruit salad.

Dixie Cookbook IV

Crater of Diamonds State Park is the world's only diamond site where the public may prospect and keep any gems they find. More than 70,000 precious gems have been recovered from the crater's kimberlite soil since the first diamond was discovered in 1906 by John Wesley Huddleston—17,000 of these have been carried home by visitors.

Vegetables

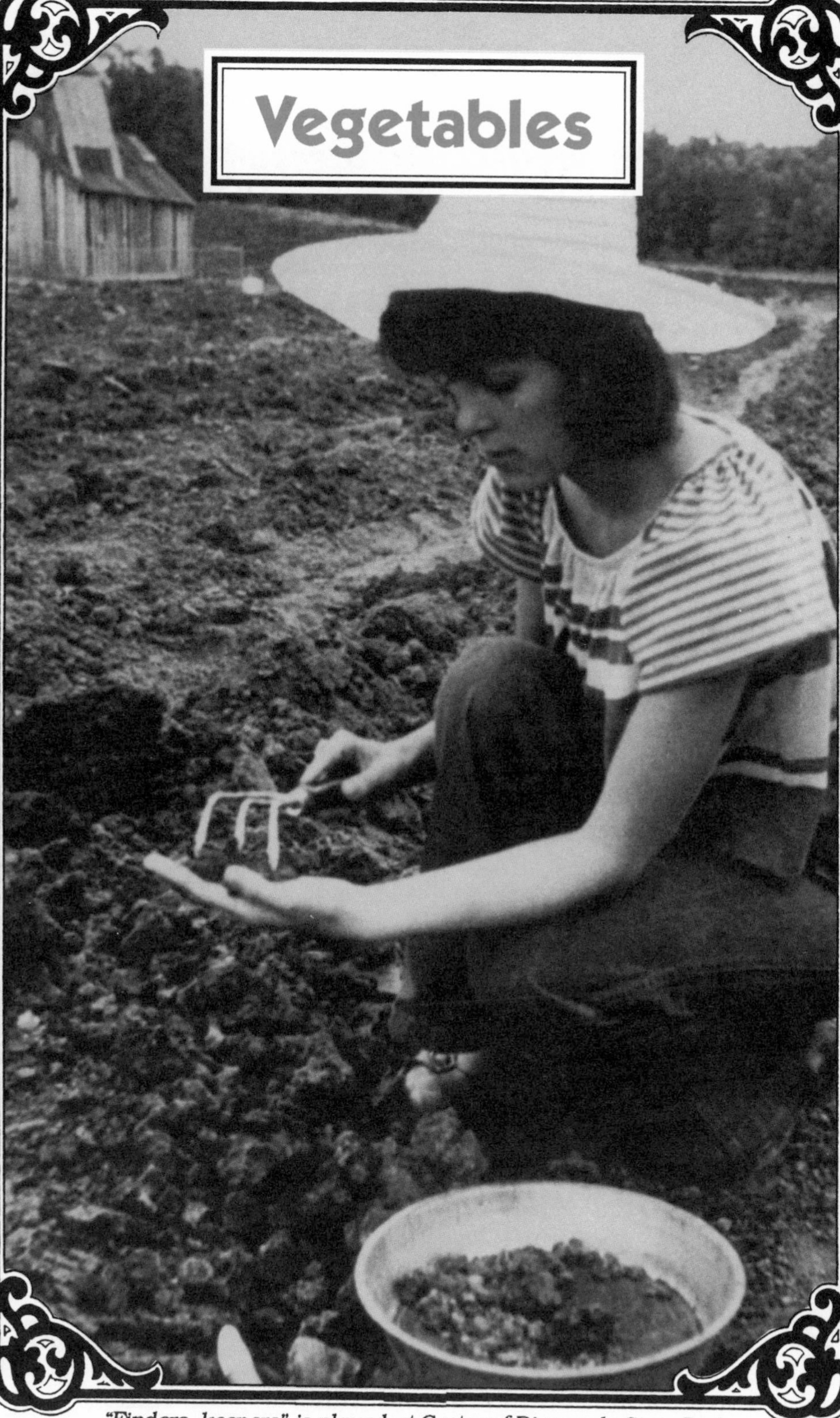

"Finders, keepers" is played at Crater of Diamonds State Park.

Artichoke Hearts au Gratin

2 (14-ounce) cans artichoke hearts
1 clove garlic, minced
1/4 cup butter
1/2 teaspoon salt
1/4 teaspoon pepper
1/3 cup flour, sifted
1 1/2 cups milk
1 tablespoon chopped pimento
1 egg slightly beaten
1/2 cup Swiss or Gruyère cheese
1 tablespoon dry bread crumbs, crushed
1 teaspoon paprika

Slice artichoke hearts into thin slices. Sauté garlic and artichokes in butter until tender. Remove hearts and place in a shallow baking dish. Stir seasoning and flour into remaining butter. Slowly add milk, stirring constantly. Cook over low heat until thickened. Remove from heat, add pimentos. Slowly add this mixture to the beaten egg and one-fourth of the cheese. Blend till nicely combined. Pour sauce over artichoke hearts. Sprinkle with remaining cheese, crumbs and paprika. Bake 450° for 15 minutes.

Nibbles Fa La La

Broccoli and Corn Casserole

1 (16-ounce) can cream style corn
1 (10-ounce) package frozen chopped broccoli (Bird's Eye brand), thawed
1 tablespoon minced onion
1 egg, beaten
Dash of salt and pepper

Combine the above ingredients then mix in the following:

1/2 cup Ritz crackers (make into crumbs)
2 tablespoons melted margarine

Combine the above together and pour into a Pam sprayed 2-quart casserole.

1/2 cup grated cheese
1/2 cup Pepperidge Farm Herb-Stuffing Mix
3 tablespoons melted margarine

Sprinkle grated cheese on top of casserole. Sprinkle herb-mix and butter on top of cheese and bake at 350° for about 40 minutes. (This recipe can be doubled very easily). Yield: 6 servings.

Betty is Still "Winking" at Cooking

English Pea Casserole

1 (10 3/4-ounce) can cream of mushroom soup
1/4 cup margarine
1 (16-ounce) can English peas, drained
1 (10-ounce) can asparagus, drained
1 (8 1/2-ounce) can sliced water chestnuts, drained

Warm soup and margarine until margarine melts. Add vegetables and bake in 350° oven for 30 minutes.

Prairie Harvest

Corn and Asparagus Casserole

2 tablespoons flour
1 teaspoon salt
2 tablespoons sugar
Pepper, to taste
2 eggs, slightly beaten
1 (5-ounce) can evaporated milk
1/4 cup margarine, melted
1 (16-ounce) can yellow creamed corn
1 (10-ounce) can cut asparagus, drained
1/2 cup grated cheese

Preheat oven to 350°. Mix flour, salt, sugar, pepper, eggs, milk, margarine and corn. Pour into buttered casserole. Place asparagus on top. Bake about 30 minutes or until firm. Cover with grated cheese and return to oven for 5 minutes more.

Prairie Harvest

Spicy Corn

1 (8-ounce) package cream cheese
2 tablespoons butter or oleo
1/4 cup milk
3 cans white shoe peg corn
1 small can chopped green chilies
Cayenne pepper to taste
Pepper to taste
Salt to taste
Garlic powder to taste

Melt cream cheese and butter in milk in saucepan. Add corn, green chilies, peppers, salt and garlic powder; mix well. Cook on top of stove until bubbly.

Cooking For Good Measure

The name Arkansas comes from an Indian tribe called Quapaw, or Oo-gaq-pa. The name has been interpreted to mean "downstream people" or "south wind."

Corn Pudding

2 tablespoons butter
1 1/2 tablespoons flour
1 cup milk
2 cups cooked or canned corn
1 tablespoon sugar
1 teaspoon salt
Dash salt
2 eggs

Melt butter, add flour and mix. Add milk gradually and bring to boil. Add corn, sugar and salt and heat thoroughly. Remove from heat, adding well beaten eggs and put in greased dish. Bake 25 minutes.

Crossett Cook Book

Cornbake

2 cans whole kernel corn
1 bell pepper, chopped
4 eggs, beaten
1 cup grated American cheese
Sugar to taste

Mix together; pour in greased casserole dish. Bake at 350° for 40-45 minutes.

Cookin' Along the Cotton Belt

Creole Corn

1 (9-ounce) package frozen whole kernel corn
1/2 cup chopped bell pepper
1/3 cup chopped celery
1/4 cup chopped onion
1 tablespoons oil
1 (8-ounce) can tomato sauce
1 (4 1/2-ounce) jar sliced mushrooms, drained
1 tablespoon chili sauce
1 teaspoon brown sugar
1/8 teaspoon garlic powder
1 small chopped tomato
Dash Tabasco

Cook corn according to pouch directions. Drain. In medium skillet, sauté pepper, celery, onion in oil until tender. Stir in corn. Add remaining ingredients. Cook until mixture comes to a boil. Continue cooking for 5 minutes.

Nibbles Cooks Cajun

Green Bean Casserole
(Microwave)

2 (9-ounce) packages frozen green beans
1 (10 3/4-ounce) can cream of mushroom soup
1/2 cup milk
1 teaspoon soy sauce
Dash of pepper
1/2 cup sliced pitted ripe olives
1 (2.8-ounce) can French fried onions

Place beans in medium micro-safe bowl. Cover. Microwave on HIGH 9 minutes or until tender. Drain. In 1 1/2-quart micro-safe casserole, stir soup until smooth. Add milk, soy sauce and pepper; stir until well blended. Stir in beans, half of the olives and half of the onions. Cover, microwave on HIGH 7 minutes or until hot and bubbling, stirring once during cooking. Let stand, covered, 5 minutes. Sprinkle with remaining olives and onions. Makes 6 servings.

Around the Bend

Steamed Green Beans Sautéed with Dill

1/2 pound fresh green beans, whole, with ends removed
1 teaspoon olive oil
1 teaspoon dill weed
1/2 teaspoon lemon juice

Steam beans until just tender. Heat oil in a large skillet over medium heat. Add beans and toss. Sprinkle with dill weed and lemon juice. Toss once more, lightly, and serve. Yields 4 servings.

Eating Healthy in the Fast Lane

Dill Bean Casserole

2 cans cut green beans or French style
1 tablespoon bacon fat
1 1/2 teaspoons dill seed
6 tablespoons oleo
6 tablespoons flour
1 cup liquid from beans
1 cup milk
3 tablespoons grated onion
Dash Tabasco
2 tablespoons Accent
Salt and pepper
Bread crumbs or French fried onions

Boil beans, bacon fat and dill seed for 30 minutes. Set aside overnight.

Drain beans, saving liquid and place them in shallow casserole. For the sauce: Melt in saucepan the oleo, add the flour, stir until smooth. Add 1 cup liquid from beans, milk, onion, Tabasco, Accent and salt and pepper to taste. Stir over low fire until thickened slightly. Pour over green beans; top with buttered bread crumbs, and bake until light brown. This may be prepared the day before, except for crumb topping. Bake at 350° for 45 minutes. For a variation, put grated sharp cheese and rolled French fried onions over the casserole the last 20 minutes of baking instead of buttered crumbs.

Dixie Cookbook IV

Spinach Madeleine

2 (10-ounce) packages frozen chopped spinach
4 tablespoons butter
2 tablespoons flour
2 tablespoons onion, chopped
1/2 cup evaporated milk
1/2 cup vegetable liquors
1/2 teaspoon black pepper
3/4 teaspoon celery salt
Salt to taste
3/4 teaspoon garlic salt
1 teaspoon Worcestershire sauce
Red pepper to taste
1 (6-ounce) roll of jalapeño cheese

Cook spinach according to directions on package. Drain and reserve liquor. Melt butter in saucepan over low heat. Add flour, stirring until blended and smooth, but not brown.

Add onion and cook until soft but not brown. Add liquid slowly, stirring constantly to avoid lumps. Cook until smooth and thick. Continue stirring. Add seasonings and cheese which has been cut into small pieces. Stir until melted. Combine with cooked spinach.

This may be served immediately or put into a casserole and topped with buttered bread crumbs. The flavor is improved if the latter is done and kept in refrigerator overnight and then reheated. This may also be frozen. Serves 4-6.

In Good Taste

Spinach Bake

2 (10-ounce) packages frozen chopped spinach
1/4 teaspoon pepper
1/2 teaspoon nutmeg
1/4 teaspoon Butter Buds
1 cup fresh mushrooms, sliced
2 ounces Cheddar/ mozzarella cheese mixture

TOPPING:
3/4 cup plain nonfat yogurt
1 tablespoon horseradish
2 teaspoons Dijon mustard
Paprika

Spray skillet with cooking spray and add frozen spinach; cook until defrosted. Add pepper and nutmeg and stir. Meanwhile, sauté mushrooms in 2 tablespoons Butter Buds. Add cheese and cook until melted. Combine with spinach mixture. Pour into casserole sprayed with cooking spray. Combine topping ingredients, except paprika. Spread over spinach. Sprinkle with paprika and bake at 350° until brown. Serves 8.

Note: If you prefer a topping not quite so tangy, reduce amount of horseradish to 1 teaspoon.

Amount per serving: Calaories 51.8; Grams of fat .3; Cholesterol .4mg; Sodium 191mg; % of Fat 5%

Eat To Your Heart's Content, Too!

Spinach Cheese Casserole

1 1/2 sticks margarine, cut up and mix with cheeses
1 pound Monterey Jack cheese, grated
1 pound mozzarella, grated
1 pound Swiss cheese, grated
2 pounds cottage cheese
6 eggs, beaten
6-8 tablespoons flour
3 packages chopped spinach, cooked and well drained

Mix together and bake at 350° for 1 1/4 hours (uncovered) in lightly greased large casserole dish.

Classroom Classics

Popeye's Pie

Tools: 1 1/2-quart casserole dish with lid, stirring spoon, medium mixing bowl, fork, rubber spatula, 9-inch pie plate, measuring spoons, measuring cups.

1 (10-ounce) package frozen, chopped spinach
1/2 cup chopped onion
2 eggs
1 1/2 cups ricotta cheese
1/4 teaspoon salt, optional
1/4 teaspoon pepper
1/4 teaspoon nutmeg
2 teaspoons flour
1/8 teaspoon paprika

1) Place spinach and onion in 1 1/2-quart casserole. Cover with lid or waxed paper.
2) Microwave at HIGH power for 3 minutes. Stir. Microwave 3 more minutes. Drain well.
3) Beat eggs with fork in mixing bowl. Stir in ricotta cheese, salt, pepper, nutmeg and flour.
4) Blend in spinach and onion. Spread mixture in 9-inch pie plate with rubber spatula. Sprinkle with paprika.
5) Microwave at HIGH for 2 minutes. Rotate dish. Microwave an additional 2 minutes.
6) Reduce power to 50% (MEDIUM). Microwave 3-11 minutes longer or until center is set. Let stand 5 minutes. Yields 8 servings (1/8 pie per serving).

Kids Cuisine

Marvell Squash

3 pounds squash, sliced
1 medium onion, chopped
1/2 stick butter
2 tablespoons flour
1 (13-ounce) can evaporated milk
1/2 pound American cheese
Potato chips, crumbled

Cook squash and onion in salted water until tender. Drain and put into buttered 2-quart casserole. In saucepan melt butter. Add the flour, gradually add milk. Stir in cheese and simmer until melted. Pour sauce over squash; sprinkle potato chips on top. Bake at 350° for 30 minutes. Even people who don't like squash like this dish!

High Cotton Cookin'

Skillet Squash

Medium onion, sliced thinly and separated into rings
2 teaspoons margarine
2 cups zucchini, sliced thinly (crosswise)
1/2 teaspoon sea salt
Dash coarsely ground pepper
1 medium tomato, cut in wedges
1 cup fresh mushrooms, sliced

Sauté onion slices in margarine until tender-crisp. Add squash and cook covered for 6 minutes, stirring occasionally. Add remaining ingredients and continue cooking about 4 minutes. Squash should be tender-crisp. Remove with slotted spoon. Serves 6.

A Great Taste of Arkansas

Squash Soufflé

6 or 8 small yellow squash, sliced but not peeled
1 large onion, sliced
2 tablespoons margarine
1/2 teaspoon salt
1/2 teaspoon pepper
2 teaspoons sugar
6 double crackers
1 egg, lightly beaten
Paprika

Simmer the squash and onion together until tender enough to mash with a fork. Drain, almost, and mash. Add margarine, salt, pepper, and sugar. Mix and then stir in crackers crumbled up in your hands, and egg. Pour into a buttered baking dish. Put cracker crumbs and a few dots of margarine over top. Sprinkle a little paprika. Bake uncovered for 20 or 25 minutes at about 375°.

I leave a little bit of water from the squash in order to keep it from being dry.

Perfectly Delicious

Stuffed Zucchini Bites

(Microwave)

Tools: cutting board, knife, teaspoon, small mixing bowl, stirring spoon, casserole dish.

2 small zucchini squash (6-8 inches)
2 slices bread, toasted and crumbled
1/2 cup Parmesan cheese, grated
1 egg, beaten
Dash pepper
Dash oregano
Dash garlic powder
Dash paprika

1) Trim off ends of zucchini. Cut in half lengthwise.
2) Scoop out center portion with teaspoon and reserve for filling.
3) Put reserved pulp and remaining ingredients, except paprika, into a mixing bowl and stir together.
4) Stuff each zucchini half with 1/4 cup of mixture. Place in casserole dish. Sprinkle with paprika.
5) Microwave at HIGH 6-8 minutes.
6) Cut each zucchini half in half; then into 3-4 pieces. Yields 4 servings (6 pieces or bites per serving).

Kids Cuisine

Zucchini in Red Sauce

3 cups zucchini, cut in cubes
1 (24-ounce) jar Ragu or your own homemade red sauce
1 (4-ounce) can sliced mushrooms, drained
Parmesan cheese

Cook squash in small amount of boiling water until tender. Drain and place in a casserole dish. Pour red sauce and mushrooms over squash and top with Parmesan cheese. Sprinkle enough cheese over top until it is covered. Place in oven and cook at 400° until the cheese on top is browned.

Classroom Classics

Eggplant-Zucchini Parmigiana

1 medium eggplant, cut in 12 1/4-inch slices, peeled
1 tablespoon mayonnaise or sandwich spread
1/4 cup Italian bread crumbs
1 cup low-fat cottage cheese
1 egg, slightly beaten
1/4 teaspoon garlic salt
1 (8-ounce) can tomato sauce
2 tablespoons Parmesan
1 cup grated mozzarella
2 small zucchini, cut in 1/8-inch slices

Put peeled eggplant on cookie sheet. Spread with mayonnaise and crumbs. Bake in preheated 475° oven for 10 minutes.

Remove and turn oven to 375°. Mix cottage cheese, egg and garlic salt. Layer all of eggplant, half of cottage cheese mixture, half of tomato sauce, half of Parmesan and mozzarella cheese. Top with zucchini and then layer the last half of the remaining ingredients. Bake uncovered at 375° for 30 minutes. Let stand for 5 minutes before cutting. Serves 6-8.

Cookin' in the Spa

Eggplant Parmesan

2 eggplants, peeled and sliced
Flour for batter
2 eggs, beaten
Oil for browning
1 large jar spaghetti sauce
Salt and pepper to taste
Parmesan and mozzarella cheese

Dip eggplant in flour and egg batter; brown in oil. Layer in baking dish with sauce, seasoning, and cheese, ending with cheese. Bake in 350° oven until bubbly.

Around the Bend

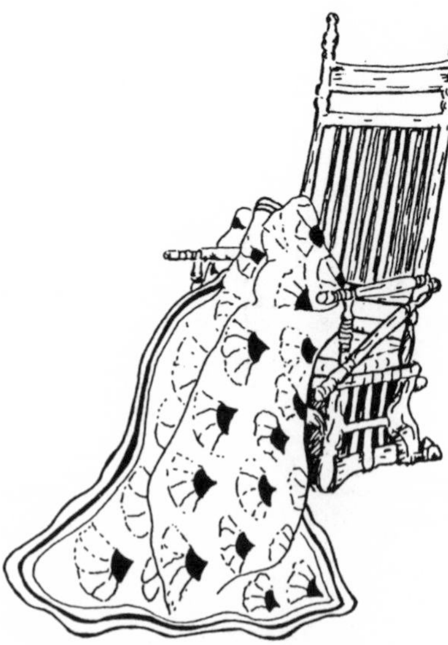

Mushroom Eggplant Casserole

3 eggplants, peeled and cubed
1 cup yellow onion, finely minced
1 1/2 tablespoons olive oil
1 pound fresh mushrooms, minced finely
3 tablespoons butter
4 1/2 ounces cream cheese
Salt and pepper to taste
4 tablespoons parsley, minced
1 1/2 teaspoons basil, minced

Soak eggplant in salted ice water 1 hour. Pour off water and boil in clear water until tender. Drain into colander and put into 3-quart mixing bowl.

Sauté onions slowly in skillet with olive oil until tender but not brown. Season lightly and add to eggplant in bowl. Twist mushrooms in a cloth to wring out juice. Sauté in butter until lightly brown, 5-6 minutes. Add to bowl.

Beat cream cheese with seasonings and add to bowl. Mix well. Pour into greased casserole dish.

TOPPING:

3 tablespoons Swiss cheese, grated
3 tablespoons bread crumbs, finely minced (we use homemade rolls)
2-3 tablespoons melted butter

Sprinkle mixture of cheese and bread crumbs over top and sprinkle that with melted butter.

Place casserole in a hot water bath about 1/8 inch deep and bake in preheated 375° oven about 20-30 minutes until hot clear through and brown on top. Serves 8-10.

The Mushroom Eggplant Casserole is one of our most-requested recipes. The homemade roll topping adds to the flavor!

Feasts of Eden

Ratatouille of Jenfo

- 2 eggplants
- 1 1/2 pounds tomatoes
- 1/4 pound pitted black olives
- 2 stalks celery
- 1/3 cup olive oil
- 2 tablespoons capers
- 1 tablespoon vinegar, or to taste
- 1 teaspoon salt
- 1 teaspoon sugar
- Pepper to taste

Peel eggplants. Cut into serving-size cubes. Salt and set aside for at least 10 minutes. Peel tomatoes and cut into cubes. Slice black olives. Clean celery, taking out the strings, and then cube. Drain eggplant on paper towels.

In a large saucepan, heat half the oil, add eggplant and lightly brown for 3 minutes. Drain and set aside. In same pan, add remaining oil. On medium heat, add tomatoes and celery and cook for 5 minutes. Add olives and capers. Add vinegar, salt, sugar and pepper. Cook for 15 minutes with lid on. Add the eggplant and cook for 15 more minutes. Serve hot or, preferably, as a cold entrée.

Arkansas Favorites Cookbook

Franke's Eggplant Casserole

- 1 medium onion, chopped
- 2 tablespoons butter
- 2 cups eggplant, cooked and drained
- 1 (#2) can tomatoes, drained (2 1/2 cups)
- 4 eggs
- 1 1/2 cups grated cheese
- 1 cup buttered bread crumbs
- Salt to taste

Sauté onion in butter. Add eggplant, tomatoes and eggs. Mash slightly. Stir over low heat until the mixture looks like scrambled eggs. Stir in cheese. Add 3/4 cup of crumbs. Salt to taste. Pour into baking dish and add the rest of the crumbs on top. Bake at 350° for 20 minutes.

Pulaski Heights Baptist Church Cookbook

Fried Green Tomatoes

1 egg
2 tablespoons water
3 green tomatoes
1/2 cup yellow cornmeal
1/2 cup flour
Salt and pepper to taste
Oil

Mix egg and water. Soak green tomatoes in egg and water while mixing cornmeal and flour. Pour small amount of oil into skillet. Heat oil. Dip tomatoes in meal and flour until fully covered. Fry in hot skillet until just brown. Drain on paper towels. Salt and pepper. Serves 4.

A Great Taste of Arkansas

Cauliflower and Tomato Bake

1 large head cauliflower
5 tablespoons butter
1/2 cup celery, finely chopped
1/4 cup onion, finely chopped
1/4 cup green pepper, finely chopped
3/4 teaspoon salt
1/4 teaspoon pepper
1/4 cup flour
2 cups milk
1 1/2 cups sharp Cheddar cheese, grated
3 large firm tomatoes, sliced

Cook cauliflower in boiling salted water for 5 minutes and drain. In a small saucepan, sauté celery, onion, green pepper, in butter until soft. Blend in salt, pepper, flour and milk. Simmer stirring until thickened. Add cheese and stir until melted. In a baking dish, layer cauliflower, half the cheese sauce, sliced tomatoes, and remaining sauce. Top with bread crumbs and bake at 400° for 25 minutes.

The Bonneville House Presents

Second Helping German Potato Bake

Excellent dish for casual buffet or picnic with a sweet and sour flavor.

6 large red potatoes, peeled, sliced into 1/4 - 1/2-inch thickness
2 large sweet yellow onions, peeled, sliced thin
8 large white mushrooms, washed and sliced (optional)
1/2 cup crumbled smoked bacon or bacon bits
1/3 cup low calorie margarine
1 1/2 cans chicken broth
1/2 teaspoon black pepper
1 1/2 teaspoons spicy brown mustard
1 1/2 teaspoons minced dried garlic
1 teaspoon prepared fresh horseradish
2 teaspoons wine vinegar
1 1/2 tablespoons brown sugar or sugar substitute
1 1/2 teaspoons garlic onion magic
1 teaspoon mustard seed
3 tablespoons cornstarch

POTATOES AND SWEET AND SOUR SAUCE:
Preheat oven to 375°. Spray oblong 3- to 4-quart baking dish or 9x12x2-inch pan lined in foil. Cook potatoes with the skins on until fork tender, approximately 20-25 minutes, on medium high heat. Cool, peel and slice into 1/4 to 1/2-inch thickness. Set aside. Peel and slice onions and mushrooms while potatoes are cooking; set aside.

In large skillet, cook bacon to crisp; remove, pat dry of grease. Wipe pan clean. Add margarine, and sauté onion slices for 5-8 minutes. Set aside in bowl. Using the skillet, add 1 can chicken broth, black pepper, mustard, garlic, horseradish, vinegar, brown sugar, garlic onion magic, and mustard seed. In remaining 1/2 can chicken broth, dissolve cornstarch. Using whisk, gradually add thickener to skillet liquid. Stir constantly on medium low heat until thickened. Remove from heat, set aside.

CONTINUED

POTATO BAKE:
In prepared baking dish or pan, arrange potato slices in a row, lengthwise. Tuck mushroom slices between potato slices. Arrange onion slices on top of potatoes and mushrooms. Sprinkle crumbled bacon or bacon bits over all ingredients. Pour the hot sauce over the entire potato, onion, mushroom mixture. Bake as directed above and until liquid has thickened and absorbed. The casserole should be quite hot and browned slightly. If browning too quickly, cover loosely with foil the last 15 minutes. Serves 10-12.

Note: Crumbled rye bread crumbs or wheat crackers are nice as a topping.

A Kaleidoscope of Creative-Healthy-Cooking

Hot Potato Salad

1 package instant potatoes
1 pint sour cream
6-8 green onions, chopped
1 cup fried bacon, crumbled
Grated cheese

Prepare potatoes according to directions. Put in buttered 9x13-inch dish. Spread sour cream on top of potatoes. Sprinkle with green onions. Add bacon; top with cheese. Bake at 350° for 20 minutes. Serves 12.

High Cotton Cookin'

Meriton Potatoes

(1920)

1 quart mashed Irish potatoes
2 raw eggs
Pepper and salt to taste
2 tablespoons chopped parsley
1 cup bread crumbs
1 large onion
2 hard-boiled eggs
Butter

Stir raw eggs into potatoes; add seasonings with part of the chopped parsley and some of the bread crumbs. Chop onions and brown in butter. Chop hard-boiled eggs and add all this to potatoes.

Mound on a pie plate or use baking dish. Before baking, make hole in center. Cover top with rest of bread crumbs, buttered. Bake about 20 minutes. When about done, place large lump of butter in center, with rest of parsley. Leave in oven until butter is nearly melted. Tastes like stuffed crabs. Serves 10-12 people.

Dixie Cook Book V

Twice Baked Potatoes

6 medium baking potatoes
1 teaspoon salt
1/8 teaspoon pepper
1/4 cup butter
1/2 cup sour cream
1 cup shredded Cheddar cheese
1 - 2 tablespoons chopped chives
2 - 4 tablespoons cooked crumbled bacon

Bake potatoes 45-60 minutes at 400° or until tender. Cut in halves lengthwise. Scoop potatoes out of shells into bowl and mash. Add ingredients and beat until light and fluffy. Spoon back into shells. Sprinkle with additional cheese and bake, uncovered, 20-25 minutes until hot. Serves 6.

Victorian Sampler

Cottage-Fried Potatoes

1/4 cup shortening or oil
6 cups potatoes, chopped
1 teaspoon salt
1/8 teaspoon pepper

Heat shortening or oil in a 10- or 11-inch pan with a tight-fitting lid. Add potatoes when fat is hot enough to simmer gently around a piece of potato. Season with salt and pepper.

Cover tightly and fry gently until potatoes are brown, turning them occasionally as they cook. Remove cover for last few minutes of cooking time to crisp potatoes. Makes 6-8 servings.

Hint: For variety, add a medium onion, finely chopped, to the potatoes when browned on one side.

Home for the Holidays

Red Potato Strips

1 stick margarine, softened
1 package dry onion soup
Black pepper
5-6 red potatoes, scrubbed and quartered

Mix margarine and soup together and spread on peppered potatoes. Put potatoes into a Pam sprayed casserole and seal with foil. Bake at 350° for 1 hour or until tender. Remove foil and bake another 10 minutes. Yield: 10 - 12 servings.

Betty is Still "Winking" at Cooking

Garlic Pommes de Terre

24 small new potatoes
1/2 cup butter
1 clove garlic, crushed
Parmesan
Parsley

Boil peeled potatoes until tender. Dry. Sauté potatoes in butter and garlic until golden brown. Sprinkle with Parmesan and parsley. Serves 6.

Nibbles Ooo La La

Sweet Potato Supreme

3 medium sweet potatoes
1 stick margarine
1 teaspoon cinnamon
1/2 teaspoon nutmeg
1 cup brown sugar
Salt to taste
Milk

Peel and cube potatoes and boil until tender. Mash potatoes well with margarine, cinnamon, nutmeg, brown sugar, and salt. Add enough milk to make mashed potato consistency. Pour into baking dish.

TOPPING:
1/4 stick margarine
1/2 cup sugar
2 tablespoons milk
1/4 teaspoon salt
1 teaspoon vanilla
1/2 cup pecans, chopped

Combine first four ingredients in a saucepan and cook over low heat, stirring until thick and bubbly. When cool, add vanilla. Sprinkle pecans on potatoes and pour topping over. Bake 400° for 15-20 minutes.

In Good Taste

Lo-Cal Carrots

4 cups sliced carrots
1 cup water
1 (15-ounce) can unsweetened pineapple tidbits, undrained
2 tablespoons cornstarch
1/2 teaspoon ginger

In a small saucepan cook carrots in water until crisp-tender; carrots may be steamed. Combine pineapple, cornstarch, and ginger in a small bowl; mix well; add to carrots. Cook over low heat, stirring constantly, until mixture thickens. (60 calories per serving.)

Celebration

Onion Fries

3/4 cup self-rising flour
1/2 teaspoon baking powder
1 tablespoon cornmeal
1/2 cup non-fat dry milk
2 teaspoons sugar
1/2 teaspoon salt
2 1/2 cups chopped onion

Combine all ingredients except onions. Add cold water a little at a time until you have a very thick batter. Add onions and mix well. Make small half-dollar size patties by dripping from spoon into hot shallow oil and flattening slightly with back of spoon. Brown on both sides.

The Farmer's Daughters

Texarkana visitors are intrigued by the Ace of Clubs House, a unique structure built in 1885 in the shape of a playing card.

County Fair Special

(Rice)

- 1 cup raw rice
- 4 1/2 cups chicken broth
- 1 can creamy chicken-mushroom soup
- 2 tablespoons chopped pimento
- 2 tablespoons chopped onion
- 2 tablespoons chopped bell pepper
- 2 tablespoons taco seasoning (Ortega, preferably)
- 1/4 cup Rotel and chili pepper, chopped
- 2 cups cooked boned chicken, cut up
- 1 1/2 cups grated cheese
- 2 cups slightly crushed regular Fritos

Cook rice in 2 1/2 cups chicken broth. When rice is not quite done, mix in soup, vegetables, taco seasoning, Rotel, and 1 1/2 cups broth. Layer half of this mixture in a greased 9x13-inch dish. Top with chicken, 1 cup cheese, and remaining rice mixture. Pour last 1/2 cup broth over top if it is too dry. Bake uncovered at 375° for 25-30 minutes. Remove from oven. Make ring of Fritos around edge of casserole. Sprinkle remaining 1/2 cup cheese in center of ring and return to oven to melt cheese. Serves 6-8.

A Heritage of Good Tastes

Jalapeño Rice and Cheese

- 1 cup uncooked rice
- 2 cups chicken broth (or 4 chicken bouillon cubes in 2 cups water)
- 1 cup sour cream (8 ounces)
- 1 1/2 tablespoons jalapeño, chopped
- 1 1/2 tablespoons jalapeño juice
- 1/3 cup creamy Italian dressing
- 1 (10-ounce) package Monterey Jack cheese

Cook rice in chicken broth until tender; combine all ingredients except cheese. Pour half of rice mixture into buttered 2-quart casserole and cover with half of cheese; add rest of rice and cover with rest of cheese. Bake at 350° for 30 minutes or until bubbly. Serves 4-6.

Betty "Winks" at Cooking

Wild Rice Casserole

1/3 cup butter or margarine
1 (10 3/4-ounce) can beef consommé
1 (10 3/4-ounce) can onion soup
1 (8-ounce) can water chestnuts, drained and sliced
1 (8-ounce) can mushrooms, drained and sliced
1 scant soup can of water
1 (6-ounce) box long grain and wild rice
1/2 cup long grain rice (white or brown)

Combine butter, beef consommé, and onion soup in a 1 1/2-quart casserole. Place in 350° oven until butter melts. Add water chestnuts, mushrooms, water, and rice with seasonings that are included in box. Stir to mix, return to oven and bake uncovered for one hour. Serves 8.

Arkansas Favorites Cookbook

Infallible Rice

1 medium onion, minced
2 tablespoons butter
2 cups chicken broth (hot)
1 cup long grain raw white rice

Sauté onion in butter until transparent. Add rice and hot broth. Bring to a boil on top of range. Cover and place in 325° oven for 20 minutes. Serve and listen to the compliments. Serves 4 hungry or 6 polite people.

Pulaski Heights Baptist Church Cookbook

Cotton was once king in Arkansas, but the flat and fertile land was perfect for growing soybeans and rice. More rice is grown in Arkansas than in any other state in the nation. Rice can be identified by the irrigation levees running through the fields.

Fried Rice

2 cups rice
4 cups cold water
1 teaspoon salt
5 strips bacon, diced
1 bell pepper, chopped
2 bunches green onions, chopped
1 can sliced water chestnuts
Soy sauce and black pepper to taste
2 eggs, beaten

Combine rice, water and salt in a covered pan. Cook until rice is tender. Remove from heat and cool thoroughly. I use a deep Dutch oven iron skillet to cook bacon in, then I add bell pepper, green onions, water chestnuts, and sauté about five minutes. Stir in the rice, add soy sauce and black pepper. Stir as it heats over low heat, then stir in eggs. It won't take long for the eggs to cook.

When ready to serve, if it needs re-heating, you can heat it in a covered baking dish in the oven or microwave. It gets better every time it's re-heated! I think all of our children or their spouses have called to ask for this recipe.

Clabber Creek Farm Cook Book

Glamour Mushroom Rice

1 small onion, chopped
1/3 cup butter or margarine
1 (6-ounce) can chopped mushrooms
1 cup uncooked long grain rice
1 (10 1/2-ounce) can beef consommé
3/4 cup water
1/2 teaspoon salt
1/4 teaspoon pepper

Sauté onion in melted butter or margarine. Add mushrooms, rice, consommé, water, salt and pepper. Pour into greased a 2-quart Pyrex dish. Cover and bake one hour at 350°.

Note: This is very good served with chopped minute steaks smothered in brown gravy. Corn bread goes well with this, also.

Prairie Harvest

Barbecued Rice

1 stick margarine
1 cup chopped celery
1 medium onion, chopped
2 cups cream of chicken soup
1 cup chicken broth
1 teaspoon liquid smoke
Salt and pepper, to taste
3 cups cooked rice
1/4 teaspoon garlic salt

Melt margarine in skillet, add celery and onion and cook until clear. Add soup, broth, liquid smoke, salt and pepper, and bring to a boil. Pour into casserole dish. Stir in cooked rice and garlic salt. Bake at 350° for 30 minutes.

A Heritage of Good Tastes

Black Beans and Rice

1 1/4 cups dried black beans
1 (16-ounce) can no-salt-added tomatoes, diced
1 3/4 cups onions, chopped
1/2 teaspoon garlic powder
1/2 teaspoon salt
1/8 teaspoon red pepper sauce
2 whole cloves
1 whole onion, peeled
1 garlic clove, minced
1 green pepper, chopped
3 cups rice, cooked

Wash beans. Place in 4 cups water; cover and soak overnight in a cool place. Combine undrained tomatoes, 3/4 cup chopped onion, garlic powder, salt, and red pepper sauce. Cover and refrigerate overnight to blend flavors of sauce.

Drain beans. Add 4 cups fresh water, bring to a boil. Cover pan, reduce heat and simmer 60 minutes. Stick whole cloves in peeled onion and add to beans along with garlic. Cover and simmer 60 minutes, adding more water if needed.

About 15 minutes before beans are done, sauté 1 cup chopped onion and green pepper in small amount of water in a skillet until onion is tender and transparent. Remove whole onion from beans; add cooked, chopped onion and green pepper and simmer a few minutes to blend flavors. Serve beans over rice and top with refrigerated sauce. Yield: 6 servings.

Per Serving (with 1/2 cup rice): Calories 230; Cholesterol 0; Fat 1gm; Sodium 215mg; ADA Exchange Value: 2 meats + 1 starch

Take It To Heart

The Great, The One and Only, Garlic Spaghetti

Garlic Spaghetti is the one recipe we have been asked for most often over the years. We would never serve it at the inn without knowing the guests extremely well; it is too bold, too assertive a dish, and, again, it doesn't quite fit the inn's ambience. But it is simply too good to leave out. Jan and I one day were talking about how, if this book reflected the way we actually ate while working on it, it would be three hundred pages of garlic spaghetti!

As far as I can tell, I must take credit for the invention of this glorious dish. It is basically an adaptation of Spaghetti à la Carbanora, made vegetarian and with a whole lot more garlic. Yes, the garlic and the egg are both raw. Don't be fainthearted about this, or about the amount of garlic, or you will miss one of the best dishes known to man or woman. What happens is the butter melts, the egg cooks ever so slightly, the cheese melts, and an indescribably heavenly amalgamation takes place.

8 ounces dry spaghetti
1 raw egg
5 to 8 cloves garlic, peeled and press—not less!
4 tablespoons butter
1/4 - 1/3 cup grated Parmesan cheese
1 teaspoon dried sweet basil
1/4 cup finely chopped parsley
Fresh coarsely ground black pepper to taste—a lot!
Red pepper flakes
Vegetarian bacon bits
More Parmesan and black pepper

Boil spaghetti in a pot of boiling water; while spaghetti is cooking, prepare the "sauce"—a thick paste, really, that you will toss over the cooked hot spaghetti. Into a blender or food processor, place the egg, garlic, butter, grated Parmesan cheese, and dried sweet basil. Whirl all together, until smooth and well blended. One can also do this by hand, if the garlic is put through a press. When spaghetti is cooked, but not

CONTINUED

overcooked, and drained, place it in a large bowl or pan and spoon over it the garlic-cheese paste and the chopped parsley and ground black pepper. Toss well. Mound this glorious concoction onto plates and serve. Pass at the table the red pepper flakes, bacon bits and more Parmesan and black pepper.

Eat this and swoon.

In the years since making the acquaintance of Garlic Spaghetti, I have tried various embellishments of this. I have sautéed onions and mushrooms, stir-fried green peppers, added cream. But nothing—nothing—except the optional red pepper flakes and veggie bacon bits adds anything special to the unadulterated blissful purity of this. You will know you used enough garlic if you wake up the next morning tasting it on your breath. Serves 2-4.

The Dairy Hollow House Cookbook

Rice with Dates and Almonds

1 cup rice
2 cups water
1/2 teaspoon salt
1/2 cup raisins
3 tablespoons margarine
1/2 onion, finely chopped
1 cup almonds, coarsely chopped
3/4 cup diced pitted dates

Combine rice, water and salt; cook till done. Remove from stove, mix raisins in with a fork, cover and set aside.

Melt margarine in skillet and sauté onions till soft; add almonds and fry till golden. (Don't burn it—it's easy to do!) Add onion and almond mixture to rice. Stir in dates.

Serves 6.

This is good served with about any kind of a meal. Those served this recipe will want it.

Clabber Creek Farm Cook Book

Harvard Beets

2 teaspoons cornstarch
2 teaspoons flour
1/2 cup sugar
1/4 teaspoon salt
 and a dash of cinnamon
A bit of grated orange peel
1 (16-ounce) can sliced
 beets, drained, reserve
 1/2 cup juice
2 tablespoons melted oleo

Mix dry ingredients. Add liquid and oleo and cook over low heat about 10 minutes. Pour over beets and let stand one-half hour before serving.

Cookin' Along the Cotton Belt

Curried Fruit

3/4 cup brown sugar
3 teaspoons curry powder
1/3 cup liquidized Butter
 Buds
1 (1-pound) can pear halves,
 drained
1 (1-pound) can pineapple
 tidbits, drained
12 maraschino cherries
1 (1-pound) can peaches,
 drained
1 (1-pound) can apricots,
 drained
2/3 cup almonds (optional)

Add sugar and curry powder to Butter Buds. Drain fruit and mix together in casserole dish. Combine sugar, curry powder, and Butter Buds; pour over the fruit mixture. Bake at 325° for 1 hour. Refrigerate overnight. If desired, sprinkle almonds on top. Reheat at 350° before serving. Serves 6-8.

Cooking to Your Heart's Content

Baked Apricots

2 large cans peeled apricots
1 or 1 1/2 boxes light brown sugar
1 box Ritz crackers
Butter—lots of it

Drain apricots well. In a greased baking dish, put a layer of apricots. Cover this with brown sugar, then a layer of crumbled Ritz crackers and dot with lumps of butter. Repeat layers to top of dish. Bake slowly—at 300° for about one hour.

Dixie Cook Book V

Scalloped Rhubarb

3 cups cubed bread, diced in 1/2 inch pieces (no crusts)
1 stick butter, melted, with red food coloring added
2 cups diced uncooked rhubarb
1 cup sugar
Water

Toast bread in oven until crisp. Add to butter and mix well. Add sugar to rhubarb and mix well. Pour bread and butter into greased oblong pan. Add rhubarb and sugar. Put 2 tablespoons water in each corner of pan. Bake 45 minutes at 325°. Serves 6.

Variation: Pineapple chunks can be used instead of rhubarb; omit food coloring and decrease sugar to 3/4 cup.

This is served in Spears Tea Room as a side dish to chicken or crepes but is often requested as dessert, hot with ice cream.

Victorian Sampler

When the barbaric practice of dueling with knives or pistols was outlawed, the islands of the Mississippi River became popular for dueling, as they were supposedly out of jurisdiction of the lawmakers.

Dilled Okra

3 pounds young okra, uncut
6 cloves of garlic
6 large heads and stems dill
1/2 teaspoon per pint, mustard seed
1 small red pepper per jar
1 quart water
1 pint vinegar
1/2 cup salt

Pack scrubbed okra into hot, sterilized pint jars with one clove garlic, one head and stem dill, one red pepper, and 1/2 teaspoon mustard seed for each jar. Make brine of water, vinegar and salt; heat to boiling. Pour over okra; seal at once. Let stand 3-4 weeks. Makes 6 pints.

Around the Bend

Chili Sauce

3 quarts ripe tomatoes, chopped
6 green peppers, chopped
4 large onions, chopped
4 tablespoons sugar
4 tablespoons salt
2 tablespoons cinnamon
3 coffee cups of vinegar (scant)

Combine chopped vegetables with other ingredients. Boil slowly 1 1/2 hours and pour into sterilized jars and seal while hot.

Perfectly Delicious

Meats

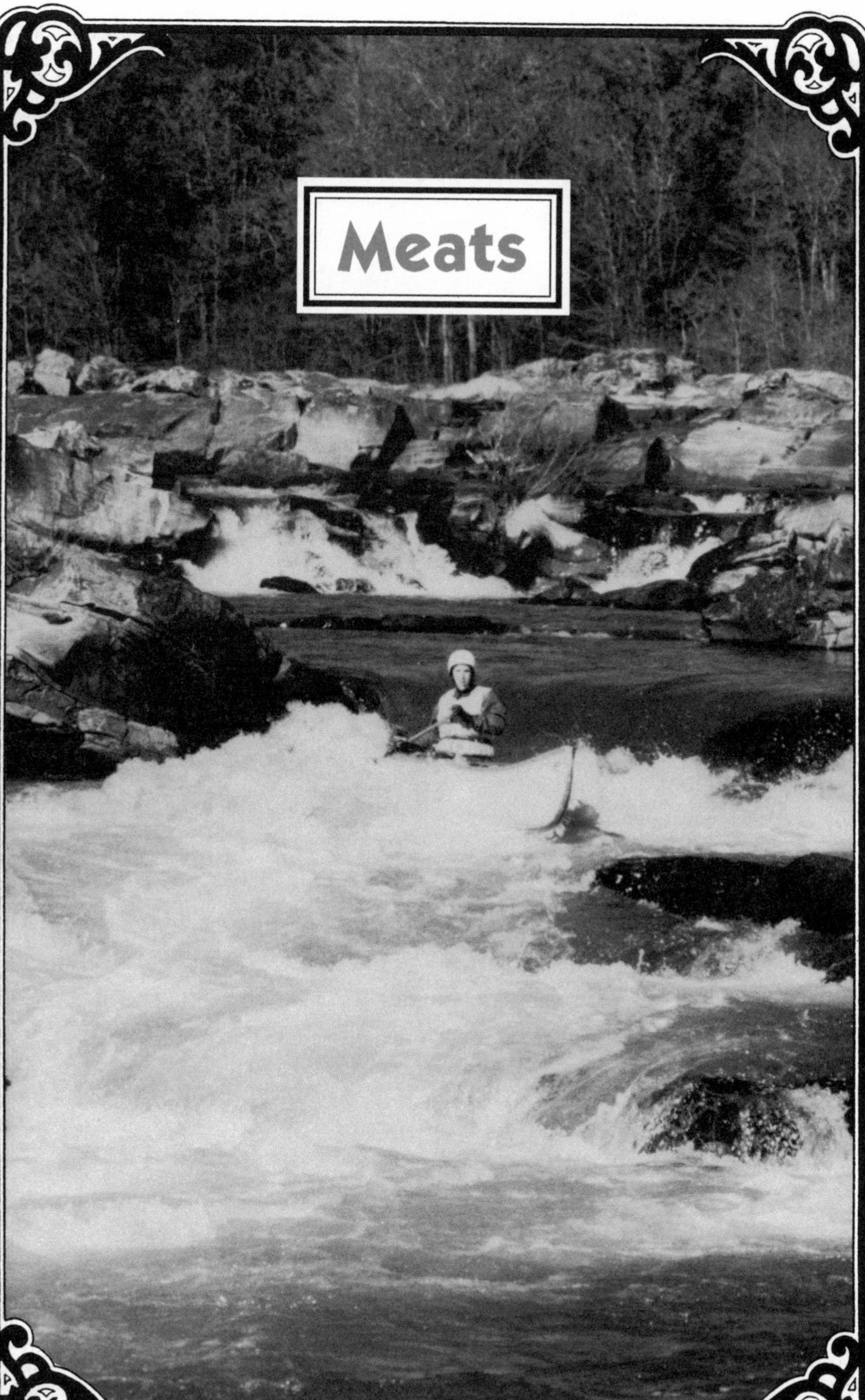

One of the most rugged and spectacular river corridors in the nation's mid-section, the Cossatot River is not for beginners.

Roast Prime Rib of Beef

6 whole celery stalks
6 whole carrots
6 onions, halved
15-pound prime rib of beef
Salt
Crushed black pepper
2 cups fresh parsley, minced or 1 cup parsley flakes

Place celery, carrots and onions in bottom of large roasting pan. Place roast on top and cover with the mixture of salt, pepper, and parsley. Cover and bake in a slow oven (250°) 4 hours until well-done on the outside, but rare in the center. Serve thick slices with natural juices poured over. About 3 servings per pound.

Feasts of Eden

Venison Roast

1 large venison roast
1 medium onion, chopped
1 clove garlic, chopped
Butter
Pepper
Cayenne pepper
Worcestershire sauce
Bay leaves (if desired)
Celery, chopped
Potatoes, chopped
Carrots, chopped
Green peppers, chopped

Place roast in crock pot with water to cover top of roast. Add onion, garlic, butter, peppers, Worcestershire sauce to taste, and bay leaves, if desired. Cook overnight. Remove and place in large baking dish. Add all vegetables, small amount of juices from roast, and salt and pepper to taste. Cover and bake at 325° until vegetables are tender. Uncover and brown slightly.

Around the Bend

Roast Beef Barcelona

3-4 pounds pot roast
1 (8-ounce) bottle French dressing
1/2 cup water
1 cup sliced stuffed olives
8 small onions
8 whole potatoes

Brown roast in 1/4 cup dressing. Add remaining dressing and water. Cover and cook slowly 2 - 2 1/2 hours on low heat. Add olives, onions, and potatoes. Cook 45 minutes longer, or until vegetables are tender. (Canned potatoes and onions can be used to shorten cooking time.) Serves 6-8.

Cookin' in the Spa

Scenic 7 has been named "one of the ten most scenic highways in America," and "one of the most fun-to-drive highways in America" by leading magazine and travel writers. There are unique places to stay, camp, shop, and stop along this scenic picture-postcard route.

Smoke-Flavored Beef Brisket

2 1/2 to 3 pounds well-trimmed boneless beef brisket
Salt to taste
1/4 cup liquid smoke
1 teaspoon onion salt
1 teaspoon garlic salt

Sprinkle brisket with regular salt and place on a large piece of foil. Set in a shallow dish or pan and pour liquid smoke over meat. Seal foil and refrigerate overnight.

Remove brisket from refrigerator, sprinkle with onion salt and garlic salt. Reseal foil, bake at 250° for 5 hours or until done. Slice thin and serve with smokey sauce.

Cookin' Along the Cotton Belt

Green Pepper Steak

2 tablespoons Crisco or oil
1 pound sirloin steak, cut into 1/8-inch slices
1 teaspoon salt
Dash pepper
2 tablespoons minced onions
1 clove garlic, minced
2 cups bouillon
2 green peppers, diced
4 small tomatoes, quartered
4 tablespoons cornstarch
4 teaspoons soy sauce
1/2 cup water
Boiled rice

Heat Crisco in heavy skillet. Add meat, salt, pepper, onion, and garlic. Cook over moderately hot heat, stirring constantly, until meat is brown.

Add bouillon and green peppers. Cover closely and cook over low heat 10 minutes. Add tomatoes and cook 1 minute longer. Blend together cornstarch, soy sauce and water. Add to skillet and cook 3 or 4 minutes longer, stirring constantly until mixture is hot and sauce is thickened. Serve at once over hot rice.

Cookin' Along the Cotton Belt

Beef Tips Over Rice

1 pound sirloin steak, cubed, sprinkled with unseasoned tenderizer
1 medium onion, chopped
2 cloves garlic, minced
2 tablespoons olive oil
1 small can of mushrooms or 8-10 fresh ones
1/2 cup white wine
2 teaspoons beef base seasoning
Salt and fresh ground black pepper to taste
1 tablespoon parsley flakes
1 tablespoon cornstarch
1/2 cup cold water
Hot cooked rice

Brown cubed steak, onions, and garlic in olive oil in a large heavy skillet. Add mushrooms, wine, beef base, salt and pepper and parsley. Let simmer 15 or 20 minutes until meat is done, then add the dissolved cornstarch-water mixture and let thicken. Takes just a few minutes.

Serve over hot cooked rice. Baked squash and fresh spinach salad completes this meal. Yield: 3-4 servings.

Betty is Still "Winking" at Cooking

Chicken Fried Steak

2 pounds tenderized round steak
Flour
1/2 cup vegetable oil

Cut steak into 6-8 pieces. Flour each piece thoroughly, and shake off excess. Dip in batter, flour again, and shake off excess flour. Preheat oil and cook meat 7-10 minutes until golden brown.

BATTER:
3 tablespoons sugar
1/2 teaspoon salt
1 egg
1 tablespoon baking powder
1 1/2 cups milk

Mix first 4 ingredients with half of the milk and stir until smooth. Add remainder of milk and mix well.

GRAVY:
1/4 stick butter or margarine
2 cups milk
1/8 cup vegetable cooking oil
1/4 cup flour
1/2 teaspoon salt
Pepper to taste

Melt butter. Add milk and mix thoroughly. Bring to a boil. Blend flour into oil; add to heated milk. Stir until smooth and thickened. Remove from heat; add salt and pepper to taste. Serves 4-6.

A Great Taste of Arkansas

Daisy Air Rifles are still made at Rogers. A museum there shows the world's largest and most complete collection of antique air guns.

Western Hash

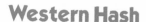

1 pound ground beef
1/2 cup chopped onion
1/2 cup chopped bell pepper
3 1/2 cups canned tomatoes
1/2 cup uncooked rice
1 teaspoon basil
1/2 teaspoon salt
Dash pepper
American cheese slices

Brown beef, onion and bell pepper in skillet. Drain. Add tomatoes, rice, basil, salt and pepper. Cover and simmer for 25 minutes, stirring occasionally. Put in casserole dish and top with cheese slices. Heat until cheese is melted and serve hot. Serves 6.

Evening Shade

Cowboy Stew

(Cooked in Dutch oven)

2-3 pounds ground beef
1 tablespoon margarine
2 (15-ounce) cans chili beans

Brown beef in margarine in skillet. Add beans and cook slowly 15-20 minutes in covered skillet. Serves 8.

Variation: Brown one medium onion, finely chopped, with the beef.

Camper's Guide to Outdoor Cooking

Excellent Meat Loaf

MEAT LOAF:
1 1/2 pounds ground beef
1/2 can tomato soup
1 cup Pepperidge Farm Herb Stuffing
2 ribs celery
1 egg
1 large onion, chopped
1/2 cup American cheese, grated
1/2 cup bell pepper, chopped
1 1/2 teaspoon salt
1/4 teaspoon black pepper
Bacon slices

SAUCE:
2 tablespoons butter, melted
2 tablespoons soy sauce
1 (8-ounce) can tomato sauce
1/4 cup water
1/4 cup vinegar
1/2 cup brown sugar

Mix all meat loaf ingredients; form into loaf and top with bacon slices. Pour sauce over top and cook at 350° for 1 hour and 15 minutes. Baste with sauce every 5 minutes.

The Bonneville House Presents

Coach Hugo Bezdek is credited with naming the University of Arkansas athletic teams "Razorbacks" in 1909 when he referred to his football players as "a wild band of razorback hogs."

Barge Rice

1 pound hamburger
1 bell pepper, chopped
1 onion, chopped
2 teaspoons Louisiana Hot Sauce
1 small can chopped green chilies
1 can tomatoes and green chilies
1 tablespoon chili powder
1 teaspoon salt
1 cup cooked rice
1 cup beer
1/2 teaspoon pepper
1 tablespoon Lea and Perrin Worcestershire
1 cup grated cheese
1 cup sour cream

Brown meat; drain. Sauté pepper and onion with meat. Add all other ingredients except sour cream. Simmer until mixed, about 5-10 minutes. Add sour cream. Heat, but do not boil. Serve with chips as a hot dip or as a main dish over rice.

A Great Taste of Arkansas

Sue's Cabbage Rolls

1 head cabbage
3 pounds ground chuck
1 large can stewed tomatoes, chopped (drain, reserve juice)
1/2 cup cooked rice
1 onion, chopped
1 teaspoon salt
1/2 teaspoon pepper
Whole carrots, washed and stemmed
Whole potatoes, scrubbed
2 cups tomato juice

Cut cabbage leaves off one at a time and peel from head. Drop in salted boiling water for 1 minute or until pliable. Drain leaves. Mix next 6 ingredients. Roll heaping spoon of meat in leaf. Begin by tucking sides of leaf to center, then rolling from the edge. Place rolls in heavy pot, place whole carrots and potatoes on top. Pour in juice from tomatoes plus 2 cups tomato juice. Cover and cook on top of stove on medium-low until large carrot on top is soft (about 2 hours). A favorite at teacher's pot lucks.

Classroom Classics

Spaghetti Casserole

2 pounds ground beef
2 onions, chopped
1/2 bell pepper, chopped
2 cloves garlic, chipped
1 tablespoon oregano
Salt to taste
Pepper to taste
1 (10 1/2-ounce) can Campbell's tomato soup
1 (3-ounce) can tomato sauce
1 (12-ounce) package vermicelli spaghetti
1 (8-ounce) package Olde English cheese slices
1 (2-ounce) bottle green stuffed olives
1 (10 1/2-ounce) can mushroom soup

Brown together beef, onions, pepper, and garlic. Drain liquid; add oregano, salt, pepper, tomato soup, and tomato sauce. Simmer 30 minutes. Cook vermicelli according to package directions. Grease a 3-quart casserole. Layer spaghetti, spaghetti sauce, cheese torn in pieces, green olives sliced. Repeat layers until bowl is full. Pour over the top 1 can undiluted mushroom soup. Cook in oven at 350° 30 minutes. Can be refrigerated or frozen before cooking.

In Good Taste

Red Beans and Rice

1 pound ground beef
1 large onion, chopped
1 large bell pepper, chopped
1 tablespoon chili powder
2 teaspoons salt
1 (16-ounce) can tomatoes or juice
1 cup water
1 1/2 cups uncooked rice
1 can red kidney beans

Brown meat with onions and peppers. Add remaining ingredients except rice and beans, and simmer for 15 minutes. Remove from heat and pour into 9x13-inch pan. Evenly distribute 1 1/2 cups uncooked rice and 1 can red kidney beans in mixture. Cover and bake at 350° for 1 hour. Take out and stir, cover, and return to oven for another 15 minutes.

The Farmer's Daughters

Blender Quick Cheeseburger Pie

Very much like a quiche, this recipe is super simple!

1 pound ground beef
1 1/2 cups chopped onions

Preheat oven to 400°. Grease a 10 x 1 1/2-inch deep pie plate or an 8 1/2 x 11-inch baking pan. Brown beef and onions. Spread in baking dish.

2/3 cup whole wheat flour
1 teaspoon baking powder
1/2 teaspoon salt
3 eggs
1 1/2 cups milk
2 tablespoons butter or margarine

Blend the above ingredients in blender on high for about 15 seconds or with a hand beater about 1 minute. Pour over hamburger. Bake 25 minutes. Add topping, bake 5 minutes longer.

TOPPING:

2 fresh tomatoes, thinly sliced
1 cup shredded Cheddar cheese

After baking 25 minutes, top with tomatoes and cheese; bake about 5 minutes longer until cheese melts. Makes 4-6 servings.

War Eagle Mill Wholegrain and Honey Cookbook

Named for the giant herds of buffalo that roamed its banks long ago, the Buffalo National River was the first river in America to receive national park protection (1972) and no wonder at all. Its beauty is highlighted by towering limestone bluffs, clear rushing waters, and wide gravel bars. A float trip on the Buffalo is an exhilarating, never-to-be-forgotten experience.

Crepes Cannelloni

- 2 tablespoons vegetable oil
- 3/4 cup minced onion
- 1 garlic clove, minced
- 1 1/2 pound ground chuck
- 1 cup chopped, drained, cooked spinach
- 1 egg, lightly beaten
- 1/4 cup grated Parmesan cheese
- Salt and freshly ground pepper to taste
- 4 tablespoons butter
- 4 tablespoons flour
- 2 cups milk
- 1/2 cup prepared spaghetti sauce
- 14 Basic Crepes (page 147)
- 1 (6-ounce) package sliced mozzarella cheese, cut into 1 1/2 x 5-inch pieces

Heat oil in large skillet. Sauté onions and garlic over medium heat until translucent but not brown. Add beef and brown, stirring frequently; drain.

Combine meat with spinach, egg, and Parmesan cheese. Season with salt and pepper; taste and adjust seasonings. Reserve 1/4 cup mixture for cream sauce.

Make the sauce by melting butter in a saucepan over medium heat; whisk in flour. Add milk, stirring constantly, until thickened and smooth. Stir in reserved meat mixture, simmer 5 minutes, season with salt and pepper to taste. Spread spaghetti sauce on bottom of greased 9x13-inch baking dish. Spread 2 tablespoons meat filling on each crepe and roll. Place crepe, seam-side-down, on spaghetti sauce. Spoon cream sauce over crepes and top each with a slice of mozzarella cheese. Bake, uncovered, at 350° for 30 minutes or until thoroughly heated. Serves 7 or 8.

Victorian Sampler

There are two mountain ranges in Arkansas, the Ozarks and the Ouachitas (*Wah-shi-taws*). Unlike most mountain ranges that run north and south, the Ouachitas run east and west.

Don't-Cook-The-Pasta-Manicotti

1 pound lean ground beef
1/2 cup chopped onion
2 cloves garlic, minced
4 cups tomato juice, divided
1 (6-ounce) can tomato paste
1 teaspoon sugar
2 teaspoons oregano
1 teaspoon salt
1/8 teaspoon pepper
3 cups shredded mozzarella cheese, divided
2 cups ricotta cheese, or cottage cheese
1 (10-ounce) package frozen, chopped spinach, thawed, drained
2 eggs, slightly beaten
1/2 cup grated Parmesan or Romano cheese
1 (8-ounce) package manicotti shells

In a large skillet brown meat with onion and garlic; drain well. Stir in 2 cups tomato juice, tomato paste, sugar, and seasonings; simmer while preparing filling.

In a large bowl combine 2 cups mozzarella cheese, ricotta cheese, spinach, eggs, and grated cheese; mix well. Stuff dry pasta shells with cheese mixture; arrange in a greased 9x13-inch baking dish. Spoon meat sauce evenly over shells; pour remaining tomato juice on top. Cover with foil; place pan on a baking sheet; bake at 350° 1 hour. Remove from oven; remove foil; top with remaining mozzarella cheese. Let stand 15 minutes before serving.

Celebration

Salami

2 pounds raw hamburger meat
1/2 teaspoon black pepper
1/2 teaspoon garlic salt
1 tablespoon mustard seed
2 tablespoons tenderquick salt
3/4 cup water
1 tablespoon peppercorns

Place all ingredients in bowl. Mix well, cover and refrigerate for 24 hours. Stir once or twice. Will change color. Roll into 1 1/2 - 2-inch thick rolls (3 or 4) 8 inches long. Bake on rack at 225° or 250° for 3 hours. Do not brown. Will turn salami color.

Prairie Harvest

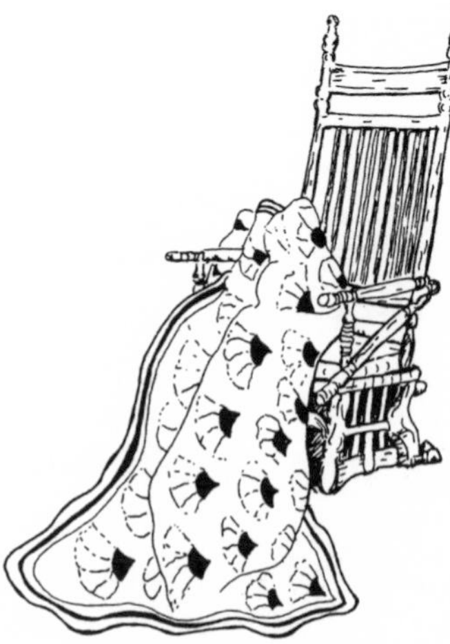

Sausage Casserole

1 pound bulk sausage
1 onion, chopped
1 green pepper, chopped
2 packages Lipton Noodle Soup
1 cup wild rice, or plain
1 cup diced celery
1 cup sliced toasted almonds
5 cups water

Sauté sausage in skillet. Remove from pan and sauté onion and green pepper. Mix these with noodle soup, rice, celery, almonds, and water. Bake in casserole 1 1/2 hours at 375°.

Dixie Cookbook IV

Sausage Pilaf

1 pound hot pork sausage
1 cup chopped celery
1/2 cup chopped onion
1/2 cup chopped bell pepper
1 cup cream of mushroom soup
3 cups cooked rice
1/2 cup chopped cashew nuts or peanuts, optional

Brown sausage; add celery, onion, and pepper. Cook 3 to 5 minutes. Stir in soup and rice. Pour into a 1-quart casserole. Cover. Bake 20 minutes at 250°. Remove from oven, sprinkle nuts on top and return to oven uncovered for 10 minutes longer.

Prairie Harvest

Zucchini Sausage Casserole

1 pound mild sausage
2 zucchinis (medium size)
1 large onion, chopped
1 tablespoon minced jalapeño pepper
1 can chicken broth
2 cups grated Jack cheese
1 (10-ounce) package macaroni

Crumble sausage in lightly greased skillet and brown. Add sliced zucchini, onion, jalapeño, and sauté. Remove from stove and mix in broth, cheese, cooked and drained macaroni. Bake at 350° for 25 minutes.

Clabber Creek Farm Cook Book

Baked Sliced Ham

1 (5-6-pound) canned ham
Whole cloves
1/4 cup honey
1/4 cup catsup
2 tablespoons prepared mustard
2 teaspoons minced onion
2 tablespoons Worcestershire sauce
1/4 teaspoon lemon peel
1/8 teaspoon ginger

Have butcher run the whole ham through his meat slicer. Set the gauge for slices of the thickness you wish. Have him push slices together and tie string securely once around sides and twice over top and bottom. Keep refrigerated until ready to bake. Press cloves in rows on top of ham slices. Place on a rack in a shallow baking pan.

HONEY GLAZE:
Mix together the honey, catsup, mustard, onion, Worcestershire sauce, lemon peel, and ginger. Spread over top and sides of ham. Bake in 350° oven about 1 hour.

Serve hot or cold. Remove string before serving. Makes 12-15 servings.

The Wonderful World of Honey

Ham Casserole

1 package frozen asparagus
1 cup cubed ham (or more)
1/4 cup grated cheese
2 tablespoons cut green pepper
2 tablespoons chopped onion
1 tablespoon minced parsley
1 tablespoon lemon juice
4 hard-cooked eggs, sliced
1 can cream of mushroom soup
1/2 cup light cream
2 slices toast, cubed

Cook asparagus, drain, and line a 1 1/2-quart casserole. Combine ham, grated cheese, green pepper, onion, parsley, and lemon juice. Alternate mixture in layers on asparagus, with hard-cooked eggs. Combine soup and light cream and pour over. Top with toast cubes. Bake 375° for 30 minutes.

Dixie Cookbook IV

Ham Loaf

1 1/2 pounds cured ham (raw)
1/2 pound fresh lean pork
Milk
1 egg, beaten

Grind ham and pork and mix together. Add egg and enough milk to moisten. Put in greased loaf pan.

DRESSING:
3 tablespoons flour
1/2 cup vinegar
1 1/2 cups brown sugar
1/2 cup water

Pour over loaf. Bake in moderate oven for 1 hour.

We were raised on this. It is sweet and wonderful. There is a lot of sauce that thickens when cold.

Perfectly Delicious

Ham Loaf and Mustard Sauce

1 1/4 pounds ground smoked ham
3/4 pound ground veal or ground beef
1 cup dry bread crumbs soaked in 1 cup milk
2 teaspoons dry mustard
2 tablespoons brown sugar
1/2 teaspoon pepper
2 eggs, slightly beaten

Mix all ingredients and let stand 1 hour or overnight if possible. Make into 2 loaves; bake 1 1/2 hours at 350°. Good plain or with a sauce such as:

GRAM'S HAM SAUCE WITH MUSTARD:
3 egg yolks
1 tablespoon flour
1/2 cup of canned undiluted Campbell's tomato soup
1/2 cup French's mustard
1/2 cup white vinegar
1/2 cup white sugar
1/2 cup vegetable/salad oil

Whisk egg yolk with flour until smooth. Combine all ingredients in top of a double boiler and whisk, over medium heat, till smooth and thickened. Cool before serving. Keeps well refrigerated.

A Great Taste of Arkansas

Barbecue Spareribs

4 pounds spareribs
1/2 cup chopped onion
2 cloves garlic
1 1/2 cups catsup
2 tablespoons vinegar
1 cup honey
1/2 teaspoon salt
1 teaspoon prepared mustard
1/2 teaspoon black pepper
2 tablespoons escoffier sauce or any steak sauce

Cut spareribs in serving-size portions. Simmer in enough water to cover plus 2 teaspoons salt for 1/2 hour. Mix the remaining ingredients and cook over low heat for 5-7 minutes. Drain ribs and place in baking pan. Pour sauce over ribs and bake in oven, 400°, for 45 minutes or until tender. Baste every 10 minutes with sauce. Makes 4-6 servings.

The Wonderful World of Honey

Stuffed Pork Chops

6 center-cut pork chops, about 1 1/2 inches thick
2 cups cornbread, crumbled
1 cup light bread, crumbled
1 can chicken broth
1 teaspoon sage
1/2 teaspoon salt
2 eggs
Pepper to taste
1/2 cup diced celery
1/2 cup diced onion

Mix stuffing ingredients together and stuff in pork chops. Roll pork chops in flour and brown in skillet. Fasten with toothpicks. Bake in roasting pan covered at 350° for two hours or until done. During the last half hour of cooking time, uncover roasting pan and thicken broth for gravy.

Thirty Years at the Mansion

Poultry

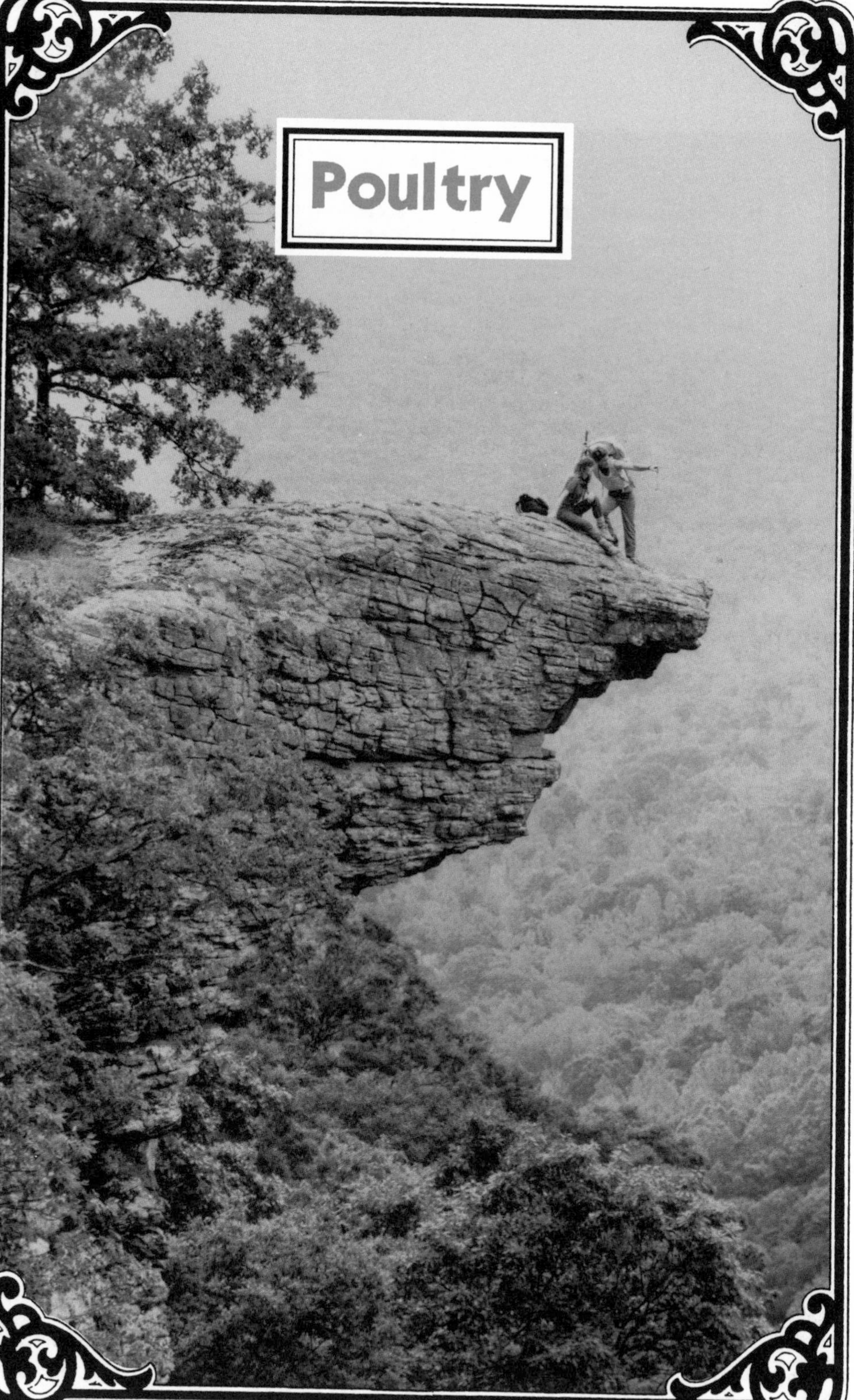

Whitaker Point in the Ozark Mountains near the Buffalo National River Park.

Champagne Chicken

2 tablespoons flour
1/2 teaspoon salt
1/4 teaspoon pepper
4 chicken breast halves, skinned and boned
2 tablespoons butter or margarine
1 tablespoon olive oil
3/4 cup champagne or white wine
3/4 cup sliced fresh mushrooms
1/2 cup whipping cream

Combine flour, salt, and pepper and rub all over chicken. Heat butter and oil in large skillet. Add chicken and brown about 5 minutes on each side. Add champagne and cook over medium heat 15 minutes or until done. Remove chicken and set aside. Add mushrooms and whipping cream to skillet. Cook over low heat, stirring constantly until thick. Add chicken long enough to heat through. Serves 4.

Arkansas Favorites Cookbook

Orange and Chicken Cashew

4 chicken breasts, (6 ounces)
1/4 cup flour
1 teaspoon salt
1 teaspoon paprika
1/4 cup butter
1 cup orange juice
1/4 cup toasted cashews or almonds

Dust chicken lightly in flour with salt and paprika. Sauté in butter until golden brown (turn only once). Add orange juice; cover and cook over low heat for 20 minutes. Uncover, remove chicken to a serving dish. Reduce liquid to a thickened sauce. Pour over chicken, sprinkle with nuts, and serve at once with rice.

Dixie Cook Book V

Chicken Breast Eden Isle

This is a recipe I devised when I was first preparing menus for the Inn. We wanted to stress Arkansas products where possible. It has stayed on the menu more than 20 years because of its popularity, and we still get requests for the recipe.

6 chicken breasts, halved, boned and skinned
Pepper to taste
6 slices bacon
1 package dried beef
2 cans cream of chicken soup
1 1/2 cups sour cream
1 package cream cheese

Pepper, do *not* salt chicken breasts. Wrap one slice bacon around each breast. Place layer of dried beef in bottom of baking dish. Place bacon-wrapped breasts in dish. Mix together chicken soup, sour cream, and cream cheese in mixer or food processor. Cover chicken breasts with mixture, and cover baking dish tightly with foil. Place in 325° oven 2 hours. When tender, remove foil and let brown well. Serve on a bed of rice. Serves 6.

Feasts of Eden

Quick Marinated Chicken

8 chicken breasts
1 bottle dark Wishbone Russian Dressing
1 package dry onion soup mix
1 (10-ounce) jar apricot, peach, or orange marmalade

Season breasts with salt and pepper. Combine rest of ingredients. Mix well. Layer half of sauce on bottom of baking dish; layer chicken on top. Pour remaining sauce over chicken. Marinate overnight, or at least 4-5 hours. Bake uncovered at 325° for 1 hour or until tender.

The Bonneville House Presents

Chicken and Dumplings

1 large fryer or 4 breasts
3 tablespoons butter
1 tablespoon salt

Boil chicken in approximately 2 quarts of salted water until tender. Remove chicken; strain, and reserve broth. Remove skin of chicken and bone. Cut meat into large pieces.

DUMPLINGS:
1 egg, slightly beaten
1/4 teaspoon salt
2 tablespoons butter
1 cup chicken broth (cooled)
2 cups flour (approximately)

Mix egg, salt, butter, and broth together. Add flour, mixing with a fork, a small amount at a time. Knead in flour until a stiff dough is formed. Roll out very thin. Cut in strips. Bring chicken broth to a boil. Pull apart and stretch strips of dough as you drop into broth. Reduce heat and cook about 10 minutes (covered), stirring occasionally. Add cut up chicken to dumplings and enjoy!. Serves 8-10.

Variation:

Pea Dumplings: If you don't have chicken but have left-over broth, make dumplings, and add a box of frozen peas. Cook until peas and dumplings are tender. Delicious!!

A Great Taste of Arkansas

Cherry Chicken

3 whole chicken breasts, halved
1/3 cup flour
1 1/2 teaspoons salt
1 1/2 teaspoons garlic salt
1 1/2 teaspoons paprika
1/4 cup oil
1 (16-ounce) can pitted dark sweet cherries
1 cup Sauterne, or other sweet dessert wine

Dredge chicken in mixture of flour, salt, garlic salt, and paprika. In a skillet, brown chicken in oil. Add cherries, including liquid, and wine; cover, and simmer about 1 hour. Serve over hot rice.

Celebration

Sunday School Chicken

1 whole fryer
1 pound fresh carrots
4 potatoes, unpeeled
4 onions
1 pound fresh mushrooms
Salt and pepper to taste

Scrub vegetables. Place chicken and vegetables in large roaster; salt and pepper to taste and cover. Add no water. Place in cold oven. Turn thermostat to 250° when you leave for Sunday School and enjoy a delicious meal when you return from church. Alter proportions as needed.

Pulaski Heights Baptist Church Cookbook

Chicken Croquettes

2 (1 1/2 - 2-pound) broilers
Boiling, salted water
1 tablespoon minced onion
1/4 cup butter
1/3 cup flour
1 1/2 teaspoons salt
1/4 teaspoon pepper
2 cups milk
1 egg, beaten
1 1/2 cups bread crumbs
Pure vegetable oil
3 tablespoons butter
3 tablespoons flour
1/2 teaspoon curry powder
1/4 teaspoon salt
1 1/2 cups chicken broth

Cook broilers in water to cover for 45 minutes, or until tender. Reserve broth—you should have 6 cups. Remove chicken from bones; chop.

Sauté onion in 1/4 cup butter until soft. Stir in flour, salt and pepper. Cook until bubbly; remove from heat. Stir in milk. Cook on medium, stirring constantly, until thickened and bubbly. Add chicken. Spread in shallow pan; cover and chill several hours.

Divide mixture into 8 portions. Shape each into a round, slightly tapered shape. Dip each croquette into egg, then roll in crumbs to coat evenly. Let dry about 15 minutes.

Fill deep fat fryer or large saucepan 2/3 full of oil. Heat to 375°. Fry croquettes for 2-3 minutes until golden brown; drain.

Melt 3 tablespoons butter in saucepan; add flour, curry powder and salt. Cook 1 minute. Add broth and stir until thickened and bubbly. Serve over warm croquettes.

Serves 6.

High Cotton Cookin'

Chicken Crepes

Served regularly in Victorian Sampler Tea Room in Eureka Springs.

2 tablespoons butter
1 tablespoon minced onion
2 tablespoons flour
1 1/2 cups half cream, half milk
1 cups diced chicken
1/4 cup sherry or white wine
1/4 cup grated Parmesan cheese
1/4 cup sliced almonds
6 or 8 Basic Crepes

Melt butter. Add onion and sauté until yellow. Add flour and cook until thick and smooth. Add milk and cream, stirring until medium thick sauce is made. Add chicken and sherry to half the sauce. Place 2 tablespoons mixture in each crepe and roll. Place in buttered pan, seam-side-down. Cover with remaining sauce, sprinkle with cheese and almonds. Bake at 450° until brown. Makes 6 crepes.

Variation: Substitute crab, shrimp, scallops or combination instead of chicken.

BASIC CREPES:

3 eggs
1 1/3 cups milk
1 cup Wondra instant blending flour
1/4 teaspoon salt
Vegetable oil

Combine all ingredients except oil, using blender. Batter should be smooth. Let stand 30 minutes (important for lighter and tender crepe). Place a greased crepe pan or 8-inch skillet over moderately high heat until hot. Brush pan lightly with oil. Pour 2-3 tablespoons crepe batter in center. Tilt pan and swirl batter to cover and form a thin crepe. Pour excess back in bowl. Cook crepe 30-45 seconds until light brown. Turn and cook briefly on other side. Remove to plate and trim any ragged edges. Cool and separate with wax paper until ready to use.

Very versatile, can be made ahead and frozen.

Victorian Sampler

Chicken Breasts in Cream Sauce

6 chicken breasts
1/2 cup chopped onions
1 clove minced garlic
1 cup heavy cream
1 cup chicken broth
2 teaspoons salt
1 teaspoon white pepper
1 tablespoon Worcestershire
2 tablespoons flour
1/2 cup water

Brown chicken breasts. Place breasts in oven dish. Add remaining ingredients except for flour and water, and bake 2 hours in 300° oven. After baking, remove breasts; strain juices into saucepan. Add 2 tablespoons flour and 1/2 cup water. Mix with whisk until thickened. Add milk if too thick. Pour sauce over breasts. Garnish with parsley or rosemary.

Serves 6.

Nibbles Ooo La La

Poppy Seed Chicken

12 chicken breasts, boiled and boned
2 cans cream of chicken soup
1 1/2 pints sour cream
1/4 cup sherry
Salt and pepper
35-40 Ritz Crackers, crumbled
2 tablespoons poppy seeds
6 tablespoons butter, melted

In 2 (2-quart) casserole dishes or 1 large baking dish, put layer of coarsely chopped chicken. Mix soup, sour cream and sherry, and season to taste with salt and pepper. Pour over chicken. Top with cracker crumbs mixed with poppy seeds. Pour melted butter over crumbs. Bake at 350° for 30 minutes. Can make a day ahead. Serves 12.

Southern Accent

Chicken Loaf

Delicious! The best chicken loaf I've ever eaten.

2 cups cooked chicken
3/4 cups milk
1 1/2 cups soft bread crumbs
2 tablespoons butter or margarine
1 small onion, chopped
1 stalk of celery with leaves, chopped
2 sprigs of parsley, chopped
1 teaspoon salt
2 eggs, beaten
1/8 teaspoon black pepper

Start oven at 375°. Cut chicken in small pieces. Heat milk until film wrinkles over top, then pour it over bread crumbs. Add butter and let stand about 5 minutes.

Meanwhile, mix onion, celery, and parsley with chicken. Season with salt and pepper. Beat eggs slightly, and stir into bread and milk mixture. Add chicken and mix thoroughly. Pour into greased medium casserole. Set in pan of warm water in the oven and bake about 45 minutes, or until a silver knife comes out clean when tested in center of loaf. Garnish with a border of sliced olives on platter, and serve with following sauce.

OLIVE SAUCE:

1/4 cup butter or margarine
2 sprigs parsley, minced
1 small onion, chopped
1 tablespoon flour
1 cup chicken broth
Salt, pepper, nutmeg
8-10 olives, sliced

Melt butter and in it cook the parsley and onion slightly (do not brown). Mix flour in and gradually add broth. Cook, stirring constantly, until sauce is creamy and slightly thick. Season with salt, pepper, nutmeg, and add olives. Bring to a boil and serve. Serves 4 generously.

Perfectly Delicious

Just south of Paris is the highest land in Arkansas, Mount Magazine, which rises to 2,750 feet. The view from its summit offers a commanding panorama of the surrounding Ozark National Forest.

Boneless Cheesy Chicken Breasts

6 chicken breasts, boneless
6 (4x4-inch) slices Swiss cheese
1 can cream of chicken soup, undiluted
1/2 cup white wine
1 cup Pepperidge Farm Herb-Seasoned Stuffing Mix, crushed
1/4 cup butter or margarine, melted

Arrange chicken in a lightly greased 9x13-inch baking dish. Top with cheese slices. Combine soup and wine, stirring well. Spoon sauce evenly over chicken and sprinkle with stuffing mix. Drizzle butter over crumbs. Bake at 350° for 45-55 minutes. Yield: 4-6 servings.

Betty is Still "Winking" at Cooking

Chicken-Spaghetti Casserole

1/2 cup diced celery
1/2 cup chopped onion
1/4 cup chopped bell pepper
2 cups chicken broth
1 (14 1/2-ounce) can tomatoes
1 (10 3/4-ounce) can mushroom soup
Salt and pepper to taste
2 cups diced, cooked chicken
1 (8-ounce) package thin spaghetti, cooked and drained

In large saucepan simmer celery, onion, and bell pepper in chicken broth until tender. Add tomatoes and soup; season to taste; bring to a boil. Remove from heat; fold in chicken and spaghetti; pour into a greased 9x13-inch baked dish; top with cheese. Bake at 400° until cheese melts.

Celebration

Sadie's Deep Dish Chicken Pot Pie

1/2 cup celery, chopped fine
1/4 cup onion, chopped fine
4 tablespoons butter
4 tablespoons flour
2 cups chicken stock
Salt and pepper
2 cups cubed, cooked chicken

Sauté celery and onion in butter until tender. Add flour and mix well. Gradually add stock, stirring and cook slowly until medium thick. Season to taste and set aside to cool.

PASTRY:
3 cups flour
1 1/2 teaspoons salt
6 heaping tablespoons shortening

Mix until dough looks like coarse meal. Sprinkle with ice water (10-12 teaspoons) until dough sticks together. Roll into ball and divide into two parts. On floured board, roll 1 part of dough to 1/4 inch thick. Line a 2-quart round baking dish with pastry, allowing it to extend a little over the sides. Add chicken and sauce. Roll other part of dough and place over top of baking dish. Handle pastry carefully to avoid holes. Trim any excess crust around edge of dish. Moisten edges of crust with ice water and stick together. Make several slashes in top crust to allow steam to escape while cooking. Bake at 350° for 1 hour.

Southern Accent

Mabel's Improved Chicken Barbecue Sauce

1 (6-ounce) can frozen lemonade concentrate
1 (6-ounce) can frozen orange juice concentrate
3 ounces wine vinegar
1 teaspoon garlic powder
1 rounded tablespoon oregano
1/2 teaspoon pepper or to taste
1 teaspoon salt or to taste
4 ounces olive oil, extra virgin or pure

Thaw lemonade and orange juice concentrate and blend with remaining ingredients. Marinate **1 (3 1/2 - 4-pound) chicken** 2 hours or overnight and then barbecue. Apply sauce generously while barbecuing.

The Sicilian-American Cookbook

Lemon Chicken for the Grill

2 chickens, cut in pieces
1 cup vegetable oil
1 tablespoon salt
2 teaspoons onion powder
1/2 teaspoon thyme
1/2 cup lemon juice
1 teaspoon paprika
2 teaspoons crushed basil
1/2 teaspoon garlic powder

Place chicken in 13x9-inch glass dish. Combine remaining ingredients, blending well. Pour over meat and cover tightly. Chill 6 hours, turning chicken occasionally. Remove from refrigerator 1 hour before grilling. Cook 20-25 minutes on medium heat on grill, basting often and turning for 20 minutes.

Pulaski Heights Baptist Church Cookbook

Oven-Fried Chicken

1 cup cornflake crumbs
1 teaspoon paprika
1/2 teaspoon garlic powder
1/4 teaspoon ground thyme
1/4 teaspoon red pepper
6 chicken breast halves, skinned
1/4 cup buttermilk

Combine first 5 ingredients in plastic bag. Shake to mix well. Brush both sides of chicken with buttermilk. Place in bag of crumbs and shake to coat. Place chicken on broiler pan which has been sprayed with vegetable spray. Bake at 400° for 45 minutes or until done. Yield: 6 servings.

Per Serving: Calories 200; Cholesterol 75mg; Fat 3gm; Sodium 110mg; ADA Exchange Value: 3 meats

Take It To Heart

Broccoli Chicken Casserole

1 pound boneless chicken breast, cut in small pieces
1/2 onion, chopped
2 cups rice
1 can cream of mushroom soup
1 package frozen chopped broccoli
4 ounces chicken stock
1 (8-ounce) carton sour cream
1 (8-ounce) package cream cheese
6 ounces sharp Cheddar cheese, shredded

Stir-fry chicken pieces in wok or skillet. Quick fry onion in a little butter until tender. Prepare rice according to package directions. Combine rice, chicken, soup, onion, broccoli, and chicken stock; mix. Bake at 350° for 30 minutes. Remove from oven. Combine sour cream and cream cheese; add to hot mixture. Bake 10 minutes more. Remove from oven; spread Cheddar cheese on top. Broil until cheese is melted. Serve.

Note: Other vegetables may be substituted for broccoli, if desired.

Cooking For Good Measure

Sour Cream Chicken Breasts

6 chicken breasts
1 can mushroom soup
1 (3-ounce) can mushrooms or 1/2 cup fresh mushrooms
1 cup sour cream
1/4 cup sherry or white wine (optional)
Hot cooked rice

Place chicken breasts in baking dish, skin-side-up. Combine soup, mushrooms, sour cream, and sherry. Mix well and pour over chicken. Bake, uncovered, at 325° for 1 1/2 hours or until fork tender. Serve over rice.

Victorian Sampler

Chicken Broccoli

2 carrots, sliced
1 onion, diced
2 stalks celery, diced
1/2 cup chicken broth
Salt to taste
1 fryer, cooked and diced
2 cans cream of mushroom soup
2 (8-ounce) cartons sour cream
2 (10-ounce) packages frozen chopped broccoli
Grated Cheddar cheese
Lemon pepper
Slivered almonds

Cook carrots, onion, and celery in chicken broth, adding water if necessary. Add salt and chicken. Combine soup and sour cream in a separate bowl. Layer chicken, broccoli, soup mixture and cheese in a 2-quart casserole, sprinkling each layer with lemon pepper. Bake at 350° for 45 minutes. Sprinkle almonds on top and bake 10 minutes longer. Serves 6-8.

Favorite Recipes from Associated Women for Harding

Chicken and Artichoke Hearts

1 large yellow onion, chopped coarse
2 tablespoons olive oil, extra virgin or pure
2 large fresh eggs, beaten
2 cups chicken broth
1/2 teaspoon flaked red pepper, more if desired
3/4 teaspoon rosemary leaves, crushed
1 teaspoon oregano
1/2 teaspoon pepper
Salt to taste
1/4 cup parsley, chopped coarse
1 cup Parmesan cheese, grated
3 cups cooked chicken, cubed
1 (14-ounce) can artichoke hearts, quartered and drained
1 (4-ounce) jar pimentos, chopped coarse
3 large cloves garlic, chopped fine

Preheat oven to 350°. Lightly brown onions in olive oil; retain. In a large mixing bowl, blend eggs, broth, spices, parsley, cheese and onions. Add remaining ingredients and blend thoroughly. Pour mixture into a lightly greased 9x11x2-inch pan and bake 40 minutes. Serve piping hot over rice. Use remaining broth for egg drop soup. Yields 8 servings.

Wine selection: California Inglenook Savignon Blanc, a dry white.

The Sicilian-American Cookbook

Chicken Provençale

Provençal, a French term, generally means a dish is made with olive oil, garlic and tomatoes. This particular dish is simple and quite elegant, a good company dish as well as a last minute meal.

2 tablespoons olive oil
2 cloves garlic, minced
1 pound of skinless, boneless chicken breasts, cut into 1-inch chunks
2 (14 1/2-ounce) cans tomatoes, chopped
1/4 teaspoon salt (optional)
2 teaspoons dried basil
1 (10-ounce) package of chopped frozen spinach
2 cups uncooked medium flat egg or spinach noodles

In a 4 to 5-quart pan, heat oil over medium-high heat. Add garlic and chicken and sauté 5 minutes or until chicken is no longer pink. Add canned tomatoes and their liquid; season. Turn heat to high and bring mixture to a boil. Add frozen spinach. When spinach has separated, add noodles. Stir gently to cover noodles with liquid. Add a small amount of water if necessary. Bring to boil and reduce heat. Simmer for 8-10 minutes or until noodles are tender. Yields 4-6 servings.

Variations: Use fresh finely chopped spinach, or use frozen Italian green beans instead of spinach.

When dish is cooked, add frozen baby green peas. Stir until they are heated, but retain their bright green color.

Eating Healthy in the Fast Lane

Arkansas Wine Country, near the town of Altus, was settled by Swiss-German immigrants because it reminded them of the wine-growing region of their homeland. Tours and tastings are available from vineyards that produce some of America's finest wines.

Chicken Rotel

1 medium hen
2 large bell peppers, chopped
2 large onions, chopped
1 1/2 sticks butter
1 (7-ounce) package vermicelli
1 (10-ounce) can Rotel tomatoes
2 tablespoons Worcestershire
2 pounds Velveeta cheese
1 (17-ounce) can tiny English peas

Season and cook hen in enough water to have at least 1 1/2 quarts broth. Sauté peppers and onions in butter. Cook vermicelli in 1 1/2 quarts broth and leave it in the broth. Add tomatoes and half the juice; add Worcestershire and cook until thick. Cut up cheese, add to vermicelli mixture and stir until melted. Add drained peas and the onion mixture. Remove chicken from bone, cut into pieces and add to vermicelli mixture. Salt and pepper well. Place in 2 or 3-quart casserole. Bake at 350° about 30-40 minutes.

High Cotton Cookin'

Mexi-Chicken Casserole

1 (8-ounce) can cream of mushroom soup
1 (8-ounce) can cream of chicken soup
1 onion, diced
1 cup green chilies, diced
1 tablespoon garlic, curshed
1/2 cup medium picante sauce
1 teaspoon ground cumin
2 cups white meat chicken, cooked, boned and skinned
9 jumbo flour tortillas
1 cup low fat Cheddar/ mozzarella cheese mixture

In a mixing bowl combine soups, onion, chilies, garlic, picante, and cumin. Add chicken and mix thoroughly. Spray 9x13-inch casserole dish with cooking spray. Arrange 3 tortillas on bottom of pan and cover with half the chicken mixture. Repeat layering with tortillas and chicken. Sprinkle cheese on top and bake at 350° until cheese melts and casserole is bubbly (about 25 minutes). Serves 8.

Amount per serving: Calories 431; Grams of fat 14; Cholesterol 68mg; Sodium 640mg; % of Fat 29%

Eat To Your Heart's Content, Too!

Chicken Enchiladas

Cooking oil
2 (4-ounce) cans green chilies
1 large clove garlic, minced
1 (28-ounce) can tomatoes
2 cups chopped onion
2 teaspoons salt
1/2 teaspoon oregano
3 cups shredded, cooked chicken
2 cups dairy sour cream
2 cups grated Cheddar cheese
15 corn tortillas

Preheat oil in skillet. Chop chilies after removing seeds; sauté with minced garlic in oil. Drain and break up tomatoes; reserve 1/2 cup liquid. To chilies and garlic add tomatoes, onion, 1 teaspoon salt, oregano, and reserved tomato liquid. Simmer uncovered until thick, about 30 minutes. Remove from skillet and set aside.

Combine chicken with sour cream, grated cheese, and other teaspoon salt. Heat 1/3 cup oil; dip tortillas in oil until they become limp. Drain well on paper towels.

Fill tortillas with chicken mixture; roll up and arrange side-by-side, seam down, in 9x13x2-inch baking dish. Pour chili sauce over enchiladas and bake at 250° until heated through, about 20 minutes. Yields 15 enchiladas.

Thirty Years at the Mansion

Mexican Chicken

2 pounds chicken, cooked and boned
1 onion, chopped
1 (5 3/4-ounce) bag nacho cheese Dorito chips, crushed
1 can cream of chicken soup, undiluted
1/2 pound grated American cheese
1/2 can Rotel tomatoes
1 can cream of mushroom soup, undiluted

Layer all ingredients in greased 9x13-inch casserole dish, beginning at top of list. Bake uncovered at 350° for 30 minutes.

Classroom Classics

Chinese Egg Rolls

MARINADE:

1/3 cup orange juice
1/4 cup teriyaki sauce
1 teaspoon sesame oil
1/4 teaspoon each cayenne pepper, ground ginger, and garlic
2 teaspoons brown sugar

INSIDES:

1 chicken breast, boned, skinned, and diced (uncooked)
4 carrots, shredded
3 celery ribs, sliced thin
1 package egg roll wrappers

Marinate the insides in the marinade for 30 minutes or overnight. Heat a non-stick skillet sprayed with cooking spray over medium heat. Cook in small batches till chicken is done. Roll into egg roll wrapper, spray the egg roll with cooking spray, covering all sides, and bake at 400° for 10-12 minutes or till golden. Serves 12.

Amount per serving: Calories 75; Grams of fat 1.9; Cholesterol 8mg; Sodium 333mg; % of Fat 23%

Eat To Your Heart's Content, Too!

Stir-Fry Chicken

- 2 whole boneless chicken breasts
- 3 tablespoons cornstarch
- 4 tablespoons soy sauce
- 1 stalk fresh broccoli
- 1 small onion, thinly sliced separated into rings
- 2 tablespoons peanut oil
- 1/4 pound mushrooms, sliced
- 2 cups fresh bean sprouts
- 1 (8-ounce) can water chestnuts, drained, sliced
- 1 cup chicken broth

Cut chicken into thin slices. In small bowl combine cornstarch and soy sauce; stir in chicken; stir to coat; marinate 15 minutes. Cut off broccoli flowerets; thinly pare stalks; slice inner stalk into thin slices. Heat oil in wok or deep skillet over high heat. Add chicken; stir-fry until browned; remove; set aside. Add broccoli and onion; stir-fry 2 minutes; add mushrooms, bean sprouts, water chestnuts and chicken. Stir in broth; cover and cook gently 5 minutes or until vegetables are crisp-tender. Serve over hot rice.

Celebration

Sweet 'n' Sour Sauce

- 1/2 cup pineapple juice
- 2 tablespoon lemon juice
- 1 tablespoon vinegar
- 2 tablespoons brown sugar
- 1 tablespoon soy sauce
- 1 tablespoon cornstarch
- 1/4 teaspoon powdered ginger
- 1/4 green pepper, chopped
- 1 (9-ounce) can pineapple tidbits, undrained

Combine all ingredients except for undrained pineapple tidbits and green pepper in a blender. Blend until mixed. Pour mixture into saucepan and add peppers and pineapple. Cook over moderate heat until thick and clear. Serve over roast lean pork or poultry. Serves 6.

Amount per serving: Calories 74; Grams of fat .02; Cholesterol 0mg; Sodium 151mg; % of Fat less than 1 %

Eat To Your Heart's Content, Too!

Roast Turkey

Regardless of how many times we've roasted turkey, the long delay between times helps us to forget exactly how we did it last time. This method can be found in the files of many Arkansas families who witness to its reliability. Good turkeys can be roasted by other methods, but with any method, the secret of tenderness and juiciness is roasting enough but not too much. Overcooking is the prime cause of dry breast meat.

To prepare turkey for roasting, remove any pinfeathers from the outside of the bird and bits of lung, liver, etc., from cavity. At this time (or preferably the day before) put the gizzard, heart, and neck in 1-2 quarts of water with salt and a small onion. Cover and simmer 2-3 hours, until gizzard is fork-tender, adding liver 20 minutes before the end of cooking time. When tender, cool, cover, and refrigerate.

Rinse turkey both inside and out with cold water. Drain, then pat dry with paper towels or a soft cloth. Sprinkle inside of cavity with salt and rub outside with soft unsalted shortening.

Stuff now if you wish to stuff your bird; though USDA researchers recommend cooking dressing separately to reduce necessary cooking time. Tie legs of stuffed or unstuffed turkey to tail with soft string; or if there is a bridge of skin under abdominal opening, pack legs under this bridge. Trim off excess neck skin, leaving just enough to fold neatly under the bird. Lay wings flat against sides and tie in place or twist wing tips under back of turkey. If you have a meat thermometer, insert it in the center of the inner portion of the thigh. Make sure that the bulb (or tip) is centered in the meaty section, not touching bone.

Set your oven to 325° for slow cooking. Place the bird on a greased rack in an open roasting pan. Do not sear and do not add water. (Turkeys are usually roasted breast up; but, if the elegant appearance of a beautifully roasted bird is not required, roasting it breast down results in more moist breast meat, because the dark meat bastes the breast as it roasts.)

CONTINUED

Cover with a fat-moistened cheese cloth. Place a loose tent of foil over the turkey and slide it into the oven.

When the turkey is about two-thirds done, release the skin or string that holds the legs in place to allow heat to reach inside thigh. While you have the turkey out of the oven, rub the skin with margarine. Roast until meat thermometer registers 180°-185°. Your turkey is done when the meat on the drumstick feels very soft when pressed between your fingers (protected by a paper towel or cloth).

Home for the Holidays

Turkey Cutlets

4 turkey breast cutlets
1/2 cup low-fat milk
1 tablespoon Dijon mustard
1/2 cup dry bread crumbs
3 tablespoons olive oil
2 large cloves garlic, crushed
1/2 pound fresh spinach, chopped
2 large tomatoes, cut in chunks
1/4 teaspoon salt
1/4 teaspoon pepper
1/4 cup imitation mozzarella cheese, grated

Put turkey cutlets between 2 sheets of wax paper and pound with rolling pin to 1/4 inch thick. Dip cutlets into milk and mustard mixture, then into bread crumbs. Heat 2 tablespoons oil in skillet and add cutlets. Cook 4-5 minutes on each side. Remove from heat, put on oven-proof plate, and keep warm.

Wipe out skillet, add 1 tablespoon olive oil, and heat; add garlic and cook about 2 minutes. Add spinach, tomatoes, salt, and pepper. Cook about 2 more minutes until spinach is wilted, stirring frequently. Sprinkle turkey with mozzarella; put under broiler about 30 seconds to melt cheese. Serve turkey with spinach and tomatoes. Serves 4.

Cooking to Your Heart's Content

Turkey-Vegetable Stir-Fry

1 (4-ounce) can sliced mushrooms, undrained
1 large onion, coarsely chopped
2 small green peppers, cut into 1-inch strips
3 cups cooked turkey, cut into 1-inch pieces
1 (8-ounce) can water chestnuts, sliced and drained
1/4 cup + 1 tablespoon lite soy sauce
2 teaspoons cornstarch
1/2 teaspoon sugar
1/8 teaspoon red pepper
3 cups cooked rice, unsalted

Drain mushrooms, reserving liquid; set aside. Spray wok or skillet with vegetable spray and allow to heat at medium high (325°) for 1 minute. Add onion and green pepper to wok: stir-fry 3-4 minutes or until vegetables are crisp-tender. Push up to sides of wok and add turkey, sliced mushrooms, and water chestnuts. Heat thoroughly. Combine lite soy sauce, reserved mushroom liquid, cornstarch, sugar and red pepper; mix well.

Reduce heat to low (225°), simmer 2-3 minutes or until slightly thickened. Serve over rice. Yield: 6 servings.

Per Serving (with 1/2 cup unsalted rice): Calories 230; Cholesterol 45mg; Fat 2gm; Sodium 560mg; ADA Exchange Value: 1 meat, 2 starches

Take It To Heart

Turkey Chili

3 pounds ground turkey
2 onions, diced
8 tomatoes, diced
1 (8-ounce) can tomato sauce
1 (8-ounce) can Rotel tomatoes
2 cups kidney beans
2 tablespoons garlic
8 ounces fresh mushrooms, diced
Splash Tabasco and Worcestershire
1 package taco seasoning
1 red bell pepper, diced
1 (16-ounce) can Budweiser beer
1 - 2 tablespoons chili powder
2 1/2 ounces shredded Lite Line Cheddar cheese (approximately 1 tablespoon for each serving)

Brown ground turkey and onions in large pan. Slice and dice all veggies, add all remaining ingredients (except cheese) to browned mixture. Cook for approximately 2 hours over low heat. Stir every 15-20 minutes. When ready to serve, sprinkle shredded cheese on top. Serves 20.

Note: Chili always tastes better after being refrigerated for 24-36 hours. Let those flavors mingle!

Amount per serving: Calories 133; Grams of fat 1.72; Cholesterol 41.4mg; Sodium 232mg; % of Fat 12%

Eat To Your Heart's Content!

"The Duck Stops Here" proclaims a Stuttgart T-shirt, and indeed the ducks do. It is situated in the Mississippi River Flyway, the main flight path for waterfowl going south for the winter. Because of its many rice fields, Stuttgart is known as "the rice and duck capital of the world."

Cornish Hens Imperial

CORNISH HENS:

2 large Cornish hens, thawed and halved
1 1/2 teaspoons garlic onion magic

SPICY TOMATO WINE SAUCE:

1/2 cup red sweet wine
1 (8-ounce) can tomato sauce
1/2 cup cocktail sauce with horseradish
2 or 3 drops hot sauce or to taste
1 teaspoon tarragon, dried and crushed
1/2 teaspoon garlic onion magic
1/2 teaspoon onion and garlic powder
1/3 cup Parmesan cheese, grated

Line broiler pan with heavy foil. Wash Cornish hens and cut in half. Rub all sides with garlic onion magic. Spray with butter-flavor cooking spray. Broil until almost tender, 15 minutes, 4 inches from coil. Make Spicy Tomato Wine Sauce while hen halves are cooking. Brush heavily on both sides and finish broiling just until tender. (The halves will be cooked more later.) Cool and refrigerate covered until total preparation and assembling time.

SEAFOOD FILLING:

1/2 pound imitation crab blend
1/4 pound baby shrimp, fresh or frozen
1 cup coarse crumbled wheat bread crumbs
1/4 cup chopped onions
1/4 cup diced celery
1/2 teaspoon dried parsley flakes
1/4 cup prepared Butter Buds or melted margarine
1 tablespoon sweet vermouth or Madeira wine
1 or 2 drops hot sauce, if desired

In a medium bowl, shred the crab blend, mix in baby shrimp, reserving a few to top each serving. Blend in the bread crumbs,

CONTINUED

onions, celery, parsley, Butter Buds or melted margarine, wine and hot sauce. Mix well with fork. Cover and reserve until 1 1/2 hours prior to serving.

Preheat oven to 325°. Cover a broiler pan with heavy foil. Arrange Cornish hens in pan, brushing both sides with Spicy Tomato Wine Sauce. Turn cavity-side up. Divide dressing between the four halves. Spoon Spicy Tomato Wine Sauce over dressing and each bird. Cover lightly with foil. Place on center rack of oven and reheat for 25 minutes, removing foil, and continue to heat for 30 more minutes. Depending on varying oven temperatures, the oven temperature may have to be increased to 350°. Brush with warm sauce just prior to serving. Arrange a few shrimp on the top of each serving and sprinkle with Parmesan cheese. Serves 4.

A Kaleidoscope of Creative Healthy Cooking

Honeyed Duck

1 duck
2 1/8 teaspoons salt
1 teaspoon ground ginger
1 teaspoon ground basil
1/2 teaspoon pepper
3/4 cup honey
1/4 cup butter (or margarine)
3 tablespoons orange juice
2 teaspoons lemon juice
1 teaspoon orange peel
1/8 teaspoon dry mustard
1/2 teaspoon cornstarch
2 oranges (for garnish)

Clean duck and dry thoroughly inside and out. Combine 2 teaspoons salt, ginger, basil, and pepper. Rub half of mixture on inside of duck. Heat honey, butter, orange juice, lemon juice, orange peel, mustard, and 1/8 teaspoon salt together until butter melts. Rub 2-3 tablespoons on inside of duck. Truss duck. Rub remaining seasoning mixture on outside of duck. Place duck on a large piece of aluminum foil. Pour remaining honey mixture over duck. Wrap and roast in a slow over, 325°, for 1 3/4 hours.

Unwrap. Baste with drippings for 20-25 minutes or until brown. Place duck on platter. Combine cornstarch with a little cold water; add to drippings. Stir and heat to boiling. Serve with duck.

The Wonderful World of Honey

Marinated Duck Breasts

4 boneless duck breasts
1/2 cup Italian dressing
1 tablespoon Worcestershire sauce
Juice of one lemon
1/4 teaspoon garlic powder
1/4 teaspoon ground cloves
Bacon slices

Soak duck in salt water for 3 hours. Remove from water and drain on paper towel, pat dry and place in shallow pan. Combine all ingredients, pour over duck breasts and marinate for 4 hours. Wrap each breast in bacon and secure with toothpick. Cook on grill over a slow fire 7 minutes per side, or until bacon is done.

The Farmer's Daughters

Duck and Wild Rice Casserole

2 medium ducks (3 cups cubed meat)
3 stalks celery
1 onion, halved
Salt
Pepper
1 (6-ounce) package seasoned wild and long-grain rice
1/2 cup oleo
1/2 cup chopped onion
1/4 cup flour
4 ounces sliced mushrooms
1 1/2 cups half-and-half cream
1 tablespoon chopped parsley
Slivered almonds

Boil ducks for 1 hour (or until tender) in water to cover, with celery, onion halves, salt and pepper; remove and cube meat. Reserve broth. Cook the rice according to the package directions.

Melt oleo; sauté onion; stir in the flour. Drain mushrooms, reserving broth; add mushrooms to the onion mixture. Add enough duck broth to the mushroom broth to make 1 1/2 cups of liquid; stir this into the onion mixture.

Omitting almonds, add remaining ingredients plus 1 1/2 teaspoons salt and 1/4 teaspoon pepper. Put into greased 2-quart casserole. Sprinkle almonds on top.

Bake covered, at 350° for 15-20 minutes. Uncover and bake for 5-10 more minutes, or until very hot. (If the casserole has been refrigerated it will take longer to heat.) If you don't have ducks, try substituting chicken—it's still good! Serves 6.

This recipe is so delicious that its fame is widespread. Certainly no collection of Pine Bluff's favorite recipes would be complete without it.

Southern Accent

Marvelous Mallard

Ducks (I allow 2 for 3 people)
Wishbone Italian Dressing
Worcestershire sauce
Soy sauce
Lemon pepper
Garlic salt
Onion (celery, apple)
Add fruit juices or wine

Place ducks in pan breast-side-up. Pour dressing over each duck. Sprinkle with next four ingredients. Let ducks marinate overnight (or at least a couple of hours).

Chop onion and whatever and place in pan. Add 1/2 inch water. Bake at 500° until breasts are brown (about 20 minutes). Turn ducks over and bake until backs are brown. Cover and cook 3 hours at 250°-300°. Baste every 30 minutes. Serve with hot fruit and add can juice to marinade.

Classroom Classics

The Natural State has over 2 1/2 million acres of national forest lands, 9,700 miles of streams and rivers, and over 500,000 acres of surface water comprising 11 big lakes and hundreds of smaller ones. The 65,000-acre Felsenthal National Wildlife Refuge in south central Arkansas features the world's largest greentree reservoir. No wonder there is such great hunting and year-round fishing.

Seafood

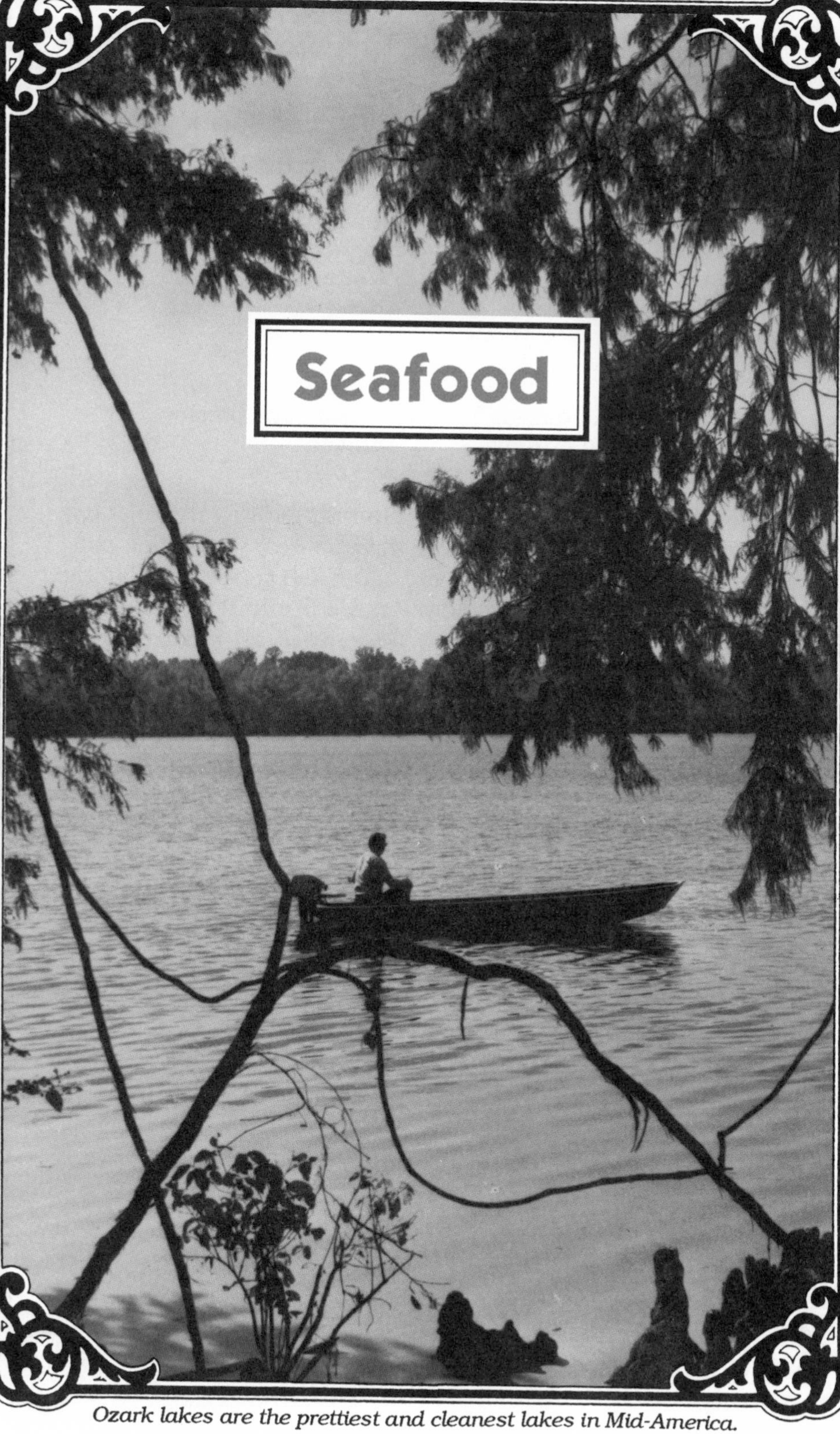

Ozark lakes are the prettiest and cleanest lakes in Mid-America.

Sautéed Flounder Fillets

4 flounder fillets (may substitute sole, catfish or turbo)
1 large egg, beaten in 1/4 cup milk
Salt and pepper to taste
Seasoned salt
1/4 cup pure olive oil

BREADING:
1/3 cup Parmesan cheese
2/3 cup dry bread crumbs
1 teaspoon garlic powder
2 tablespoons parsley, minced

Season flounder fillets to taste. Dip in egg mix and then coat with crumb mix. Shake off excess. In a heavy nonstick skillet over medium heat, add oil and sauté fish gently until lightly brown. Turn and cook an additional 2-3 minutes. Drain on paper towels and keep warm. Serve with an Italian veggie frittata and a fresh lettuce and onion salad. Yields 4 servings.

Wine selection: Centine Bianco, a dry white with a touch of spritziness.

The Sicilian-American Cookbook

Oven-Poached Rainbow Trout with Cucumber-Dill Cloud

Rainbow trout is one of our guests' all-time favorite entrées. Partly this is because we serve it only when we can get it really fresh-fresh. There are those who still like their trout dipped in milk, rolled in cornmeal and pan-fried, a classic Ozark treatment, but we prefer the sweet and delicate flavor of this oven-poached trout. With white wine for a poaching liquid and a grated cucumber and fresh dill garnish, this recipe fairly sparkles.

4 small rainbow trout, about 10 ounces each
1/2 cup white wine
1 cup water
Juice of 2 lemons
Paprika

Preheat oven to 325°. Wash and pat dry the rainbow trout; place them in a buttered baking dish and pour over them the wine and water; sprinkle with lemon juice and paprika.

Bake for 35-40 minutes, or until fish is firm to the touch a flakes easily with a fork.

Gently spoon Cucumber-Dill Cloud over each trout and serve, garnished with a large sprig of fresh parsley. A tomato provençal and a heap of tiny steamed and buttered new potatoes works very well with this, as with so many fish dishes.

CUCUMBER-DILL CLOUD:
1/2 cup sour cream
1/4 cup plain yogurt
1 teaspoon Tamari soy sauce
1 tablespoon minced fresh dill (or 1 teaspoon dried)
1/4 cup finely grated cucumber

Blend together well, preferably several hours in advance so flavors have a chance to marry. Serves 4.

The Dairy Hollow House Cookbook

Mammoth Bull Shoals Lake boasts 1,050 miles of shoreline; its neighbor Lake Norfork, 550.

Catfish Sesame

Crispy and flavorful

3 pounds fresh or frozen catfish fillets or steaks
3 cups water
1/4 cup vinegar
1 cup fine dry bread crumbs
3 tablespoons sesame seeds
2 tablespoons Greek seasoning
1/8 teaspoon white pepper
1 teaspoon salt
1/4 cup all-purpose flour
1 egg, beaten
2 tablespoons milk
Vegetable oil
Lemon wedges

Place catfish in a bowl and cover with water and vinegar. Prepare more solution, using same proportions, if needed. Soak for an hour or more.

Place bread crumbs on wax paper and mix in sesame seed, Greek seasoning, pepper, salt, and flour.

Mix egg and milk in a shallow dish. Drain and dry catfish. Dip in egg mixture and coat with bread-crumb mixture.

Fry in 1-inch deep hot oil (360°) 4-5 minutes to the side. Drain on paper towels and keep hot in a 200° oven. Garnish with lemon wedges. Makes 8 servings.

Hint: If preferred, bake fish on an oiled cookie sheet 15-20 minutes at 375° only until fish flakes easily with a fork.

Home for the Holidays

Salmon Patties with Wheat Germ

1 (15-ounce) can salmon, drained
1/2 cup raw wheat germ
1/2 teaspoon salt
1/4 teaspoon black pepper
1 egg
1/2 cup onion, chopped
2 tablespoons green pepper, chopped
3 tablespoons vegetable oil for frying

In medium-size mixing bowl, stir together salmon, salt, pepper, egg, onion, green pepper, and wheat germ.

Shape into small patties. Fry in large skillet over medium-high heat until golden brown; turn. Makes about 9 patties.

War Eagle Mill Wholegrain and Honey Cookbook

Lemon Baked Fish with Vegetables

2 pounds fish fillets*
3 lemons
1 tablespoon reduced-calorie margarine
1 tablespoon polyunsaturated oil
2 bell peppers, chopped
3 tomatoes, chopped
1 onion, chopped
1/4 teaspoon salt (optional)
Pepper, as desired

Rinse fish in cold water. Soak for 1 hour in ice water with juice of 1 lemon. Drain and pat fillets dry.

In 9x13-inch baking dish, melt margarine and oil. Separately layer tomatoes, peppers, and onions on bottom of baking dish. Sprinkle lightly with salt and pepper. Squeeze 1 lemon over mixture. Place fillets over vegetables. Garnish with lemon slices.

Bake in preheated 500° oven for 20 minutes or until fish flakes easily with a fork. Yield: 10 servings.

*Suggested fish: Orange Roughy, Sole or Cod

Per Serving (3 ounces): Calories 11; Cholesterol 55mg; Fat 3gm; Sodium 90mg; ADA Exchange Value: 1 meat + 1 vegetable

Take It To Heart

Tuna Patties

2 cans tuna, packed in water, drained, reserve 1/4 cup liquid
1/2 cup unbleached flour
2 egg whites, beaten
Cavender's All-purpose Greek Seasoning, to taste
1 heaping teaspoon baking powder

Mix tuna, flour, egg whites and Cavender's. Mix tuna liquid and baking powder until it foams. Add to tuna mixture. Make into patties and fry in Puritan oil. Use within 15 minutes of mixing (any longer and baking powder won't work).

Asbury United Methodist Church Cook Book

Shrimp Etouffée

ROUX:

6 tablespoons oil
6 tablespoons flour

Make roux, medium brown. Keep stirring until brown, 20 minutes.

2 cups chopped onions
1 cup chopped bell pepper
1 cup chopped celery
5 crushed garlic cloves
1 small can stewed tomatoes
2 (10 1/2-ounce) cans chicken broth
2 cups water
2 bay leaves
1 teaspoon basil
1 teaspoon chili powder
1/2 teaspoon cayenne
1/4 teaspoon black pepper
1 teaspoon Season-all
3-4 pounds peeled shrimp
1 cup chopped green onions
2 tablespoons chopped parsley

Add to roux the onions, bell pepper, celery and garlic. Add canned tomatoes, mixing well. Add chicken broth and water. While simmering, add spices. Let simmer 1 hour. Now add shrimp, green onions, and parsley. Cook 20 minutes, on very low heat, until shrimp is done. Serve over rice.

Nibbles Cooks Cajun

Herbed Italian Shrimp

With Italian Wine Marinade

1 1/2 tablespoons salt or salt substitute
1 tablespoon garlic onion magic
2 bay leaves
1 tablespoon lemon juice, plus rind halves
5 pounds fresh or frozen shrimp
1 (6-ounce) package shrimp and crab boil

Fill an 8-quart kettle half full of water and add all of the above seasonings except the shrimp boil. Bring to a full rolling boil and add the shrimp and shrimp crab boil. Bring water to boil again and cook for 10 minutes, or until the shrimp curl and are pink. (Do not overcook!) Drain and rinse in cool water. Peel if desired. Refrigerate in a large bowl covered with plastic wrap. If in a hurry, chill down in the freezer for at least 1 hour.

MARINADE:

1 (16-ounce) bottle low calorie Italian dressing
1/2 teaspoon sweet basil, dried, crushed
1/2 teaspoon crushed thyme, fresh or dry
1 teaspoon minced dried garlic
1 tablespoon garlic onion magic
1/2 cup white semi-sweet wine

Mix all of the above ingredients together in a quart jar. Shake vigorously and pour over chilled shrimp. Marinate, stirring shrimp every 30 minutes for 2 hours. The shrimp will absorb the flavors. Serve on a chilled platter or large bowl with picks. Serves 6.

A Kaleidoscope of Creative Healthy Cooking

Shrimp and Mushroom Shells

- 2 pounds shrimp, cooked and peeled
- 4 tablespoons butter
- 4 tablespoons flour
- 1 egg yolk, slightly beaten
- 1 cup chicken broth
- 1 teaspoon salt
- 1/8 - 1/4 teaspoon cayenne pepper
- 1 tablespoons lemon juice
- 3 tablespoons dry sherry
- 1/2 cup grated sharp Cheddar cheese
- 1/2 pound fresh mushrooms
- 1/4 cup butter
- Fine bread crumbs

Melt butter, add flour, and cook a few minutes, stirring constantly. With a wire whisk, stir in combined egg yolk and broth. Add salt and cayenne, and cook until very thick. Slowly add lemon juice, sherry, and cheese. Add shrimp, then mushrooms that have been sautéed in butter. Simmer 5 minutes. Put in 4 buttered sea shells or ramekins and cover with bread crumbs. (Or make 8 if using as appetizer.) Bake at 350° for about 20 minutes. Serves 4.

Southern Accent

Impossible Seafood Pie

- 1 (6-ounce) can crabmeat, drained
- 1 cup shredded sharp Cheddar cheese
- 1 (3-ounce) package cream cheese, cut into 1/4 inch cubes
- 1/4 cup chopped green onion
- 2 cups milk
- 1 cup baking mix
- 4 eggs
- 3/4 teaspoon salt
- Dash nutmeg

Preheat oven to 400°. Lightly grease 10-inch deep dish pie plate. Mix crabmeat, cheeses and onion in pie plate. Beat remaining ingredients until smooth (15 seconds in blender or 1 minute with hand beater). Pour into pie plate. Bake until golden brown 40-45 minutes. Let stand 5 minutes before cutting. Serves 4-6.

Cookin' in the Spa

Shrimp and Chicken Jambalaya

1/4 cup oil
1/2 pound smoked sausage, diced
1/2 pound ham, cubed
3 chicken breasts, de-boned, chopped
1 cup chopped onion
1 cup chopped bell pepper
1 cup chopped celery
1 cup chopped green onion
2 cloves minced garlic
1 (16-ounce) can tomatoes
1 teaspoon thyme
1 teaspoon black pepper
1/4 teaspoon cayenne pepper
1 teaspoon salt
1 cup rice, uncooked
2 tablespoons Worcestershire
1 1/2 cups chicken stock
2 pounds peeled shrimp

Sauté sausage and ham in the oil until lightly browned in big Dutch oven. Remove from oil. Add chicken, sauté till it looks done. Remove from oil.

Sauté onion, bell pepper, celery, green onion, and garlic in meat drippings until tender. Drain tomatoes, saving the juice. Add tomatoes, thyme, pepper, and salt. Cook 5 minutes. Stir in rice.

Mix liquid from tomatoes, Worcestershire, and stock to equal 2 1/2 cups. Add to pot and bring to a boil. Reduce to simmer. Add raw shrimp, ham, sausage, and chicken. Cook uncovered, stirring occasionally for 30 minutes or until rice and shrimp are done.

Nibbles Cooks Cajun

Scalloped Oysters

1 cup coarsely rolled cracker crumbs, divided in thirds
1 quart drained raw oysters
2 eggs
1 3/4 cups milk
3/4 cup butter
1 teaspoon salt
Pepper to taste

In buttered casserole, put a layer of cracker crumbs, layer of oysters. Make 2 layers. Beat eggs, add to milk and pour over casserole. Top with buttered crumbs; dot with butter. Bake in 350° oven 20-30 minutes. Serves 6-8.

Dixie Cookbook IV

Seafood Casserole

- 1/2 cup bell pepper chopped
- 1/2 cup onion, chopped
- 4 cups rice, cooked
- 3 tablespoons butter
- 2 (6 1/2-ounce) cans crab meat
- 1 pound shrimp, cooked (may use more)
- 1 (10 3/4-ounce) can cream of celery soup
- 1 (8 1/2-ounce) can water chestnuts, sliced
- 1/2 cup Hellman's mayonnaise
- 1 egg, beaten
- 1/2 pound sharp Cheddar cheese, grated
- 1 tablespoon Worcestershire sauce
- 2 tablespoons lemon juice
- Salt and white pepper to taste
- Bread crumbs, buttered

Sauté bell pepper and onion in butter until soft. Combine all ingredients except bread crumbs; mix gently. Put in buttered casserole and top with bread crumbs. Bake 30 minutes. May be made ahead, baked later. If so, increase baking time about 10 minutes. Yield: 10-12 servings.

In Good Taste

Steamed Mussels with Garlic and Wine

- 2 - 2 1/2 pounds mussels, scrubbed and washed
- 1/4 cup fresh parsley, chopped coarse
- 4-5 cloves garlic, chopped coarse
- 1 cup dry white wine
- 2 tablespoons lemon juice
- 3 tablespoons olive oil, extra virgin or pure

Place washed mussels in a large pan with a tight cover. Add the parsley, garlic, wine, and lemon juice. Toss gently with a wooden spoon until all the mussels are coated. Sprinkle olive oil over mussels and cover. Heat to a boil; reduce heat and steam 10 minutes. Makes a great appetizer. Juices may be spooned over toasted Italian bread and sprinkled with Parmesan cheese for an additional treat.

Wine selection: BV Sauvignon Blanc, a crisp dry white.

The Sicilian-American Cookbook

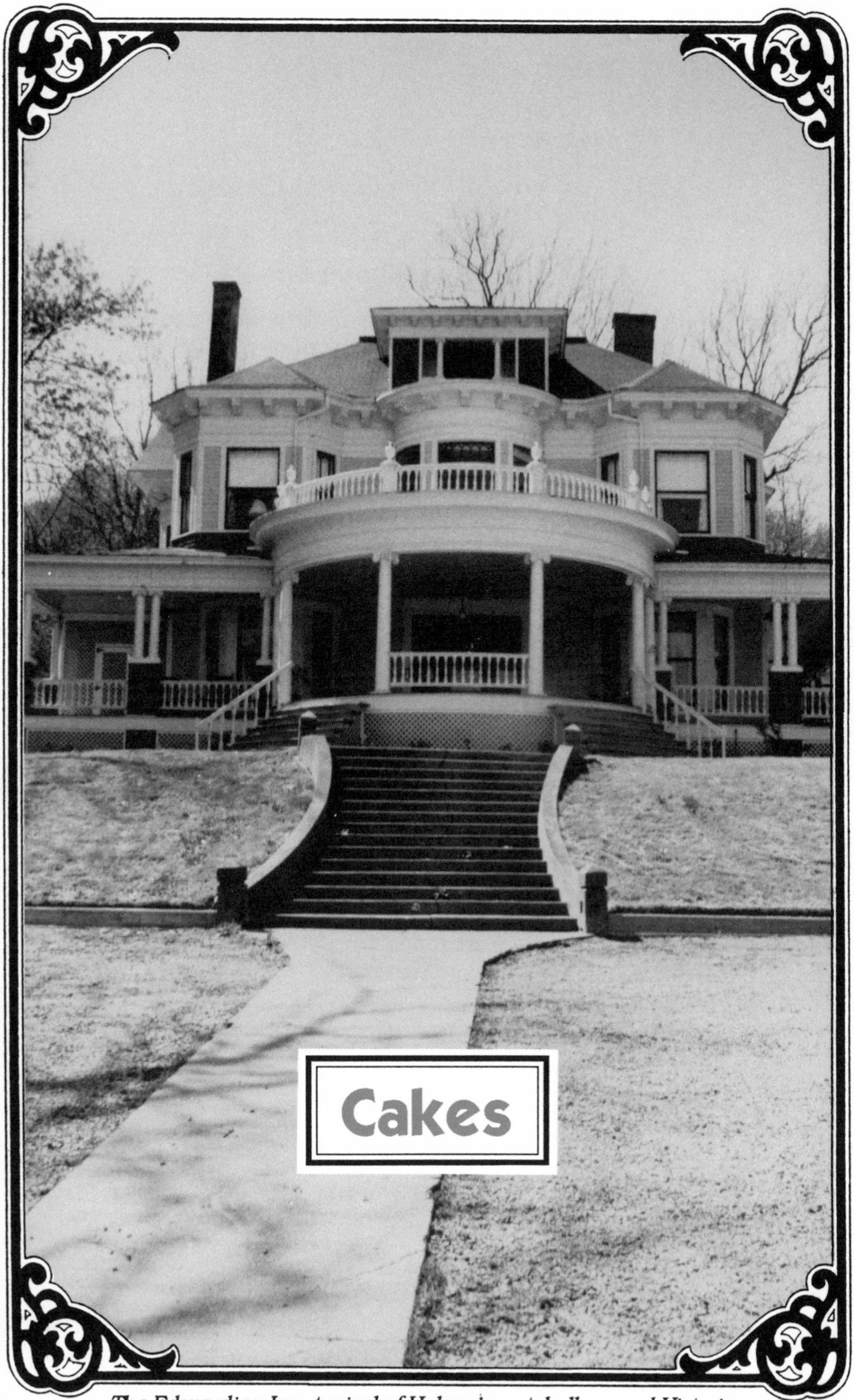

The Edwardian Inn, typical of Helena's antebellum and Victorian structures.

Without Rival Chocolate Fudge Kahlua Cake

(With Chocolate Kahlua Glaze)

1 (18.25-ounce) chocolate fudge*, with pudding in the mix, cake mix
16 ounces sour cream
1 (12-ounce) package real semi-sweet chocolate morsels
1/4 cup cooking oil
2 eggs
1/2 cup kahlua
1 cup powdered sugar
2 tablespoons unsweetened cocoa
1 tablespoon margarine, softened
1 tablespoon light corn syrup
2 tablespoons kahlua
1 tablespoon water

Preheat oven to 350°. Grease and flour a 12-cup Bundt pan. With electric mixer, combine first 6 ingredients; beat 4 minutes; pour into Bundt pan; bake for 50 minutes or until cake tester (or toothpick) inserted comes out clean. Cool in pan 10-15 minutes; turn onto cake plate.

To make glaze, away from burner but in small saucepan, combine rest of ingredients; stir until smooth and creamy; over low heat, warm glaze 3-5 minutes; stir often. Drizzle over warm cake. Allow glaze to cool before serving. Yields 12-16 servings.

This unbelievably easy to make cake is sinfully delicious. It is wonderful topped with whipped cream, vanilla ice cream, or kahlua ice cream for a sublime chocolate repast!!!

*You may also use one 18.25-ounce chocolate butter, with pudding in the mix, cake mix. Just as delicious!

Southern Flavors' Little Chocolate Book

Chocolate Ice Box Cake

1 dozen lady-fingers
1/2 pound sweet chocolate
3 tablespoons sugar
3 tablespoons water
4 eggs, separated
1/2 pint whipping cream

Line sides and bottom of mold with lady-fingers. Melt chocolate in double boiler; add sugar and water and yolks of eggs, well-beaten. Cook until smooth and thick, stirring constantly. When cool, add stiffly beaten egg whites. Cover lady-fingers with filling, place in refrigerator twelve hours or more before serving. When ready to serve, remove to chop plate and cover with whipped cream, sweetened if desired.

Dixie Cook Book V

1-2-3-4 Cake

Great Grandmother Price's Cake and Sauce—a tradition at the Teacher's Christmas Party.

1 cup butter or margarine, softened
2 cups sugar
3 cups flour
1 teaspoon baking powder
4 eggs
1/2 teaspoon soda in 1 cup buttermilk
1 teaspoon vanilla

Cream **1** cup butter with **2** cups sugar for 10 minutes. Sift **3** cups flour with baking powder. Add **4** eggs one at a time to the creamed mixture, then add dry ingredients alternately with milk mixture, beating until smooth. Beat in vanilla. Reserve 1 cup batter for sauce! Bake in 9x13-inch greased and floured pan at 325° until golden brown, about 1 hour.

HOT SAUCE:
1 cup reserved cake batter
2 eggs
1 cup sugar
2 tablespoons flour
3 cups milk
1/2 cup butter
1 teaspoon vanilla
Nutmeg

Add eggs to batter while beating. Mix the flour into the sugar, then add to the batter. Slowly add the milk and cook in a double boiler. Add the butter when the liquid is warm. Add the vanilla as the sauce thickens. Continue to cook in the double boiler until the sauce is thick.

Serve warm over warm cake. This sauce is sufficient for half of the cake. Double the sauce for the whole cake. Sprinkle with nutmeg.

Classroom Classics

Lake Ouachita, created in 1953 by Blakeley Mountain Dam, is the largest lake in Arkansas with almost 50,000 surface acres. It is fed from such remote areas that it is one of the two cleanest man-made lakes in the nation.

Milk Chocolate Candy Bar Cake

CAKE:

2 1/2 cups flour
1/4 teaspoon salt
2 sticks butter or margarine
2 cups sugar
4 eggs
8 (1.65-ounce) milk chocolate bars
1 cup chocolate syrup
1/4 teaspoon soda
1 cup buttermilk
2 teaspoons vanilla

Grease and flour tube pan. Sift together the flour and salt. In a mixer bowl cream butter and sugar. Add 4 eggs one at a time, mixing between each addition. Melt 8 chocolate bars, add 1 cup chocolate syrup. Mix soda and buttermilk and add to butter, sugar and egg mixture. Blend in flour, then chocolate mixture and add 2 teaspoons vanilla. Pour into prepared pan and bake 2 hours at 300°.

ICING:

1 1/2 cups sugar
1 cup evaporated milk
1/4 stick butter or margarine
1 teaspoon vanilla
4 (1.65-ounce) milk chocolate bars

Put sugar, evaporated milk and butter in a saucepan over medium heat and bring to a boil. Boil 10 minutes. Add chocolate bars and vanilla. Beat until smooth and well mixed. Spread or pour over cooled cake. Serves 24.

Cookin' in the Spa

Brownie Cake

I sure wish I could remember where I got this one, cause it is a dandy!

1 cup water
1 stick oleo
1/4 cup cocoa
1/4 cup oil

Melt. I usually put all this in a 4-cup measurin' cup and stick it in the microwave for a couple of minutes. When the oleo is melted and the whole mess is good and hot, add **1 teaspoon of soda**. This is gonna bubble up, so stir it up good and pour it over:

2 cups flour
2 cups sugar
1/2 teaspoon salt

Mix all that together—I use the mixer. (In the 36 years that I have been married, I wore out 2 big mixers, so my sweet thing got me a Kitchen Aid and it is a dandy.) After that's all mixed up add:

1/2 cup buttermilk
2 eggs
Vanilla

Pour this into a jelly roll pan and cook it for 20 minutes at 400°. Ice it while it's hot. You just leave it in the pan.

ICING:
1 stick oleo
1/4 cup cocoa
1/3 cup buttermilk
1 box powdered sugar
Chopped nuts
Coconut

Melt oleo, cocoa, and buttermilk. Pour this over a box of powdered sugar, and add some chopped nuts and some coconut and slap it on the cake.

This is one of my bunch's all-time favorites. It's sure good to carry to folks when there has been a death in the family or if some new folks have moved in close by, they'd sure like this.

CONTINUED

Now for a different wrinkle on this cake, after you put the batter in a pan, open up a can of cherry pie filling and spoon out that stuff over the top of the cake batter. Try and do it so there will be a dab of cherries in every piece of cake. When this gets to cookin', it may run over just a little dab, but don't worry bout it, cause it will turn out ok.

When you make the icing, instead of coconut, put in about 1/3 cup of maraschino cherries that's been chopped up. This will sure make you the hit at the church supper, and if it happens that you ain't cute, you might better give some thought to bein' a good cook, cause who of us is it what don't like a little attention now and then.

Sunday Go To Eatin' Cook Book

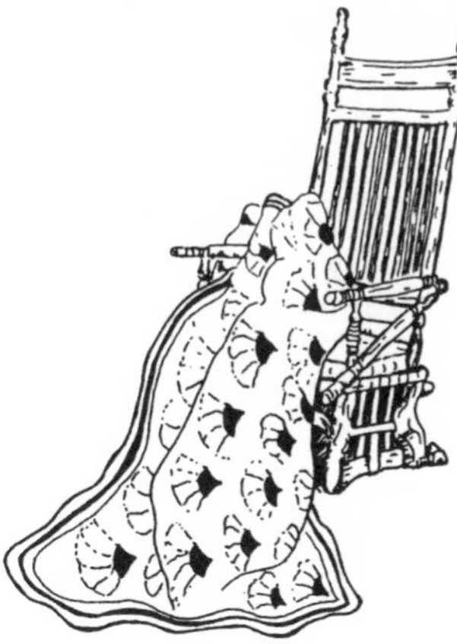

Cherry Chocolate Cake

First Place Best of Show Mid-South Fair 1989

1 package Duncan Hines Devil's Food Cake Mix
2 cups Cool Whip, thawed
1/2 cup chopped maraschino cherries
1 can Duncan Hines Chocolate Frosting

Heat oven to 350°. Grease and flour two 9-inch layer pans. Prepare batter as directed on package. Divide batter evenly between pans. Bake and cool as directed on package. Fold cherries into Cool Whip. Spread between cake layers. Frost with frosting. Store in refrigerator.

Cooking For Good Measure

Burnt Sugar Cake

SYRUP:

3/4 cup sugar
3/4 cup boiling water

Melt sugar in copper-bottomed skillet over low heat, stirring constantly until dark brown, but not actually burned. Remove from heat and add the boiling water, stirring constantly. Return to heat and boil until thoroughly mixed and has the consistency of thin syrup. Divide into two measuring cups, half in each cup.

CAKE:

Buttermilk
1 teaspoon vanilla
1/2 pound margarine
2 cups sugar
3 eggs
2 egg yolks
3 cups cake flour
1 teaspoon baking soda
1/4 cup boiling water

Add enough buttermilk to half the Burnt Sugar Syrup to make one cup of liquid. Add the vanilla. Cream together the margarine and sugar, mixing until light and fluffy. Beat in the eggs and egg yolks one at a time. Sift, then measure the cake flour and add alternately with the buttermilk mixture beginning and ending with the flour. Last, add the soda dissolved in 1/4 cup boiling water. Bake in 3 (9-inch) greased and floured pans in 350° oven for 30 minutes.

FROSTING:

Milk
3 cups sugar
1/3 stick margarine

Add enough milk to the rest of the Burnt Sugar Syrup to make 1 1/2 cups of liquid. Place in saucepan with the sugar and margarine. Cook, stirring often, until it makes a soft ball when tested in cold water, or soft ball stage on candy thermometer. Pour into mixing bowl and cool to lukewarm before beating to spreading consistency. Cool the cake completely before frosting.

In Good Taste

Pistachio Bundt Cake

Color coordinates with Christmas. Flavor, texture, and appearance make one think that making it takes lots more time and skill than it does.

1 (18 1/4-ounce) package butter-recipe golden cake mix
1 (3 3/8-ounce) package pistachio instant pudding-and-pie-filling mix
4 eggs
1 cup orange juice
1/2 cup oil
3/4 cup chocolate syrup

Place cake and pudding mixes in large bowl of electric mixer. In a separate bowl, beat eggs, orange juice, and oil together until well mixed. Pour into mixer bowl and beat on low speed 1 minute, then on high for 3 minutes. Pour two-thirds of batter into a buttered and floured 10-inch tube or bundt pan.

Pour chocolate syrup evenly over batter. Pour remaining batter into pan and run a knife through it to distribute syrup. Bake at 350° 1 hour or until toothpick inserted in center comes out clean. Serve without icing or ice with:

FUDGE CAKE ICING:
3 tablespoons cocoa
3 tablespoons butter or margarine, softened
5 tablespoons water
2 cups powdered sugar
1 teaspoon vanilla extract
1/8 teaspoon salt

Mix cocoa, butter, and water. Simmer for 2 minutes in a heavy saucepan on range top or in a large bowl in a microwave oven. Stir as needed to prevent sticking.

Remove from heat and beat in powdered sugar, vanilla, and salt. Add a few drops of water, if needed, to make icing just thin enough to run down sides when spread on top of cake.

Home for the Holidays

Coon Cake

1 package Duncan Hines Butter Cake Mix (take out 2/3 cup of the cake mix)
1 stick butter or margarine
1 egg

Mix well and press in the bottom of a 9x13-inch pan. Bake at 350° for about 15-20 minutes. Do not get too brown.

2/3 cup cake mix
1 tablespoon flour
3 eggs
1 1/2 cups dark Karo syrup
1/2 cup brown sugar
1 teaspoon vanilla
2 cups pecans, chopped or whole

Mix well and pour on baked, cooled cake portion. Cook about 30-35 minutes. Start cooking at 350° until it gets hot; then turn the oven down to 325° and continue to cook until center of cake is like a pecan pie. *Do not overcook!*

Asbury United Methodist Church Cook Book

Miracle Butter Cake

1 Duncan Hines Yellow Cake Mix
2 eggs
1 stick butter, melted

Mix and spread in bottom of 9x13-inch pan.

TOPPING:
1 (8-ounce) bar cream cheese
2 eggs
1 box powdered sugar

Let cream cheese sit until soft or sit in oven while it is getting warm for a few minutes (do not let it sit in oven too long, for it will stick and burn). Mix all ingredients and pour over cake mixture. Bake at 350° for 35-40 minutes only.

Asbury United Methodist Church Cook Book

Carrot Cake

3 cups flour
2 teaspoon baking soda
1 teaspoon salt
2 teaspoons cinnamon
1 cup vegetable oil
1 1/2 cups honey
4 eggs
3 cups grated carrots
1 cup chopped pecans

Sift flour, soda and salt with cinnamon. Add oil, honey and eggs; mix well. Fold in carrots; add nuts. Pour into 2 layer pans. Bake at 325° for 30 minutes or until done.

FROSTING:
1 (8-ounce) package cream cheese
1/3 cup honey
1 teaspoon vanilla

Cream cheese with honey and vanilla until smooth. Spread on cake when cool.

The Wonderful World of Honey

German Apple Cake

- 3 eggs
- 1 cup cooking oil
- 2 cups sugar
- 1 teaspoon vanilla
- 2 cups all-purpose flour
- 2 teaspoons cinnamon
- 1/2 teaspoon salt
- 1 teaspoon soda
- 4 cups raw apples, chopped
- 1 cup nuts

Beat eggs and oil until foamy. Add sugar and vanilla. Sift together flour, cinnamon, salt and soda and add to above mixture. Add apples and nuts; mix well. Bake in 13x9x2-inch pan at 350° for 50-60 minutes.

ICING:

- 2 (3-ounce) packages cream cheese
- 3 tablespoons melted butter
- 1 teaspoon vanilla
- 1 1/2 cups powdered sugar (more, if necessary)

Mix all ingredients together and ice cake while still hot.

Favorite Recipes from Associated Women for Harding

Lemon-Pecan Fruitcake

- 1 (1-pound) box brown sugar
- 1 pound margarine
- 6 egg yolks, beaten
- 2 cups all-purpose flour
- 1 teaspoon baking powder
- 1 (2-ounce) bottle lemon extract
- 1 quart chopped pecans
- 1/2 pound candied pineapple, chopped
- 1/2 pound candied cherries, chopped
- 2 cups all-purpose flour
- 6 egg whites, beaten

Cream sugar and margarine until smooth. Add beaten egg yolks and mix well. Combine 2 cups flour and baking powder; add to creamed mixture. Add lemon extract. Coat pecans and candied fruit with other 2 cups of flour, and add to creamed mixture. Fold in beaten egg whites.

Cover and let stand overnight. The next day put mixture into a greased tube pan; bake at 250° for 2 1/2 hours, or until cake tests done.

Asbury United Methodist Church Cook Book

Squash Cake

3 cups squash
3 cups sugar
1/2 cup oil
4 eggs
1 teaspoon vanilla
3 cups flour
2 teaspoons baking powder
2 teaspoons baking soda
1 teaspoon cinnamon
1 teaspoon salt
1 cup pecans

Grate squash (or cook and strain). Beat sugar and oil. Add squash. Add eggs, one at a time, beating after each. Add vanilla. Sift together the dry ingredients. Add sifted flour; mix and beat well. Add nuts. Pour into greased and floured 9x13-inch pan.

TOPPING:
3/4 cup brown sugar
3 teaspoons cinnamon
3 tablespoons butter or oleo

Crumble together. Sprinkle on top and bake at least one hour in 350° oven. Check before removing to see if completely done in center.

The Pink Lady...in the Kitchen

Walnut Crunch

This easy recipe won a first place in the 1977 Arkansas Dairy Recipe Contest. With the variations included here, I have used it many times since.

1 cup sugar
1 cup English walnuts, chopped
1 egg, beaten
2 tablespoons butter or margarine, softened
1 (3 5/8-ounce) package vanilla-flavored instant-pudding-and-pie-filling mix
1 cup sour cream
1 (3-ounce) package cream cheese, softened
1 cup milk
2 medium bananas, sliced
Mint sprigs for garnish

Combine sugar, walnuts, egg, and butter. Spread thinly on buttered baking sheet. Bake at 350° 18-20 minutes or until golden brown. Cool to room temperature; crush and set aside.

Combine pudding-and-pie-filling mix, sour cream, cream cheese, and milk. Beat on low speed of electric mixer 1-2 minutes, until well blended. Fold in sliced bananas. Sprinkle half of crumb mixture on bottom of an 8x8x2-inch pan.

Spoon milk mixture over crumbs, then top with remaining crumbs. Chill several hours before serving. Garnish with mint sprigs. Makes 9 (2 2/3-inch) squares.

Hint: Double the recipe and make in a 13x9x2-inch pan for 24 (2 1/4-inch) squares.

Home for the Holidays

Texarkana is named for the states it borders, Texas and Arkansas, and also for Louisiana, whose border is about 30 miles south. The Bi-State Justice Center at Texarkana—the only such facility in existence—houses facilities for both Arkansas and Texas.

Whole Wheat Oatmeal Cake

1 1/2 cups boiling water
1 cup oatmeal
1 stick butter or margarine
1 3/4 cups sifted whole wheat flour
1 teaspoon cinnamon
1 teaspoon baking soda
1/2 teaspoon salt
1 cup honey
2 eggs
1 teaspoon vanilla
1 cup raisins
1/2 cup chopped nuts

Pour boiling water over oatmeal; add butter or margarine; let cool. Mix dry ingredients. Stir honey, eggs, and vanilla together. Add to dry mixture; stir in raisins and nuts. Pour in a greased and floured 9x13-inch pan. Bake in a preheated 350° oven 45 minutes or until inserted toothpick comes out clean.

TOPPING:
1/2 cup honey
1/4 cup evaporated milk
4 tablespoons butter or margarine
1 cup coconut

Bring honey, evaporated milk and butter to a boil. Add coconut; cool and spread on cooled cake.

War Eagle Mill Wholegrain and Honey Cookbook

Jam Cake

3/4 cup butter
1 cup sugar
3 eggs, separated
1/2 cup buttermilk
1 teaspoon soda
1 teaspoon each: salt, cinnamon, allspice
2 cups flour
1 cup strawberry jam
1/2 cup chopped pecans

Cream butter and sugar, and add egg yolks, beating after each one. Add buttermilk. Sift soda, spices and flour together and add to mixture, mixing well. Fold in jam and pecans. Fold in stiffly beaten egg whites. Bake in a greased 9x13-inch pan at 350° for 30-40 minutes, or until top springs back when tapped. Allow to cool. Ice with Caramel Icing.

CARAMEL ICING:

1/2 cup sugar
2 1/2 cups sugar
2 eggs
2 tablespoons butter
3/4 cup milk
1/2 teaspoon salt

Brown 1/2 cup sugar in heavy iron skillet. Mix 2 1/2 cups sugar, 2 whole eggs, and beat well. Add butter, milk, salt. Add the browned sugar. Cook slowly until it forms soft ball in cold water, stirring all the time. Take from fire and beat until ready to spread on cake. Serves 10.

Feasts of Eden

Fallen-Down Cake

2 cups Bisquick mix
1 box brown sugar (dark or light)
4 eggs
1 teaspoon vanilla flavoring
1 cup chopped pecans

Mix Bisquick mix, brown sugar and eggs; add flavoring and pecans. Bake very slowly (about 325° for 40 minutes) in oven in greased sheet pan (9x13). Cake will rise then fall—reason for the name of the cake.

Asbury United Methodist Church Cook Book

Cake That Doesn't Last

3 cups flour
2 cups sugar
1 teaspoon soda
1 teaspoon salt
1 teaspoon cinnamon
1 1/2 teaspoons vanilla
3 eggs
1 1/2 cups oil
2 cups mashed bananas
1 (15-ounce) can crushed pineapple, with juice
1 cup nuts

Combine all ingredients by hand until well blended. Pour into a large greased and floured Bundt pan. Bake at 350° for 1 hour and 20 minutes.

High Cotton Cookin'

Mammy's Strawberry Shortcake

1 1/2 tablespoons butter
1/2 cup sugar
1 egg
3 tablespoons water
1 heaping cup flour
1/6 teaspoon soda
1/4 teaspoon baking powder
2 quarts strawberries
Whipped cream

Melt butter; add sugar, egg and water. Mix well. Sift flour, soda, and baking powder. Add to mixture to make batter the consistency of soft biscuit dough. Bake at 375° in 8-inch square pan greased with butter for 20 minutes. This recipe may be doubled. To serve, split cake when cool, through the middle. Crush 2 quarts of strawberries and put part between the layers, the remainder on top. Serve with whipped cream, if desired. This recipe has been a specialty of the family for seven Southern generations.

Dixie Cookbook IV

Hawaiian Wedding Cake

2 cups flour
2 cups sugar
2 teaspoons baking soda
2 eggs
1 cup nuts, chopped
1 cup coconut
1 (20-ounce) can crushed pineapple

Mix ingredients and pour into 9x13x2-inch pan. Bake at 350° for 30-40 minutes.

ICING:

1 (8-ounce) package cream cheese, softened
2 teaspoons vanilla
1 1/2 cups powdered sugar
1 stick oleo, softened

Mix and spread on cooled cake. Sprinkle with chopped nuts.

Southwest Cookin'

Granny's Applesauce Fruit Cake

1/2 cup shortening
1 1/2 cups sugar
2 eggs, beaten
1 cup applesauce
2 1/2 cups flour
1/2 teaspoon nutmeg
1/4 teaspoon cloves
1/2 teaspoon cinnamon
1 teaspoon soda
1 cup chopped walnuts
1 cup raisins
1 (1-pound) package seeded chopped dates

Beat together shortening, sugar and eggs. Add applesauce and beat. Combine flour, spices, soda and mix with above.

Dust walnuts and raisins with flour and add with dates to above mixture, stir in well. Bake in a greased floured tube pan at 350° until done, about 1 hour.

Clabber Creek Farm Cook Book

Fruit Cocktail Cake

1 1/2 cups sugar
2 cups flour
1 teaspoon vanilla
2 eggs
1/2 teaspoon soda
1/2 teaspoon baking powder
1 can fruit cocktail
1/2 cup coconut
1/2 cup chopped nuts

Mix well in order given; pour into 9x13-inch pan and bake for 30-35 minutes at 350°.

FRUIT COCKTAIL CAKE ICING:

1 1/2 cups sugar
1 stick butter
1 small can evaporated milk
1 teaspoon vanilla
1/2 cup coconut
1/2 cup chopped nuts

Combine first 4 ingredients and cook until well mixed. Add coconut and nuts. Ice cake while hot.

The Farmer's Daughters

Ambrosia Cake

1 Duncan Hines yellow cake mix with pudding
1 cup orange juice, divided
1 can condensed milk
1 large container Cool Whip
Fresh coconut

Cook by instructions for sheet cake, but substitute 1/2 cup orange juice for 1/2 cup liquid. While warm, punch holes in cake and pour 1 can condensed milk over cake. Then pour 1/2 cup orange juice over cake. Let cool and frost with large container Cool Whip. Top with fresh coconut.

Cookin' Along the Cotton Belt

Post Office Cake

1 Duncan Hines Butter Cake Mix
1/2 cup oil
2 eggs
1 small can mandarin oranges with juice

Mix thoroughly and bake in 3 layers.

ICING:
1 large carton Cool Whip
1 small box vanilla instant pudding mix
2 small cans crushed pineapple (drained)

Mix and spread between layers; refrigerate.

Evening Shade

Fresh Raspberry and Peach Shortcake Supreme

Light, pretty, and refreshing summer dessert.

1 (5x9-inch) loaf angel food cake, cut lengthwise
1/3 cup naturally sweet fruit spread
3 fresh peaches, skinned, sliced thin, soaked in 1/2 cup orange juice
1 pint fresh red raspberries
1 (8-ounce) carton whipped topping

Place bottom piece of cake on serving platter. Spread with fruit spread. Drain peach slices from orange juice and pat dry using paper towels. Reserve orange juice for another use. Layer half of the peach slices over fruit spread. Place half the raspberries over peach slices. Spread 1/3 cup whipped topping over fruit. Set second (top) layer of cake over fruit, with cut side down. Ice entire assembled cake with whipped topping on the sides and top. Arrange remaining peach slices and raspberries in a row on the top. Serve within 15 minutes of assembling. Cut at the table, so this can be enjoyed. Serves 4-6.

A Kaleidoscope of Creative Healthy Cooking

No Cook Cake

2 small boxes (or 1 large) French Vanilla pudding
1 (8-ounce) container sour cream
1 can pie filling (I like strawberry)
1 angel food cake

Mix pudding according to package directions. Break or cut cake in pieces. Pour sour cream and pudding mix over cake, then pour pie filling on top of cake pieces. Use 13x9-pan. Chill.

Southwest Cookin'

Elsie's Gingerbread

There is no doubt in our minds that this is the world's best gingerbread. Moist and sweet and dark, tinged with molasses but not too molasses-y, sprinkled with a crisp streusel topping, this is outstanding, perhaps one of our ten all-time favorite recipes. Try it plain, with ice cream, with whipped cream, accompanying a baked apple or pear; make it with a few variations, as muffins; try it as upside-down cake. A wonderful, can't-go-wrong dessert, perfect for fall.

1 1/2 cups unbleached white flour
1 cup sugar
2 teaspoons ginger
1 teaspoon cinnamon
1/2 cup butter or shortening
1 egg, well beaten
3 tablespoons molasses
1 teaspoon baking soda
1 scant teaspoon salt
1 cup buttermilk

Preheat oven to 350°. Combine flour, sugar, ginger and cinnamon. Cut in butter or shortening. Reserve 1/4 cup of crumbled mixture for topping. Add egg to the flour mixture. Stir in molasses. Dissolve soda and salt in 1 cup buttermilk. Add to the other mixture. Pour into a Pam-ed 9-inch square pan, sprinkle with the reserved topping, and bake for 30 minutes.

The Dairy Hollow House Cookbook

Company Cheesecake

1 1/4 cups graham cracker crumbs
2 tablespoon sugar
3 tablespoons butter or margarine, melted
2 (8-ounce) packages plus 1 (3-ounce) package cream cheese, softened
1 cup sugar
2 teaspoons grated lemon peel (or lemon juice)
1/4 teaspoon vanilla
3 eggs
1 cup dairy sour cream or Strawberry Glaze

Heat oven to 350°. Stir together cracker crumbs and 2 tablespoons sugar. Mix in butter thoroughly. Press mixture evenly in bottom of 9-inch springform pan. Bake 10 minutes. Cool. Reduce oven temperature to 300°.

Beat cream cheese in large mixer bowl. Gradually add 1 cup sugar; beat until fluffy. Add lemon peel and vanilla. Beat in eggs, one at a time. Pour over crumb mixture. Bake 1 hour or until center is firm. Cool to room temperature. Spread with sour cream or Glaze. Chill at least 3 hours. Loosen edge of cheesecake with knife before removing side of pan. Serves 12.

STRAWBERRY GLAZE:

1 cup strawberries
1 cup sugar
3 tablespoons cornstarch
1/3 cup water

Mash enough fresh strawberries to measure 1 cup. Blend 1 cup sugar and 3 tablespoons cornstarch in small saucepan. Stir in 1/3 cup water and the strawberries. Cook, stirring constantly, until mixture thickens and boils. Boil and stir 1 minute. Cool thoroughly.

Loni Anderson (Mrs. Burt Reynolds)
Evening Shade

Italian Cheese Cake

1 pound ricotta cheese, room temperature
1 pound cream cheese, room temperature
1 1/2 cups sugar
1 teaspoon fresh lemon juice
1 teaspoon lemon rind, grated
1 tablespoon pure vanilla
3 tablespoons flour
3 tablespoons cornstarch
1 stick butter, melted
1 pound sour cream
4 large eggs, slightly beaten

Do not preheat oven. Important to add ingredients as instructed. Blend ricotta and cream cheese. Gradually add sugar and blend. Stir in lemon rind and juice, vanilla and flour mixed with cornstarch. Add butter and blend well by hand. Add sour cream and eggs and mix by hand. Spray 9-inch springform pan with Pam. Fill with mix, place pan on cookie sheet and set the pan on a flat surface several times to remove air bubbles. Bake at 325° 1 1/2 hours. Do not open oven door. Turn off heat and leave cake in oven 2 hours.

The Sicilian-American Cookbook

Cheesecake Pie

Easy and Delicious!

1 (9-inch) graham cracker pie crust
1 (8-ounce) package cream cheese, soft
3/4 cup sugar
1 cup sour cream
2 teaspoons vanilla
1 (8-ounce) carton of Cool Whip
1 small box frozen sweet strawberries, thawed, or 1 can blueberry pie filling, or 1 can cherry pie filling

Beat cream cheese until smooth; gradually beat in sugar. Blend in sour cream and vanilla. Fold in Cool Whip, blending well. Spoon into crust (the crust may be bought—makes it even easier). Chill at least 4 hours. Garnish with strawberries or other topping. Yield: 6-8 servings.

Betty is Still "Winking" at Cooking

Pumpkin Cheesecake Bars

1 (16-ounce) package pound cake mix
3 eggs
2 tablespoons margarine or butter, melted
4 teaspoons pumpkin pie spice
1 (8-ounce) bar cream cheese, softened
1 (14-ounce) can sweetened condensed milk
1 (16-ounce) can pumpkin
1/2 teaspoon salt
1 cup chopped nuts

Preheat oven to 350°. In a large mixer bowl, on low speed, combine cake mix, 1 egg, margarine and 2 teaspoons pie spice until it is crumbly. Press into bottom of 15x10-inch jelly roll pan. In a large mixer bowl, beat cheese until fluffy. Gradually beat in sweetened condensed milk, then remaining 2 eggs, pumpkin, remaining pie spice and salt. Mix well. Pour over crust, sprinkle with nuts. Bake 30-35 minutes or until set. Cool, chill and cut into bars. Store in the refrigerator. Yield: 48.

Cookin' in the Spa

America's only national park located in a city, Hot Springs has been famous for its healing waters from thermal springs for over a century. The "Valley of the Vapors" has long been a destination for tourists from around the world, beginning with the Spanish explorer, Hernando DeSoto, who discovered the famous hot springs.

Cookies and Candies

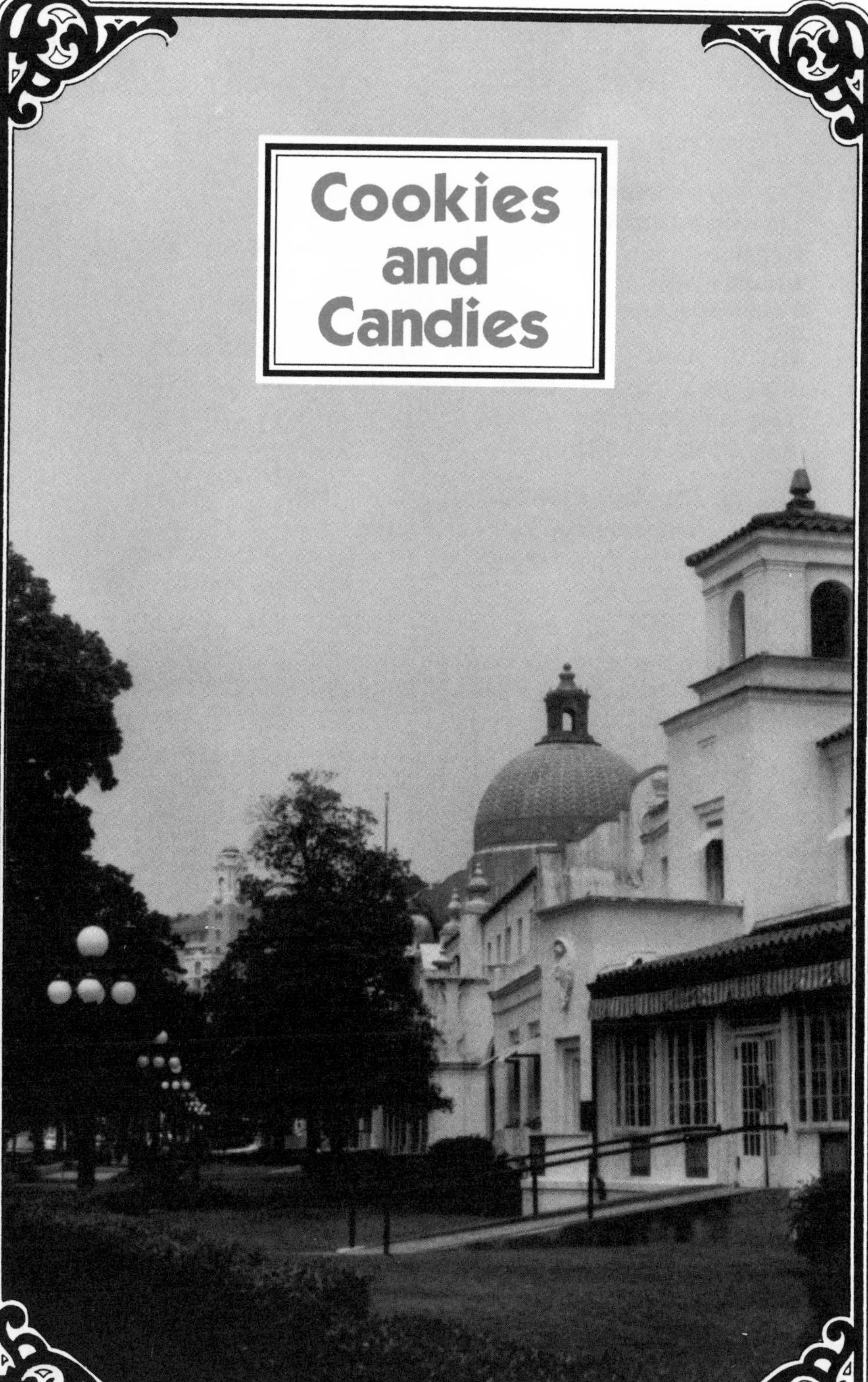

Bathhouse Row in Hot Springs.

Cream Cheese Fudge Brownies

1/2 cup shortening
1/2 cup butter or oleo
4 eggs
2 cups sugar
4 tablespoons cocoa
1 cup flour
1/2 teaspoon salt
1 cup coconut
1 cup pecans
2 teaspoons vanilla

Mix in order given. Spread one-third of batter in 13x9-inch pan. Spoon cream cheese filling over it. Spoon remaining batter over cheese mixture. Spread carefully. Bake at 350° for 35 minutes.

CREAM CHEESE FILLING:

2 tablespoons butter
1 (3-ounce) package cream cheese, softened
1/4 cup sugar
1 egg
1 tablespoon flour
1/2 teaspoon vanilla

Cream cheese and butter together. Add sugar, a spoonful at a time. Mix well. Add egg, flour, and vanilla. Stir until mixed well.

The Pink Lady...in the Kitchen

German Chocolate Brownies

1 (1-pound) package Kraft Caramels
2/3 cup Pet Milk
3/4 cup oleo, melted
1 package German Chocolate Cake Mix
1 cup chopped nuts
1 (6-ounce) package Nestle's Chocolate Chips

Melt Kraft Caramels (about 50) with 1/3 cup Pet Milk. Set aside to cool. Mix melted oleo, 1/3 cup Pet Milk with cake mix. Add chopped nuts. Mix well. Put half of cake mixture in greased 13x9-inch pan. Pat evenly on bottom of pan. Bake 6 minutes at 350.°

Remove from oven and sprinkle with the chocolate chips.

CONTINUED

Being very careful, pour caramel mixture over chips. Pat remainder of cake mixture flat with hands, then place on top of caramel mixture. Bake 20 minutes at 350°. When you remove from oven, run knife around edges so caramel won't stick.

Southwest Cookin'

Miss America Brownies

4 eggs, beaten
2 cups sugar
2 sticks oleo (or 1 oleo and 1 butter)
3 squares chocolate
1 1/2 cups flour
2 teaspoons vanilla
1 cup chopped pecans

Gradually add sugar to beaten eggs. Melt oleo (or oleo and butter) with chocolate. Cool slightly and add to beaten egg-sugar mixture. Add flour, vanilla, and pecans.

Bake in greased 10x14-inch pan about 30 minutes in preheated 350° oven. Let brownies cool and cover with icing.

ICING:

1/4 cup butter
1 1/2 squares chocolate
2 cups confectioners sugar
1 teaspoon vanilla
2 tablespoons milk

Melt the butter and chocolate together and pour over the sugar. Mix well. Add vanilla and milk and beat well. Spread icing thinly over the brownies and cut into squares.

The Pink Lady...in the Kitchen

Jam Diagonals

1/2 cup butter or margarine, softened
1/4 cup granulated sugar
1 teaspoon vanilla
1/8 teaspoon salt
1 1 /4 cups flour
1/4 cup strawberry jam
3/4 cup powdered sugar
4 teaspoons lemon juice

In a large mixing bowl, cream butter, granulated sugar, vanilla and salt until fluffy. Gradually stir in flour until blended. Divide dough into thirds. On lightly floured surface, with hands, roll each in a 9-inch rope. Place 3 inches apart on a lightly greased cookie sheet. With finger, make 1/2-inch depressions down center of each rope. Ropes will flatten to about 1-inch wide strips. Fill depressions with jam. Bake in preheated 350° oven 12-15 minutes or until golden. Cool on cookie sheet. Blend powdered sugar and lemon juice until smooth; drizzle over jam. When icing is set, cut diagonally in 1-inch cookies. Makes 24.

Prairie Harvest

English Toffee Cookies

1/2 cup butter
1/2 cup margarine
1 cup sugar
1 egg yolk
1 teaspoon vanilla
2 cups flour
1/2 teaspoon salt
1 egg white, beaten
2 cups chopped pecans

Blend butter, margarine, and sugar in food processor or electric mixer until creamy. Add egg yolk and vanilla and blend. Add flour and salt and blend. Let dough stand in refrigerator at least 30 minutes. With the palm of your hand, spread very thin on cookie sheet, covering it completely. Lightly brush with beaten egg whites. Sprinkle with chopped pecans. Bake at 375° 12-15 minutes or until light brown. Let cool about 5 minutes and cut into small rectangles.

Feasts of Eden

Lemon Sour Cookies

1 cup sifted cake flour
2 tablespoons sugar
1/8 teaspoon salt
1/3 cup butter or margarine, softened
2 eggs, slightly beaten
1 cup firmly packed brown sugar
1/2 cup chopped pecans
1/2 cup grated coconut
1/2 teaspoon vanilla

Sift flour, sugar, and salt into bowl. Cut in butter until mixture resembles coarse meal. Press firmly over the bottom of greased 9-inch square pan. Bake at 350° for 15 minutes, or until pastry is lightly browned.

Meanwhile, mix eggs, brown sugar, nuts, coconut and vanilla. Pour over partially baked pastry. Bake 30 minutes or until topping is firm. Cool 15 minutes. Spread Lemon Glaze on top. Cut into 32 small bars. Cool.

LEMON GLAZE:

2/3 cup sifted powdered sugar
1 tablespoon lemon juice
1 teaspoon grated lemon rind

Blend all ingredients until smooth and spread over bars.

Arkansas Favorites Cookbook

Chocolate-Chocolate Chip Cookies

Huge, cake-like, chocolaty, and good!

1/2 cup (1 stick) butter or margarine, melted
1 cup sugar
1 teaspoon vanilla extract
2 medium or large eggs
1/4 cup cocoa
1 7/8 cups all-purpose flour, as measured from canister
1 teaspoon baking powder
1/2 teaspoon soda
1/3 cup buttermilk
1 (6-ounce) package semi-sweet chocolate chips
1/2 cup pecans, chopped

Mix melted margarine and sugar. Add vanilla and eggs and beat well. Sift together cocoa, flour, baking powder, and soda. Stir the dry ingredients and the milk alternately into the sugar mixture. Add chocolate chips and nuts. When the batter is well mixed, drop large tablespoonfuls about 2 inches apart onto a baking sheet. Bake at 350° about 12 minutes. Cool. Makes 18 (3-inch) cookies.

Home for the Holidays

Sugar Cookies

World's Best

2 sticks margarine, softened
1 1/2 cups powdered sugar
1 egg
1/2 teaspoon almond extract
1 teaspoon vanilla
2 1/2 cups flour
1 teaspoon soda
1 teaspoon cream of tartar
1/4 teaspoon salt

Cream margarine and sugar; add egg and extracts. Sift dry ingredients and add to mixture. Roll into small balls and place on Pam-sprayed cookie sheets. Bake at 375° about 7-8 minutes. Yield: 4 1/2 dozen.

Betty is Still "Winking" at Cooking

Special "K" Cookies

1 cup sugar
1 cup + 1 tablespoon white Karo syrup
1 (12-ounce) jar of chunky peanut butter
4 1/2 cups Special "K" cereal
1 (12-ounce) package milk chocolate morsels

Bring sugar and syrup to a boil and boil 1 minute. Remove from heat and fold in peanut butter and Special "K" cereal. Spread on cookie sheet—don't pack it much. Melt the chocolate chips over very low heat. When melted, pour over above mixture. Let chocolate set up, then cut into squares. Delicious! Yield: 3 1/2 dozen squares.

Betty "Winks" at Cooking

Horney Toads

1/2 cup sugar
1/2 cup brown sugar
1 cup white syrup
Pinch of salt
1 cup peanut butter
3 cups corn flakes

Blend sugars, syrup and salt. Let come to a boil. Turn to warm and add 1 cup peanut butter. Blend well. Blend in 3 cups of corn flakes and drop by teaspoonfuls onto waxed paper.

Note: Good using crunchy or creamy peanut butter.

Asbury United Methodist Church Cook Book

Oatmeal Cookies

3/4 cup flour
2/3 cup sugar
1/2 teaspoon salt
1/2 teaspoon soda
1 teaspoon cinnamon
1 1/4 cups oats
1 cup chopped pecans
1 cup raisins
1/3 cup vegetable oil
2 unbeaten eggs
3 tablespoons Karo (dark)

Sift dry ingredients (except oats) into mixing bowl. Add remaining ingredients and beat at medium speed until well blended.

Drop on ungreased cookie sheet and bake at 350° for 10-12 minutes. Do not overbake. Delicious and chewy.

The Pink Lady...in the Kitchen

Dishpan Cookies

2 cups light brown sugar
2 cups white sugar
2 teaspoons vanilla
2 cups oil
4 eggs
4 cups flour
2 teaspoons soda
1 teaspoon salt
1 1/2 cups quick-cooking oats
4 cups corn flakes

Cream first 5 ingredients together well. Add flour, soda and salt. Fold in oats and corn flakes. Drop from spoon onto cookie sheet and bake at 350° for 7-8 minutes. Do not overbake; these are better soft.

The Farmer's Daughters

Sam and Helen Walton opened their first variety store in 1945 in Bentonville. A visitor center museum maintained by Wal-Mart Stores traces the history of this marketing giant.

Fruit Cake Cookies

1 1/2 pounds pecans, chopped
1/2 pound candied cherries, chopped
3/4 pound raisins
2 1/2 cup flour, divided
1 cup brown sugar
1/4 pound butter, softened
4 eggs, beaten well
3 scant teaspoons soda
3 tablespoons milk
1 teaspoon each, cloves, nutmeg and 1 cup cinnamon
1 1/2 ounces whiskey
1/2 to 1 pound jar pineapple preserves

Mix together pecans, cherries, raisins and 1 cup flour; set aside. Cream brown sugar and butter. Add well-beaten eggs. Dissolve soda in milk and add alternately with remaining flour and spices which have been sifted together. Add whiskey and preserves to this mixture, and then add nuts and fruits. Drop onto greased cookie sheets and bake at 350° about 12 minutes. Makes a large batch of cookies that stores well in air-tight container.

Around the Bend

Snickerdoodles

1 cup butter or shortening
1 1/2 cups sugar
2 eggs, lightly beaten
2 3/4 cups flour
2 teaspoons cream of tartar
1 teaspoon baking soda
1/2 teaspoon salt
2 tablespoons sugar
2 tablespoons cinnamon

Cream butter and sugar; beat well and add eggs. Sift dry ingredients (except sugar and cinnamon) together and combine. Chill dough several hours or overnight. Mix 2 tablespoons sugar and 2 tablespoons cinnamon. Roll dough to size of walnuts and coat in sugar and cinnamon before baking 10 minutes at 400° on well greased cookie sheet. Do not overbake. Cookies will puff up and fall after cooling.

Victorian Sampler

Pecan Puffs

1 cup butter
4 tablespoons sugar
1 tablespoon vanilla
2 cups cake flour
2 cups finely ground pecans
Powdered sugar

Cream butter and sugar. Add vanilla. Stir the flour and ground pecans in the butter mixture. Roll dough into small balls. Place on greased cookie sheets. Bake in oven 300° for 45 minutes. Roll the puffs while hot in confectioner's sugar. When cold, roll again in confectioner's sugar.

Nibbles Fa La La

Melt-in-Your-Mouth Cookies

3 egg whites
1 teaspoon lemon extract
1 cup sugar
2 cups chopped walnuts
Cooking spray

Preheat oven to 350°. Beat egg whites until stiff. Add lemon extract. Gradually add sugar. Fold in nuts. Drop by teaspoons onto sprayed cookie sheet. Bake 2-3 minutes. Turn off oven and leave for one hour. Makes about 6 dozen cookies.

Cooking to Your Heart's Content

Almond Crunch

1 cup blanched slivered almonds
1/2 cup butter
1/2 cup sugar
1 tablespoon light corn syrup

Line bottom and sides of an 8- or 9-inch cake pan with aluminum foil. Set aside. Combine all ingredients in 10-inch skillet. Bring to a boil over medium heat, stirring constantly. Boil until mixture turns golden brown—about 6 minutes. Quickly spread in prepared pan.

Cool about 15 minutes. Break into bite-size pieces. This makes a great home-made gift item!

Arkansas Favorites Cookbook

Chocolate Dipped Candy

1/2 pound butter
1 large can sweetened condensed milk
2 pounds confectioner's sugar
2 cups chopped pecans
1 (12-ounce) package semi-sweet chocolate morsels
2/3 block paraffin

Mix butter, milk and sugar. Add pecans and roll into small balls. Chill balls at least 2 hours. Melt chocolate and paraffin in top of double boiler. Dip balls in chocolate mixture. Place balls carefully on waxed paper.

Nibbles Fa La La

Lazy Millionaires

2 (14-ounce) packages vanilla caramels
1 tablespoon evaporated milk
1 cup semi-sweet chocolate chips
1/3 bar paraffin
8 cups chopped pecans

In a heavy saucepan melt first 4 ingredients; stir in pecans; drop on greased waxed paper; cool.

Celebration

Old Fashioned Fudge

2 cups sugar
1/4 teaspoon salt
1/3 cup cocoa
2 tablespoons light corn syrup
2/3 cup evaporated skim milk
2 tablespoons corn oil margarine
1 teaspoon vanilla extract
1/2 cup nuts, coarsely chopped

Spray 9x5x3-inch loaf pan with vegetable spray. In 2-quart saucepan, mix sugar, salt, cocoa, corn syrup and milk. Cook over medium heat, stirring constantly, until cocoa and sugar are dissolved. Cook, stirring occasionally, to 234° on a candy thermometer, or until small amount of mixture dropped into very cold water forms a soft ball which flattens when removed from water.

Remove from heat; add margarine. Cool mixture to 115° without stirring; bottom of pan will be lukewarm. Add vanilla. Beat vigorously for 5 minutes with wooden spoon until candy is thick and no longer glossy. Mixture will hold its shape when dropped from spoon. Quickly stir in nuts. Spread mixture evenly in pan. Cool until firm. Cut into 1 inch squares. Yield: 28 (1-inch pieces).

Per Serving (1 piece): Calories 85; Cholesterol Tr; Fat 3 gm; Sodium 35 mg

Take It To Heart

Peanut Butter Fudge

2 cups sugar
1/2 cup light corn syrup
1/2 cup evaporated milk
1/4 teaspoon salt
1 cup peanut butter

Combine sugar, syrup, milk, and salt in 2-quart saucepan. Cook to softball stage (235°). Cool 10 minutes. Add peanut butter. Beat and pour into buttered 8-inch square pan. Cut in squares.

Favorite Recipes from Associated Women for Harding

German Sweet Fudge

4 1/2 cups sugar
Pinch salt
4 tablespoons butter
1 large can evaporated milk
12 ounces semi-sweet chocolate
12 ounces German sweet chocolate
1 pint marshmallow cream
2 cups nuts

Boil sugar, salt, butter, and milk for 6 minutes. (Start timing after it comes to a boil.) Remove from fire. Add chocolates, marshmallow cream, and nuts. Beat until everything is melted. Pour into jelly roll pan that has been buttered. Cut when cool.

Nibbles Fa La La

Chocolate Fudge

Tools: large mixing bowl, stirring spoon.

3 cups powdered sugar
1/4 cup cocoa powder
1/2 cup peanut butter
1/4 cup skim milk

1) Put all ingredients in a large bowl and stir together until thoroughly mixed.
2) Shape into one-inch squares.
Yields 50 pieces (1 piece per serving).

Kids Cuisine

Pecan Pralines

1 cup buttermilk
2 cups sugar
1 teaspoon baking soda
1 tablespoon butter
1 teaspoon vanilla
2 cups pecan halves

Use large (6-8-quart) pot—mixture foams. Place buttermilk, sugar and baking soda in pot and cook over medium heat. Stir constantly while cooking. Cook until soft ball stage. Test small amounts in cool water until forms soft ball. Remove from heat and add remaining 3 ingredients. Return to stove and heat until mixture becomes glossy and starts to crystallize.

Quickly spoon out candy into 2-inch patties on waxed paper or greased baking sheet. Candy hardens when cooled.

Tip for ease of removing patty: if using waxed paper, place towel under paper.

Southwest Cookin'

Pecan Pralines

1 cup light brown sugar
1 cup white sugar
1/2 cup evaporated milk
2 tablespoons butter
2 tablespoons white corn syrup
Pinch of salt
1 teaspoon vanilla
2 cups pecan halves

In saucepan, mix sugars, milk, butter, corn syrup and salt. Cook to soft ball stage (10 minutes). Remove from heat. Add vanilla and nuts. Beat mixture until it begins to thicken (1 minute).

Drop by teaspoonfuls onto buttered waxed paper. Allow to harden. Wrap individually.

Nibbles Cooks Cajun

Orange Candied Pecans

2 cups sugar
1 cup water
3 teaspoons orange juice
Grated rind of 1 orange
3 cups chopped pecans

Cook sugar and water to soft ball stage. Add orange juice and rind; beat until it begins to thicken, add pecans, stir until sugared. Separate on wax paper. (Don't make on rainy day.)

Crossett Cook Book

Peanut Brittle

3 cups sugar
1 cup Karo
1/2 cup water
3 cups raw peanuts
1 tablespoon butter
2 teaspoons soda

Put on stove: Sugar, Karo and water. Cook to medium stage or 240°. Add peanuts. Stir and cook to 290° or hard ball stage. Remove from fire. Add butter and soda. Stir well. Pour out thin on 2 cookie sheets (well-buttered). When cold, break into pieces.

Cookin' Along the Cotton Belt

Cracker Jacks

2 sticks plus 2 tablespoons oleo
1/2 cup plus 2 tablespoons Karo
1 pound light brown sugar
1/2 teaspoon baking soda
1 teaspoon vanilla
6 quarts popped popcorn
Peanuts (optional)

Combine oleo, Karo, and brown sugar in saucepan. Bring to a boil and boil for 5 minutes. Remove from heat; add baking soda and vanilla. Mix well. Pour over popped corn and mix to coat. Bake at 250° for 30 minutes. Turn oven off and leave corn in oven for about 10 minutes. Corn will break apart as it cools.

Variation: Mix peanuts with popcorn before adding sugar mixture.

Cooking For Good Measure

Pine Ridge is the home of the Lum and Abner Museum and Jot 'Em Down Store. Chester Lauck and Norris Goff entertained radio listeners during the '40s with their down-home humor.

Pies and Desserts

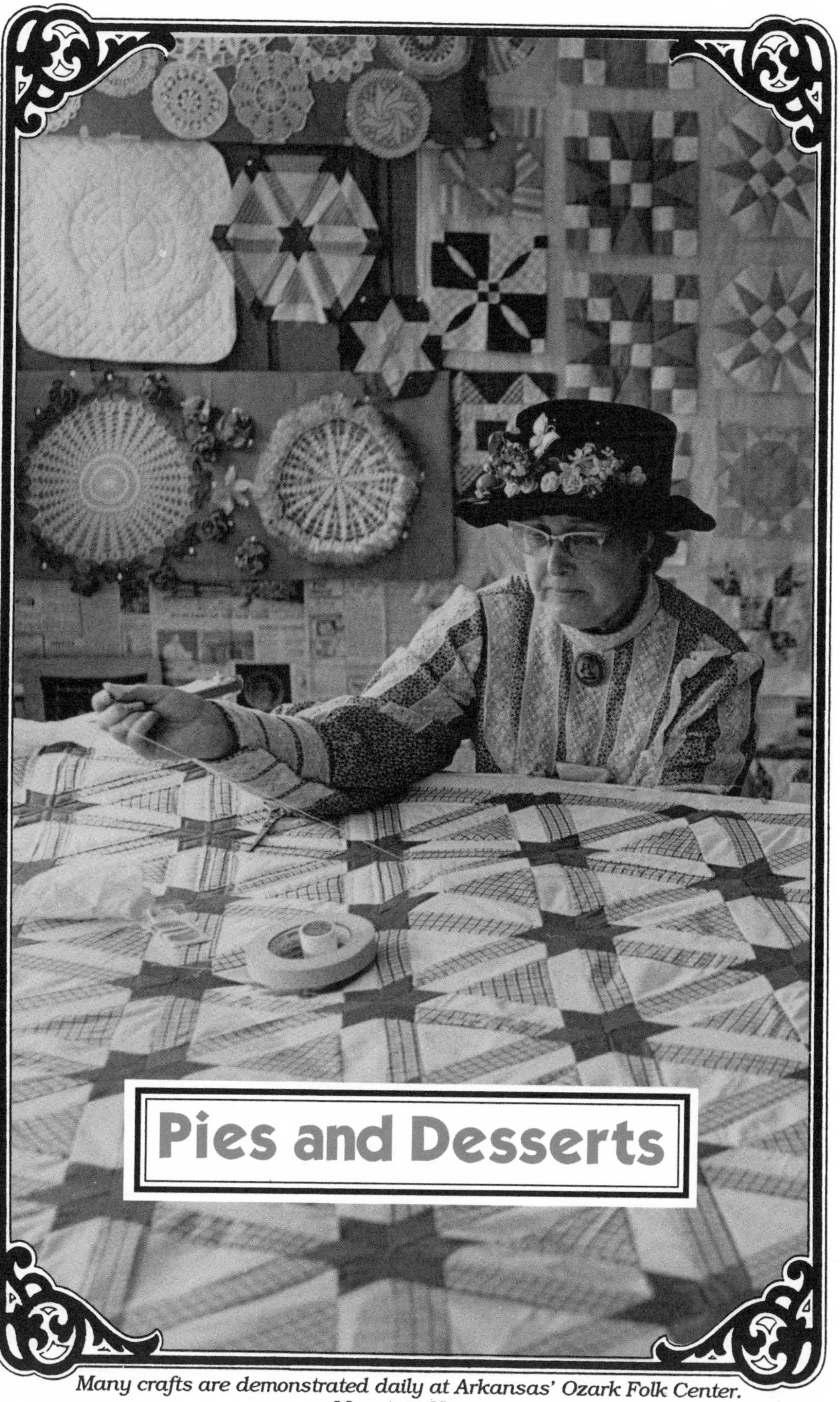

Many crafts are demonstrated daily at Arkansas' Ozark Folk Center. Mountain View.

Orange Chiffon Pie with Coconut Shell

You need fresh, very sweet orange juice to make this pie best. Its flavor recalls those days when oranges were such a special treat that children looked forward to finding one in their Christmas stockings.

1 envelope unflavored gelatin
1/4 cup cold water
4 egg yolks
1/2 cup freshly squeezed orange juice
1/2 cup granulated sugar
1 teaspoon grated orange peel
4 egg whites at room temperature
1/2 cup granulated sugar
1 baked Coconut Pie Shell (below)
1 orange, thinly sliced

Soften the gelatin in the cold water. Beat the egg yolks with the orange juice and 1/2 cup sugar. Cook the mixture in the top of a double boiler over (not in) boiling water until thick and smooth, 8-10 minutes. Remove from heat.

Add the gelatin and stir until dissolved. Add the grated orange peel. Cool.

Beat the egg whites until foamy, then begin beating in the remaining 1/2 cup sugar, a spoonful at a time. When the whites are glossy and stand in peaks, as for meringue, fold them into the cooled orange custard mixture. Pile the filling into the pie shell and chill for several hours or overnight. This pie may be made a day ahead and kept in the refrigerator. Do not cover it. Garnish with thin slices of fresh orange just before serving.

COCONUT PIE SHELL:

Use this pie shell instead of pastry for any baked or chilled pie filling that holds its own shape when prepared. It's good, easy and light.

Softened butter
Granulated sugar
1 cup (6 ounces) shredded, sweetened coconut

CONTINUED

Heavily butter a 9-inch pie plate. Sprinkle it with sugar. Firmly press the coconut against the sides and bottom of the plate.

For baked fillings, pour the mixture into the uncooked crust and proceed with baking.

For cold fillings, bake the empty shell in a preheated 375° oven for 10 minutes. Cool before filling.

Enjoying the Art of Southern Hospitality

Franke's of Little Rock Egg Custard Pie

2 tablespoons butter, softened
1 cup sugar, less 3 tablespoons
Dash of salt
6 eggs
1 pint and 2 tablespoons milk
1 unbaked pie shell

Cream butter and sugar and salt by using medium speed on electric mixer. Add 3 eggs, beat one minute; change to high speed and add 3 eggs. Beat 3 minutes. Remove from mixer and add milk. Pour into uncooked crust and cook 10 minutes at 450°. Turn heat down to 325° and bake 25 minutes longer or until set. If desired, sprinkle top with nutmeg just before baking.

Crossett Cook Book

Chocolate Decadence

(Fudge Pie Supreme)

We do not think there is a dessert on this earth that can top this one for pure unadulterated enjoyment!

1/2 stick butter, softened
1/3 cup sugar
1 tablespoon flour
1 cup pecans, finely chopped
1 stick butter, softned
1 cup sugar
2 ounces unsweetened chocolate, melted and cooled
1/8 teaspoon salt
1/4 cup flour
2 eggs, beaten
1 teaspoon vanilla
1 quart vanilla ice cream, softened
1 cup Kahlua or to taste

Preheat oven to 325°. To make crust, combine first 4 ingredients; press into sides and bottom of 9-inch pie plate.

To make filling, cream butter and sugar; add next 5 ingredients; mix well; pour into pie crust; bake 35-40 minutes or until filling is set. Do *not* overbake! To make ice cream topping, stir Kahlua into ice cream; put in plastic container; freeze.

To serve, pie should be warm or room temperature; stir ice cream well; spoon over each slice of pie. Serves 6-8 marvelously!!

Southern Flavors' Little Chocolate Book

Coconut Cream Pie

1 pie shell, baked
1/4 cup sugar
1/2 cup cake mix (yellow)
3 egg yolks
1 1/2 cups milk
1/4 stick butter
3/4 cup coconut

Mix sugar, cake mix, and egg yolks. Blend in enough milk to mix well. Add remaining milk; cook until thick. Add butter, then coconut, and pour into baked curst.

Evening Shade

Tollville Strawberry Pie

1 (3-ounce) package cream cheese, room temperature
2-3 tablespoons milk
1 (9-inch) baked pie crust
1 quart ripe fresh strawberries, washed, capped and drained
3/4 cup sugar
2 tablespoons cornstarch
1/3 cup water
Red food coloring
Whipped cream

Mix cream cheese with milk until smooth. Spread on baked pie crust with back of teaspoon, until entire pie crust is covered. Cut half of the strawberries in half and put in a saucepan with sugar, cornstarch, and water. Cook over medium heat until thickened, adding a few drops of red food coloring. Place remaining strawberries (whole) in the pie crust and pour cooked berry mixture over whole berries. Chill. Serve with whipped cream or Cool Whip.

Prairie Harvest

Pumpkin Pie

3 eggs, slightly beaten
2 cups pumpkin, canned
1 1/2 cups sugar
1 large can Pet milk
1/2 teaspoon salt
1/2 teaspoon ginger
1/4 teaspoon cloves, or less
1 teaspoon cinnamon
1/4 teaspoon nutmeg
1 (9-inch) unbaked pie crust

Mix eggs, pumpkin, sugar and milk. Add rest of ingredients and pour in pie shell (have edges on crust crimped high). Bake in hot oven 425° for 10 minutes; reduce to slow (325°) and bake 30-35 minutes longer or until firm. Use Festive Nut Topping on top of pie.

FESTIVE NUT TOPPING:
1/2 cup chopped pecans
1 tablespoon margarine
2 tablespoons brown sugar
1 1/2 teaspoons grated orange rind

Mix together until crumbly. After 45 minutes baking time, take pie from oven and spoon mixture around edge. Bake 15 minutes more.

Betty "Winks" at Cooking

Frozen Pecan Pie

1 (8-ounce) package cream cheese, softened
3/4 cup light Karo
1/4 cup brown sugar, packed firm
3/4 cup milk
1 teaspoon vanilla
1 cup chopped pecans

Mix first 3 ingredients in large bowl with mixer at high speed. Beat until smooth. Add (with mixer at medium speed) milk and vanilla until blended. Add pecans. Pour in 9-inch graham cracker crust. Freeze for 6 hours. Remove 15 minutes before serving. Cool Whip or whipped cream topping, optional.

A Heritage of Good Tastes

Karo Pecan Pie

1 cup sugar
3/4 cup light corn syrup
1/2 cup butter
3 eggs, beaten
1 3/4 cups pecan halves
1 teaspoon vanilla
1/8 teaspoon salt

Blend sugar, syrup and 1/2 cup butter in saucepan. Cook over medium heat, stirring constantly, until mixture comes to a boil. Blend mixture slowly into eggs. Stir in pecan halves, vanilla, and salt. Pour into 9-inch pie shell. Bake at 350° for 40 minutes.

High Cotton Cookin'

Arkansas Pastries

Delightful flakiness that comes from both fat and yeast.

1 (1/4-ounce) package active dry yeast
1/2 cup warm water (115-120°)
2 sticks pie crust mix
1 tablespoon sugar
1 egg yolk
1/2 cup strawberry preserves
1 cup powdered sugar, sifted
1 tablespoon milk
1 teaspoon vanilla extract

Dissolve yeast in warm water; set aside. Crumble pie-crust mix into bowl; stir in sugar, egg yolk, and dissolved yeast. Mix well. Roll dough into balls the size of a large marble and place on ungreased baking sheet. Make deep indention in the center and shape into shells. Spoon 1/2 teaspoon preserves into each shell. Let rise in a warm place for one hour. (Pastries do not double in bulk.)

Bake 12-15 minutes at 375°. Cool slightly and remove from baking sheet. Blend powdered sugar, milk, and vanilla for icing. Drizzle or brush over pastries while still warm. Makes 50 bite-sized pastries.

Home for the Holidays

Crumb Top Apple Pie

(1939)

4 medium-size tart apples
1 tablespoon butter
1/2 teaspoon nutmeg
3 tablespoons water
1/2 cup sugar

CRUST:
1 cup flour
1/2 cup butter
1/2 cup brown sugar

Peel, core and slice apples in pie dish. There is *no* bottom crust. Dot with butter and sprinkle nutmeg and water and sugar. Mix flour and butter and brown sugar with fork until crumbly and spread over top. Bake in 400° oven for 20 minutes; then 350° oven for 15 minutes. Serve warm with whipped cream or ice cream.

Dixie Cook Book V

Apple Pecan Pie

1 cup sugar
1 tablespoon flour
1 teaspoon cinnamon
Dash of salt
4 cups coarsely grated apples
1 1/2 cups grated Cheddar cheese
1 egg, beaten
6 tablespoons melted butter
1 (9-inch) unbaked pie shell
1 cup chopped pecans

Combine first 4 ingredients; add apples and cheese; toss gently. Stir in egg and butter; spoon mixture into pastry shell; sprinkle with pecans. Bake 10 minutes at 400°; reduce heat to 350°; bake 50 minutes. (If using food processor to prepare apples; do not peel.)

Celebration

Fried Apple Pies

This recipe comes from the Pioneer Crafts Festival held in Rison annually. It has been a festival secret for over 70 years!

8 ounces dried apples
5 cups water
1 cup sugar
1 teaspoon cinnamon
2 1/2 tablespoons cornstarch
2 tablespoons lemon juice

Cook apples in water for 20 minutes. Combine sugar, cornstarch, and cinnamon. Add to apples. Add lemon juice. Cook until thickened. Cool.

PASTRY:
3 cups flour
1 cup + 2 tablespoons shortening
1 egg, beaten slightly
7 tablespoons water
1 teaspoon salt
1 teaspoon vinegar

Cut shortening into flour. Combine egg, water, salt, and vinegar. Pour into flour mixture and mix.

Pinch small amount of dough and roll out on floured board. Cut out, using a saucer as a guide. Put 1 tablespoon apple mixture on dough. Wet edges of dough with iced water. Fold dough over apple mixture and seal by pressing a floured fork around edges. Fry in 1-2 inches of oil in an electric skillet on highest setting. Cook until golden brown, turning only once. Glaze with a mixture of powdered sugar and water. Yields about 24 pies.

A Great Taste of Arkansas

Ding Dong Days festival, named for the song, "I'm a Ding Dong Daddy from Dumas," is held the last weekend in July in...you guessed it...Dumas!

Mountain Cobbler

[Cooked in Dutch oven]

1 cup Sourdough Starter
1 1/2 cups flour
1/2 cup brown sugar
1/2 cup sugar
2 teaspoons cinnamon
1/2 cup cooking oil
2 cans cherry pie filling

Mix starter, flour, sugars, cinnamon and oil in a bowl. Place cherry filling in bottom of [Dutch] oven; then spread the bowl of mix on top. Bake 25-30 minutes in covered [Dutch] oven. Serves 8.

Variations:

1) Use blueberry filling instead of cherry filling.
2) Add 1 cup of raisins with the fruit filling.
3) Add 1/2 cup of chopped pecans.

SOURDOUGH STARTER:

1 envelope yeast
1 1/2 cups warm water (not hot)
2 cups flour
1 tablespoon sugar
1 teaspoon salt

Dissolve yeast in warm water; then mix in other ingredients. Set aside in a covered dish in a warm place for 1 or 2 days.

Always leave at least 1 cup of starter for seed. Replenish with 1 cup flour and 1 cup milk or water. Starter action may be delayed for several days by storage in refrigeration.

Dutch Oven Cooking

Crusty Peach Cobbler

3 cups sliced fresh peaches
1/4 cup sugar
1 teaspoon almond extract
1 tablespoon lemon juice
1 teaspoon grated lemon peel
1 1/2 cups enriched emergency flour
1/2 teaspoon salt
3 teaspoons baking powder
1 tablespoon sugar
1/3 cup shortening
1/2 cup milk
1 well-beaten egg
2 tablespoons sugar

Arrange peaches in greased, 8-inch square baking pan. Sprinkle with mixture of 1/4 cup sugar, almond extract, lemon juice, and lemon peel. Heat in oven while preparing shortcake.

Sift together flour, salt, baking powder, and 1 tablespoon sugar; cut in shortening until mixture is like coarse crumbs. Add milk and egg at once; stir just until flour is moistened. Spread dough over hot peaches. Sprinkle with 2 tablespoons sugar. Bake in hot oven (400°) 40 minutes.

Serves 6.

Perfectly Delicious

Peach Cobbler

3/4 cup flour
1/8 teaspoon salt
2 teaspoons baking powder
2 cups sugar
3/4 cup milk
1/2 cup margarine
2 cups fresh sliced peaches

Sift flour, salt, and baking powder. Mix with 1 cup sugar; slowly stir in milk to make batter. Melt butter in 8x8x2-inch pan. Pour batter over melted butter. Do not stir. Mix peaches with remaining 1 cup sugar and carefully spoon over batter. Bake 1 hour at 350°. Serve hot or cold, with cream if desired.

Southwest Cookin'

Peach Kuchen

1/2 cup butter
2 cups flour
2 tablespoons sugar
1/2 teaspoon salt
1/4 teaspoon baking powder
6-8 Freestone peaches
1/2 - 3/4 cup cinnamon sugar (1/2 teaspoon cinnamon to 1 teaspoon sugar)
1 cup whipping cream
2 egg yolks

Melt butter and mix together with next 4 ingredients, until crumbly. Pat firmly into pan. Peel 6-8 Freestone peaches; put on top of crust. Mix and sprinkle the cinnamon sugar over the top.

Bake 15-20 minutes at 350°. Mix the whipping cream and egg yolks and pour over all. Bake 30 minutes more. Cool and serve with ice cream. (Double for a larger group.)

Arkansas Favorites Cookbook

Divine Torte

8 egg whites
1 teaspoon vinegar
1 teaspoon vanilla
2 cups sugar

Add vanilla and vinegar to egg whites after you start beating. Beat until mixture forms peaks. Add sugar gradually, about 1 tablespoon at a time, beating constantly. Beat long time. Have ready 2 (9-inch) cake pans, lightly greased and lined with brown paper. Bake at 300° for 1 hour and 15 minutes. Remove from oven, remove paper and let cool.

3 (1/2-pint) cartons whipping cream
12 Heath bars

Whip cream and grind candy bars. Cover 1 layer with cream and half the candy. Put on second layer and ice all over with cream. Sprinkle rest of candy on top. Put together about 2 hours before serving, or torte may be made the day before serving.

Dixie Cookbook IV

Blueberry Torte

1 cup flour
1/2 cup chopped pecans
1/4 cup brown sugar
1/2 cup butter
1 (8-ounce) package cream cheese
1 cup powdered sugar
1 teaspoon vanilla
2 packages Dream Whip
1 can blueberry pie filling

Mix flour, pecans, brown sugar, and butter together. Pat into 9x13-inch pan. Bake at 400° for 15 minutes or until done. Mix cheese, sugar, and vanilla together. Beat Dream Whip by directions and mix into cheese. Pour into cooled crust. Spread top with fruit filling. Chill at least 8 hours or overnight.

Thirty Years at the Mansion

Rice Pudding

2 cups rice, cooked
5 eggs
1 cup sugar
1/4 cup butter or oleo, melted
2 cups milk
1 teaspoon vanilla
1/4 teaspoon nutmeg
1/2 cup raisins (optional)

Beat eggs; add sugar, butter, milk, vanilla, and nutmeg. Add rice, and raisins, if desired, and pour into a greased 2-quart casserole. Bake at 350° for 45 minutes.

LEMON SAUCE:
1 cup sugar
1 tablespoon cornstarch
1/2 teaspoon salt
3 eggs, slightly beaten
Juice of 2 lemons
Rind of 2 lemons, grated
1 cup water
2 tablespoons butter

Mix sugar, cornstarch and salt. Add eggs, lemon juice, grated rind and water. Cook in double boiler until thick, stirring constantly. Add butter and let cool.

Thirty Years at the Mansion

Rice Pudding

1 cup cooked rice
1 cup milk
2 well-beaten eggs
1/3 cup sugar
1/2 teaspoon salt
Dash mace

Mix ingredients. Spread in pan 1-inch deep. Bake until light brown on top. Cut in squares.

A Heritage of Good Tastes

Impressions of dinosaur tracks taken from an archealogical dig are on display at the Howard County Courthouse in Nashville.

Apricot-Apple Steamed Pudding

A tart, dense pudding with great flavor and texture.

2 1/2 cups white flour
1 teaspoon salt
1 teaspoon baking powder
1 teaspoon cinnamon
1/4 teaspoon nutmeg
1/4 cup butter
3/4 cup brown sugar
1 egg, beaten
1/2 cup milk
1 cup peeled, finely chopped apple
1/2 cup snipped, dried apricots
1/2 cup walnuts, chopped

Combine flour, salt, baking powder, and spices. In separate bowl, cream butter and sugar; add egg and milk; blend well. Add dry ingredients to creamed mixture and stir in nuts and fruit. Beat until well blended.

Pour batter into a well-greased and floured 6-cup mold or 2 (1-pound) coffee cans. Cover top of mold or cans tightly with aluminum foil. Steam in crockpot or large pan. Pour hot water 2 inches deep in crockpot and place covered cans in pot. Cover pot with lid; steam 3 hours. In kettle, on top of the stove, pour in hot water to a 2 inch depth. Place cans in kettle, steam for 2 - 2 1/2 hours or until pudding is firm.

Remove from pot when done; let stand 5 minutes. Invert on serving plate. Serve warm or cold. Slice and serve plain or with ice cream or butter.

Arkansas Celebration Cookbook

Bread Pudding with Raspberry or Brandy Sauce

1 (8-ounce) long loaf French or Italian bread (not sourdough), or 8 slices firm white bread, crusts removed
1/4 cup butter, softened
4 eggs
2 egg yolks
3/4 cup sugar
1 1/2 teaspoons vanilla
1/2 teaspoon cinnamon
1/4 teaspoon nutmeg
1/8 teaspoon salt
3 cups milk
2/3 cup heavy cream
Powdered sugar
Whipped cream

Spread butter on one side of bread. Layer slices, buttered side up, in a greased 2-quart baking dish or soufflé dish. In large bowl, beat eggs, yolks, sugar, vanilla, cinnamon, nutmeg and salt. Heat milk and cream until small bubbles appear around edge of pan. Gradually add to egg mixture. Pour over bread. Place baking pan in another shallow pan which has 1 inch of water up sides of baking dish. Bake for 45-50 minutes, until set, at 375°. Cool slightly and dust with powdered sugar. Broil 1 minute until sugar melts and forms glaze.

RASPBERRY SAUCE:

2 (10-ounce) packages frozen raspberries
1 tablespoon cornstarch
1/2 cup cold water
1 tablespoon lemon juice
Sugar (if needed, to taste)

Purée raspberries, strain and discard seeds. In pan, mix cornstarch and water until smooth. Add purée and cook until thickened, stirring constantly. Cool and add lemon juice. Serve warm sauce on plate or bowl, bread pudding on top, and garnished with whipped cream.

BRANDY SAUCE:

3 egg yolks
1 cup sugar
1 teaspoon vanilla
1 1/2 cups milk
1 tablespoon cornstarch
1/4 cup water
1 1/2 ounces brandy (whiskey or rum may be used)

CONTINUED

In saucepan slightly beat egg yolks and add next sugar, vanilla, and milk. Blend well. Cook over low heat until mixture comes to boil. Blend cornstarch in water and stir into hot mixture. Continue cooking until thickened. Remove from heat and stir in brandy. Serve warm or chilled.

Option: Add 1/2 cup raisins to hot mixture.

Victorian Sampler

Brownie Pudding

Tools: dry measuring cups, liquid measuring cup, measuring spoons, medium mixing bowl, stirring spoon, small mixing bowl, 8x8-inch square baking pan, no-stick cooking spray.

1 cup all-purpose flour
1/2 cup granulated sugar
2 tablespoons cocoa powder
2 teaspoons baking powder
1/2 teaspoon salt
1/2 cup skim milk
2 tablespoons vegetable oil
1 teaspoon vanilla extract
1/2 cup brown sugar
1/4 cup cocoa powder
1 3/4 cups hot water (from tap)

1) Place first 5 ingredients in a medium mixing bowl. Stir together. 2) Add milk, oil, and vanilla. Stir until smooth. Stir in nuts. 3) Pour into pan sprayed with cooking spray. 4) Preheat oven to 350°. 5) Put brown sugar and cocoa powder in small bowl. Mix together. Sprinkle over batter. 6) Pour hot water over entire batter. Do not stir. 7) Bake about 45 minutes. Yields 9 servings.

Kids Cuisine

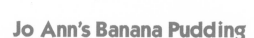

Jo Ann's Banana Pudding

2/3 cup sugar
1/4 teaspoon salt
5 tablespoons flour
2 1/2 cups milk
3 eggs, separated
1 tablespoon butter
2 teaspoons vanilla
1/4 teaspoon rum flavoring
5-6 small ripe bananas
1 small box vanilla wafers, crumbled
1/4 cup sugar

Mix dry ingredients. Add milk; cook until hot. Add a little of hot mixture to beaten egg yolks, then add egg yolk mixture to milk mixture and cook, stirring constantly, until thick. Add butter, 1 teaspoon vanilla, and rum. Cool. Layer bananas, crumbled wafers, and pudding; repeat.

Beat egg whites until stiff and add 1/4 cup sugar slowly and 1 teaspoon vanilla. Spread meringue on top. Bake at 350° until meringue is golden brown.

Note: Do the pudding 1 1/2 times for a 9x13-inch casserole.

MICROWAVE INSTRUCTIONS FOR PUDDING:
Mix dry ingredients. Add milk, cook on MEDIUM-HIGH (#8) for 8 minutes, stirring a couple of times, then add a little of the hot mixture to beaten egg yolks, then add egg mixture to hot milk mixture. Cook an additional 5 minutes on MEDIUM-HIGH, stirring frequently with wire whisk. After removing from micro, add butter and flavorings. Cool.

Betty "Winks" at Cooking

Apricot Sour-Cream Dessert

Light and refreshing. With a cup of coffee or a glass of milk, the perfect end to the hearty venison meal.

GRAHAM-CRACKER CRUST:

3 cups graham-cracker crumbs
1/2 cup (1 stick) butter or margarine, melted
1/2 cup brown sugar
1/8 teaspoon salt
2 tablespoons milk

Blend together crumbs, butter, sugar, and salt. Sprinkle milk over crumb mixture and mix well. Press mixture onto bottom and sides of an 8-inch square baking dish. Bake at 350° 10 minutes, until lightly browned. Cool.

APRICOT FILLING:

1 (16-ounce) can apricots
1 (3-ounce) package orange-flavored gelatin
1 (8 1/2-ounce) can crushed pineapple
1 cup sour cream

Drain apricots, chop, and refrigerate. Measure 1 cup apricot juice, add water if needed to fill cup, and bring to boil. Dissolve gelatin in boiling apricot juice. Refrigerate until the consistency of egg whites. Drain pineapple and reserve juice to use in topping. Blend in sour cream, apricots, and pineapple. Pour into cooled crust and chill until set.

TOPPING:

1/4 cup sugar
1 1/2 tablespoons flour
1/2 cup pineapple juice
1/2 cup whipping cream, chilled

Combine sugar and flour. Mix with pineapple juice and cook until thickened, stirring as needed to prevent lumping. Cool thoroughly. Whip cream and fold cooled pineapple mixture into it. Spread over apricot filling. Cover and refrigerate until serving time. Makes 8 (2- x 4-inch) servings.

Home for the Holidays

Mousse au Chocolate

4 bars German sweet chocolate
1/4 pound butter
6 egg yolks
6 tablespoons white corn syrup
1 cup sugar
1/4 cup water
6 egg whites
2 cups whipped cream
Shaved chocolate (for garnish)

Place butter and chocolate in a double boiler and melt slowly. Set aside and cool. Beat egg yolks until thick and creamy. In pan combine corn syrup, sugar and water until it spins 8-inch thread, or 232°-234° on a candy thermometer. Pour hot syrup into egg yolks, beating constantly with electric mixer. (Pour slowly.) Add melted chocolate and butter. Fold in stiffly beaten egg whites. Chill for 2 hours. Beat furiously. Fold in 2 cups of whipped cream. Chill for at least 4 hours before serving. Serve in parfait glasses with shaved chocolate for garnish. Incredible!

Nibbles Ooo La La

Maple Mousse

4 eggs, separated
1 cup maple syrup
1 pint of whipping cream

Beat yolks of eggs very light. Boil the maple syrup 5 minutes; pour very slowly over beaten eggs. Return this to pot on stove and cook for 5 minutes or so, stirring constantly. Pour into a large mixing bowl and let cool (stir often). Whip cream and, when custard is cool, fold in cream, and last the 4 eggs whites beaten very dry. Turn into large refrigerator tray.

Serves 8.

Dixie Cookbook IV

French explorers found a tribe of Indians, probably the Osage, whom they name "Aux Arcs" (bow carriers)—hence the name "Ozarks."

Fresh Coconut Bavarian

1 1/2 tablespoons gelatin
1/4 cup cold water
1 cup milk
1 cup sugar
2 cups whipping cream, whipped
2 cups grated fresh coconut
1 teaspoon vanilla
1/8 teaspoon salt

Soften gelatin in cold water; set aside. Scald milk, add sugar; add softened gelatin. Combine the remaining ingredients. Carefully fold both mixtures together. Refrigerate until firm in large ring mold.

SAUCE:

1 cup brown sugar, packed
1 cup granulated sugar
1 tablespoon flour
1 tablespoon butter
1 1/3 cups milk

Combine sugars and flour; add butter and milk. Bring to a boil. Serve hot over the Bavarian. May be made ahead and reheated.

Note: This is an elegant dessert. Bavarian may be poured into champagne glasses or individual peau de créme pots. This is a traditional Christmas dessert in our home.

Prairie Harvest

Freddie's Tasty Apples

1 large can pineapple tidbits, drained, but save juice
4 tablespoons flour
1/2 teaspoon salt
1 1/2 cups sugar
2 eggs, beaten
2 tablespoons butter
6 apples
1 teaspoon lemon juice
1/2 cup chopped pecans, (optional)

Add water to the pineapple juice to make 2 cups of liquid. Mix flour, salt, and sugar—add liquid and cook until thick, then add a little of the hot mixture to the beaten eggs, then add eggs into hot mixture. Add butter. Let cool.

Chop apples (leave peeling on) and sprinkle with lemon juice. Pour cooled mixture over apples, pineapple and pecans. Chill.

Betty "Winks" at Cooking

Purple Monster Applesauce

Little people enjoy crazy-looking things. They think they are funny.

1 (12 1/2-ounce) can applesauce, sweetened or unsweetened
1 teaspoon honey
1 1/2 tablespoons grape juice, frozen concentrate
1/2 teaspoon cinnamon

Mix in medium bowl the applesauce ingredients. Blend well. Spoon into small serving dishes.

1/2 cup red or green grape halves (eyes)
6 banana slices, halved (mouth)
1/2 cup shredded coconut, sweet or unsweetened (Tint green with 2 or 3 drops of food coloring)

Arrange fruit on top of applesauce to make faces. (Let the kids help. They love to dream up faces.) Serves 4-6.

A Kaleidoscope of Creative Healthy Cooking

Baked Bananas with Strawberry Flambé

This creation makes its own sauce as it bakes. If you are in a hurry or want to keep things simple, omit the flambé step.

6 medium-sized bananas
1 tablespoon soft butter
30 whole strawberries, fresh or frozen
1/4 cup brown sugar
1/4 cup Grand Marnier (optional)

Preheat oven to 350°. Peel the bananas and arrange them, whole, side by side in a buttered baking dish. Lightly spread the butter on top of the bananas. Rinse and hull the strawberries, if they are fresh. Arrange them in rows in the spaces between the bananas. Sprinkle the brown sugar over the berries and bananas.

Bake for about 25 minutes, or until the bananas are just cooked through. Do not overbake.

To serve flambéed, warm the Grand Marnier and pour it over the bananas and berries. Light immediately. For the most impressive effect, do this at the table with the lights dim so the flame will show. Serve as soon as the fire goes out. Makes 6 servings.

Enjoying the Art of Southern Hospitality

Peach Melba

1 cup sugar
1 cup water
1/4 teaspoon salt
1 teaspoon vanilla
6 fresh ripe peaches
1 box frozen red raspberries
1/3 cup sugar
6 meringue shells

Put sugar, water, and salt in pan and stir over low heat until sugar dissolves. Bring to boil for 3 or 4 minutes. Remove from fire and stir in vanilla.

Take 3 of the peaches and remove skins by dipping in hot water. Put these in the sugar syrup. Simmer until tender, 5-8 minutes. Remove peaches. Repeat this process with other 3 peaches. Put all these in the syrup and cool in refrigerator until some syrup is absorbed—even overnight.

Shortly before serving, mash raspberries through extra fine sieve to remove seeds only. Into this stir the 1/3 cup sugar and chill.

To serve, put drained peach in meringue shell or on slice of vanilla ice cream. Cover each serving with 2 or 3 tablespoons of raspberry sauce. This may be made 2 or 3 days beforehand. (Peach Melba is the famous dessert named in honor of opera star Nellie Melba.)

Dixie Cookbook IV

Peaches and Cream Soufflé

- Butter
- Sugar
- 1 cup water
- 1 cup sugar, divided
- 6 eggs, separated
- 2 envelopes unflavored gelatin
- 2 teaspoons grated lemon peel
- 1/2 teaspoon almond extract
- 1/2 teaspoon vanilla
- 1/4 teaspoon ground ginger
- 4 cups sliced ripe peaches
- 3 tablespoons lemon juice
- 3/4 teaspoon cream of tartar
- 1 cup whipping cream, whipped
- Peach slices, optional
- Mint leaves, optional

Make a 4-inch band of triple-thickness aluminum foil long enough to go around 1 1/2-quart soufflé dish or casserole, and overlap 2 inches. Lightly butter 1 side of band and sprinkle with sugar. Wrap around outside of dish with sugar-side in. Fasten with tape, paper clip or string. Collar should extend 2-inches above rim of dish. Set aside.

In medium saucepan, combine water, 1/4 cup sugar and egg yolks. Sprinkle with gelatin and let stand 1 minute. Cook over medium heat, stirring until gelatin is dissolved, about 5 minutes. Stir in lemon peel, flavorings and ginger.

Combine peaches with lemon juice, and mash to form a pulp mixture. Stir into gelatin mixture. Chill, stirring occasionally, until mixture mounds slightly when dropped from spoon.

In large mixing bowl, beat egg whites with cream of tartar at high speed until foamy. Add remaining 3/4 cup sugar, 1 tablespoon at a time, beating constantly until sugar is dissolved and whites are glossy and stand in soft peaks.

Gently but thoroughly, fold chilled gelatin mixture and whipped cream into whites. Carefully pour into prepared dish. Chill until firm, several hours or overnight. Just before serving, carefully remove foil band. Garnish with peach slices and mint leaves, if desired. Serves 6.

A Very Special Treat

Strawberry Luscious

2 small packages strawberry Jello
2 cups boiling water
1 large (16-ounce) package frozen strawberries
1 (15 1/2-ounce) can crushed pineapple
2 large bananas
1/2 cup sour cream

Dissolve Jello in boiling water. Add strawberries and pineapple, undrained. Add whipped bananas. Pour half into 8x12-inch pan; chill until set.

Spread sour cream over top and cover with remaining gelatin. Chill until firm. May use Cool Whip.

Asbury United Methodist Church Cook Book

Fraises à la Neige

2 pounds frozen strawberries, puréed
1 cup sugar
16 egg whites
1/2 teaspoon salt

Purée strawberries; add sugar. Beat egg whites with salt until stiff peaks form. In large pot, heat 2 quarts water. Using a scoop, place a scoop of egg white in water, 30 seconds on each side. Place on paper towel. Place the meringue balls in a pretty dish. Pour strawberry purée over this and serve. Serves 6-8. May be served in individual dishes also.

Nibbles Ooo La La

Millions of guests have been welcomed to *The Great Passion Play*, a premier outdoor religious drama performed on a multi-level staging area from May to November in Eureka Springs.

Faubus Fruit Fluff

2 pounds red grapes, seeded
1 (#303) can crushed pineapple
1 package salad marshmallows
1 cup chopped pecans
1 package plain gelatin
3 egg yolks
Juice of 3 lemons
1/2 cup sugar
1 pint whipping cream

Mix grapes, pineapple, marshmallows, and pecans. Sprinkle lightly with gelatin and set aside. Combine egg yolks, lemon juice, and sugar in a saucepan and cook until thick. Cool completely, then mix with fruit. Fold in whipping cream and chill.

Thirty Years at the Mansion

Joe T. Robinson (1902-1937) was the last US senator in the nation elected by a state legislature. He also holds the unique record of being congressman, governor, and senator-elect all within 14 days. Orval E. Faubus served the longest time of any governor of the state of Arkansas—six terms (1955-67).

Peppermint Pie with Rice Krispies Crust

CRUST:

1 (4-ounce) bar German Sweet Chocolate
4 tablespoons margarine
3 cups Rice Krispies

Break chocolate into pieces in saucepan; add margarine; heat until melted. Take off fire and add Rice Krispies. Mix well and press in bottom and sides of a 10-inch pie pan. Refrigerate.

FILLING:

1/2 gallon vanilla ice cream, softened
3/4 cup crushed peppermint candy

Break candy into very small pieces; stir into softened ice cream. Put filling in crust and freeze until firm, 3-4 hours. Serves 8.

Southern Accent

Paradise Pie

3 egg whites
1 cup sugar
20 soda crackers (small squares)
1 cup pecans, chopped
1/2 pint heavy cream, whipped
1 teaspoon vanilla
6 ounces grated coconut

Beat egg whites until almost stiff. Add sugar gradually, continuing to beat. Fold in crumbled crackers and nuts. Scrape into 9-inch pie pan that has been well buttered. Bake 20 minutes at 325°. Cool. Top with whipped cream flavored with vanilla, and sprinkle with grated coconut.

I first had this simple but delicious dessert 30 years ago in Bonneville, Arkansas. It is still a favorite at the Red Apple. It is quickly made and freezes well. Serves 6.

Feasts of Eden

Butter Brickle Ice Cream Pie

1/2 cup brown sugar
1/4 cup butter
1 tablespoon water
4 cups cornflakes
1/2 gallon vanilla ice cream

Bring to boil the first 3 ingredients, stirring constantly. Pour the mixture over the cornflakes in a large bowl. Using a 9-inch pie tin or plate, press around two-thirds of the mixture in the bottom and up the sides of the pie plate. Soften the ice cream by setting out for a brief time. Spread the ice cream into the cornflake-lined pie plate. When it is filled, spread the remaining cornflake mixture over the top of the ice cream and return to the freezer. Serves 8.

Cookin' in the Spa

Frozen Cream Cups

1 (8-ounce) package cream cheese
1 cup sifted powdered sugar
2 cups whipping cream
1 teaspoon vanilla
Fresh fruit

Beat softened cream cheese until smooth; blend in powdered sugar, then whipping cream and vanilla. Pour into 8 paper-lined muffin tins and freeze. Remove paper liners; spoon fresh fruit on top of each cream. Serves 8.

Southern Accent

Arkansas' only authentic Japanese Garden was a gift from Pine Bluff's "sister city" - Iwai, Japan.

Quick Strawberry Ice Cream

It doesn't need an ice-cream freezer!

I didn't expect much from this recipe when I tried it, but the ice cream is surprisingly good, definitely superior to packaged ice cream, and embarrassingly easy. You need a blender or food processor to make it.

3 cups whole frozen strawberries
1/2 cup whipping cream
2 eggs
1/3 cup granulated sugar
2 teaspoons lemon juice
1/2 teaspoon vanilla

Soften the berries a few minutes before beginning. Mix the cream, eggs, and sugar in the blender or food processor. Turn the machine on and off quickly, processing just enough to mix the ingredients.

With the motor running, feed in the frozen strawberries one at a time. Blend or process until the mixture is smooth, stopping to stir with a spatula if necessary. Add the lemon juice and vanilla in the last few seconds of processing.

Serve at once or store in your freezer. If you store the ice cream in the freezer, remove it about 15 minutes before serving to soften it slightly. Makes about 4 servings. (To double the recipe, prepare in two batches.)

Enjoying the Art of Southern Hospitality

Buttermilk Sherbet

1 cup buttermilk
1 cup sugar
1 (8-ounce) can crushed pineapple, undrained
1 teaspoon vanilla
1 pint heavy cream, whipped

Mix buttermilk, sugar, pineapple with juice and vanilla. Freeze until mushy. Fold whipped cream into chilled mixture. Place in freezer trays and stir once or twice while freezing.

Betty "Winks" at Cooking

Homemade Strawberry Ice Cream

3 cups non-fat dry milk powder
6 tablespoons margarine, melted
1 cup boiling water
24 packages Equal
1 small package Nutra-Sweet Vanilla Pudding
4 cans sugar-free strawberry soft drink
16 ounces frozen, unsweetened strawberries, sliced
3-4 cups skim milk

Blend dry milk powder, margarine, water, and Equal in blender. Pour into ice cream freezer container. Slowly stir in pudding. Mix well. Slowly mix in soft drink and strawberries. Add milk to fill line. Freeze. Yield: 4 quarts.

Per Serving (1/2 cup): Calories 55; Cholesterol 0; Fat 2gm; Sodium 80mg; ADA Exchange Value: 1 skim milk

Take It To Heart

Chunky Watermelon Sherbet

1 cup sugar
3 tablespoons lemon juice
4 cups diced, seeded watermelon
1/8 teaspoon salt
1 envelope unflavored gelatin
1/4 cup cold water
1 cup whipping cream

Combine sugar, lemon juice, watermelon, and salt; refrigerate 30 minutes. Spoon mixture into container of electric blender; process until smooth.

Soften gelatin in cold water; place over low heat, and stir until gelatin is dissolved. Add to watermelon mixture, stirring well. Add whipping cream, and beat until fluffy.

Pour into freezer can of a 1-gallon size ice cream freezer. Freeze according to manufacturer's instructions.

Yield: 1 quart.

Cooking with Ms. Watermelon

Bing Cherry Sauce

For Ice Cream
(1939)

1 (#2) can bing cherries
1 jar currant jelly
2 tablespoons cognac or good whiskey
1/4 pound blanched almonds, slivered

Drain cherries. Let juice and jelly come to a boil and simmer about 10 minutes. Then add cherries cut in halves, and slivered almonds, and reheat in oven in Pyrex dish. Just before serving, pour cognac on top and send to the table lighted.

Dixie Cook Book V

Praline Parfait

SAUCE:
2 cups dark corn syrup
1/3 cup sugar
1/3 cup water
2 cups chopped pecans

In medium saucepan heat all sauce ingredients. Stir to boil. Remove from heat. Cool.

PARFAITS:
Vanilla ice cream
Whipped cream
Chopped pecans

In parfait glass alternate ice cream and sauce, ending with sauce. Top with whipped cream and chopped pecans.

Nibbles Cooks Cajun

Lemon Sherbet

1 1/4 cups lemon juice (juice of 8 or 9 lemons)
1 lemon rind, grated, may be used in juice
4 cups sugar
2 quarts half-and-half

Freeze lemon juice and sugar 10 minutes in freezer. Add half-and-half and freeze in 1-gallon freezer until heavy. Put in the deep freeze overnight to mellow. Will keep well for weeks in the freezer.

In Good Taste

Strawberry Granite

2 1/2 cups strawberries, washed and stemmed
4 1/2 tablespoons sugar
1 1/2 tablespoons lemon juice
3-4 cups water

In blender or food processor, purée all ingredients until smooth. Pour into ice-cube tray and freeze solid. Remove cubes from tray and put back in blender or processor. Process until completely crushed. Spoon into dishes to serve. Makes 4 cups.

Cooking to Your Heart's Content

The 25 stars around the border of the diamond on Arkansas' state flag indicate Arkansas as the 25th state admitted to the Union. The diamond signifies Arkansas as the only diamond-producing state in the Union.

Index

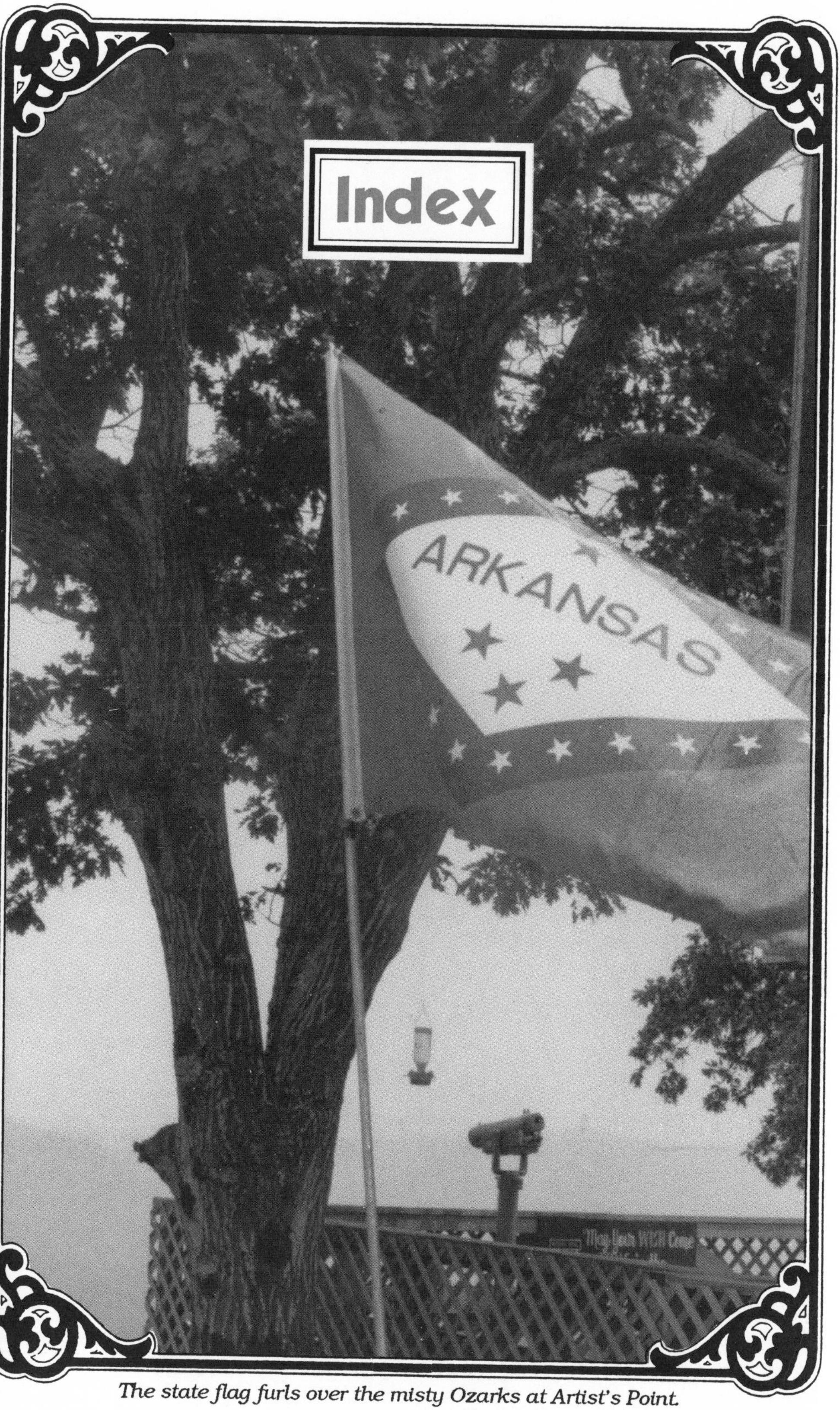

The state flag furls over the misty Ozarks at Artist's Point.

Index

C

D

E

F

G

H

I

J

Catalog of Contributing Cookbooks

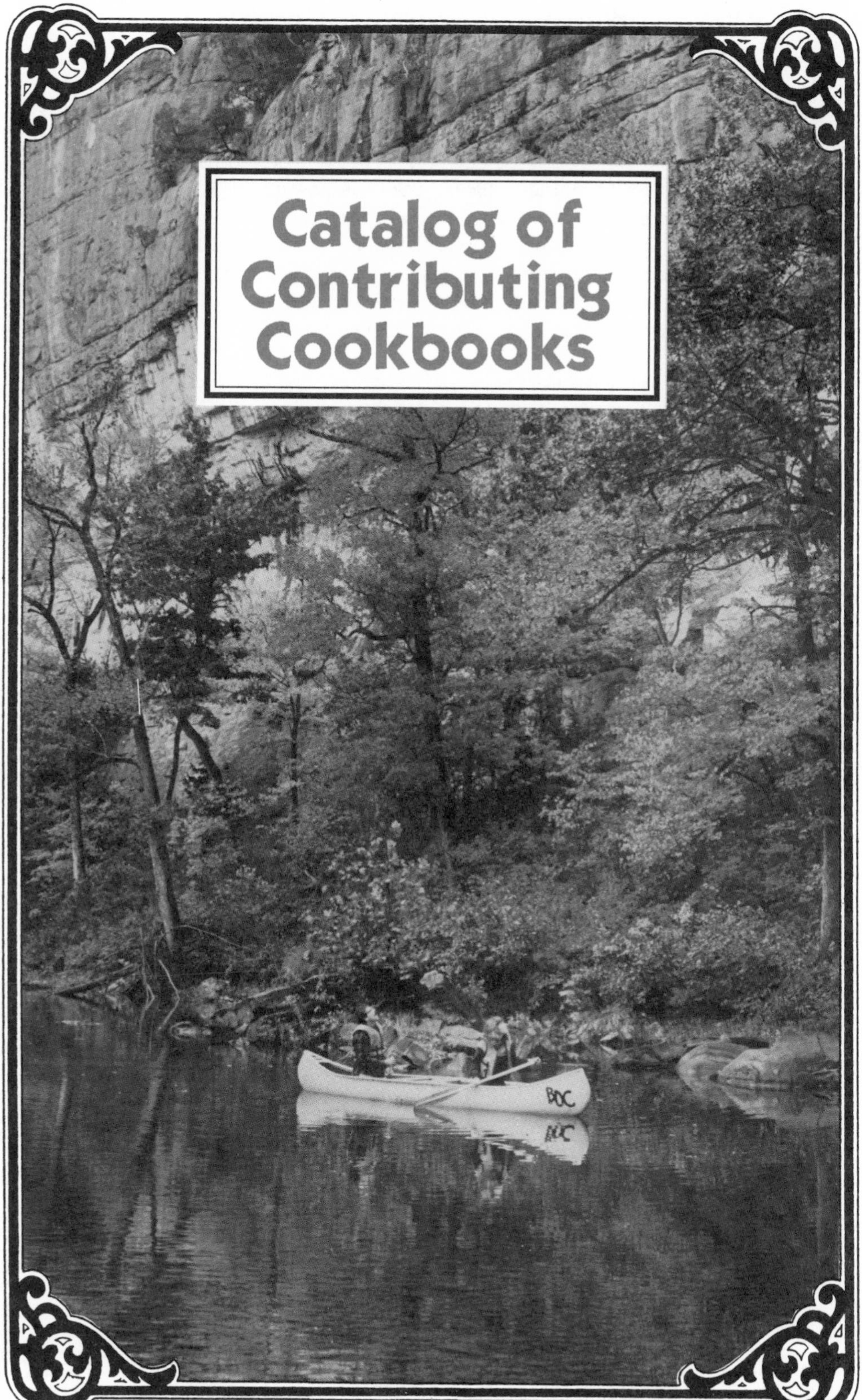

The Buffalo National River, looking much the same as it did when inhabited by Indians, has long been a favorite of canoeists, campers, and hikers.

Catalog of Contributing Cookbooks

All recipes in this book have been submitted from the cookbooks shown on the following pages. Individuals who wish to obtain a copy of a particular book can do so by sending a check or money order to the address listed. Prices are subject to change. Please note the postage and handling charges that may be required. State residents add applicable sales tax. Retailers are invited to call or write to the same address for wholesale information. Some of these contributing cookbooks may have gone out of print since the original publication of this book. Quail Ridge Press is proud to preserve America's food heritage by keeping many of their recipes in print.

ARKANSAS CELEBRATION COOKBOOK

by Zoe Medlin Caywood
War Eagle Mill
11045 War Eagle Road
Rogers, AR 72756 501/789-5343

Curl up with a light history of Arkansas and the pioneer homestead—short synopsis on the origin of recipes—as old-fashioned as they are delicious. Over 100 recipes and home remedies pack 72 pages. A cookbook to read and use—simple one-pot dishes like "Arkansas Hash" or "Beef Pot Pie with Cornmeal Pastry" will be requested again and again.

$ 5.00 Retail price
$ 4.75 Postage and handling
Make check payable to War Eagle Mill
ISBN 0-9616521-2-8

ARKANSAS FAVORITES

J and J Collections
201 San Mateo Drive 501/525-3190
Hot Springs, AR 71913 or 525-1639

Discover the "Natural State" through this unique cookbook profiling favorite Arkansas places and their histories, delicious recipes, and fine line drawings by famous artist Gary Simmons. Recipe collection includes special restaurant recipes, and a nostalgia section. Endorsed by celebrities on back cover. Perfect Arkansas souvenir! 126 pages with 166 recipes.

$12.00 Retail price
$ 1.75 Postage and handling
Make check payable to J and J Collections
ISBN 0-9628165-1-5

AROUND THE BEND

Around the Bend Arts & Crafts Association
Marshall, AR

Around The Bend Arts & Crafts Association is a combined effort of many members striving to be a productive asset to our state. Our cookbook is a fund-raising item compiled by our members, with down-home cooking and anecdotes for the country at heart. "Sample the flavor of the Ozarks, you'll be glad you did!" 106 pages. Currently out of print.

ASBURY UNITED METHODIST CHURCH COOK BOOK

Asbury United Methodist Church
Magnolia, AR

The recipes in this book are only a small sampling of delicious creations from our church family and friends. In addition to the 640 recipes, its 240 pages contain 14 topics of very helpful information, helpful hints for each recipe section, and an index. Currently out of print.

BETTY "WINKS" AT COOKING

Betty J. Winkler
2925 Millbrook Road
Little Rock, AR 72227 501/227-4784

Wonderful, easy scratch cooking with readily available ingredients at your local grocery. Microwave and diabetic recipes also. Written so young brides can understand. 648 recipes, 298 pages.

$12.00 Retail price
$ 2.00 Postage and handling
Make check payable to Betty Winkler

BETTY IS STILL "WINKING" AT COOKING

Betty J. Winkler
Little Rock, AR

More good, easy scratch recipes with readily available ingredients. Low cholesterol section. Easy for young brides to understand. Diabetic and microwave recipes also. Currently out of print.

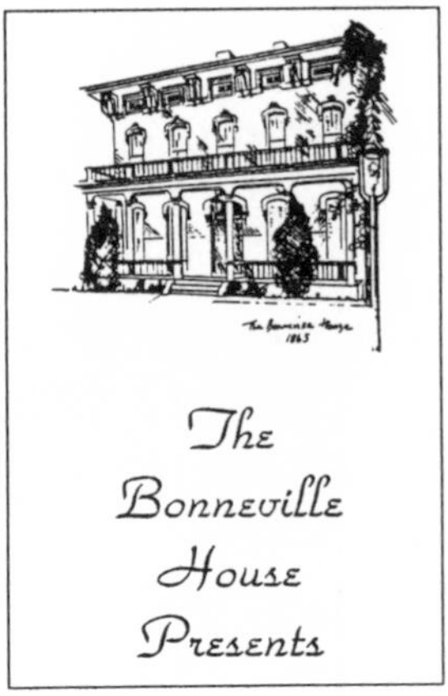

THE BONNEVILLE HOUSE PRESENTS

The Bonneville House Association
Fort Smith, AR

The Bonneville House is used as a setting for social and cultural events. Our cookbook, *The Bonneville House Presents*, is a collection of 300 recipes, tested and recommended by our members and the managing caterer of the House, and our recipes specialize in beautiful food for entertaining. Currently out of print.

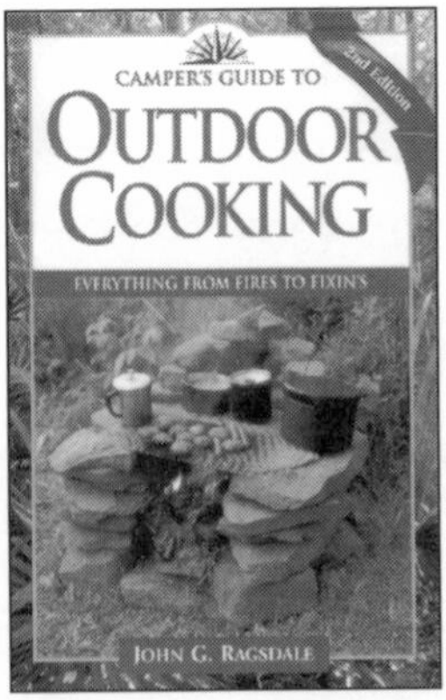

CAMPER'S GUIDE TO OUTDOOR COOKING

Camp Cookery
122 Neel
El Dorado, AR 71730 870-863-0880

If you are cooking outdoors, this book will cover selecting firewood, starting fires, using different ovens and utensils, and even cleanup chores. It provides for meal planning, food preparation, construction of a chuck box, and support for your outdoor cooking. Over 200 field-tested recipes include a variety of great things to cook.

$ 9.95 Retail price
$ 2.00 Postage and handling

Make check payable to Camp Cookery
ISBN 0-87201-626-9

CELEBRATION, A TASTE OF ARKANSAS

Sevier County
Lockesburg, AR

The official book of the Arkansas Sesquicentennial, this beautiful hardcover, ringbound cookbook is filled with 352 pages of Arkansas recipes contributed by people from all over the state. With historical facts scattered throughout, this book abounds with every imaginable type of recipe. Currently out of print.

CLABBER CREEK FARM COOKBOOK

Bill and Betty Rotramel
676 CR 403
Berryville, AR 72616 870/423-2744

This large 240-page family cookbook is filled with tested recipes (some unusual), anecdotes, photos, quotes, and cartoons by Betty. It was released in 1991 by authors and publishers, Bill and Betty Rotramel.

$10.00 Retail price
$ 3.50 Postage and handling
Make check payable to Clabber Creek Farms®

CLASSROOM CLASSICS

Trinity Episcopal School
708 W. 2nd Avenue
Pine Bluff, AR 71601 870/534-7606

Designed to be an on-going source of income for Trinity School, our cookbook has 296 pages, 1000 proven favorite recipes, and a section just for kids! The children designed the divider pages for each section; the cover design was created by Father Joseph Tucker, the school's religion instructor.

$ 6.00 Retail price
$ 1.50 Postage and handling
Make check payable to Trinity Episcopal School

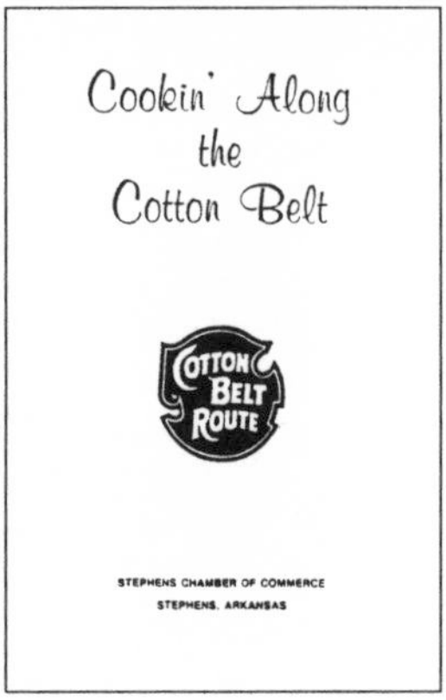

COOKIN' ALONG THE COTTON BELT

Stephens Chamber of Commerce
P. O. Box 572
Stephens, AR 71764 870/786-5221

A collection of over 600 new and old recipes that reflect the history of Stephens and the State of Arkansas. Learn how to not only "bake a possum" but also "How To Cook A Husband." Enjoy Ginger Cakes from Grandma Wright's recipe from the 1800s and Gov. Bill Clinton's Pepper Steak. Each recipe has a history of its own and could become a tradition in any family.

$10.00 Retail price
$ 2.00 Postage and handling

Make check payable to Stephens Chamber of Commerce

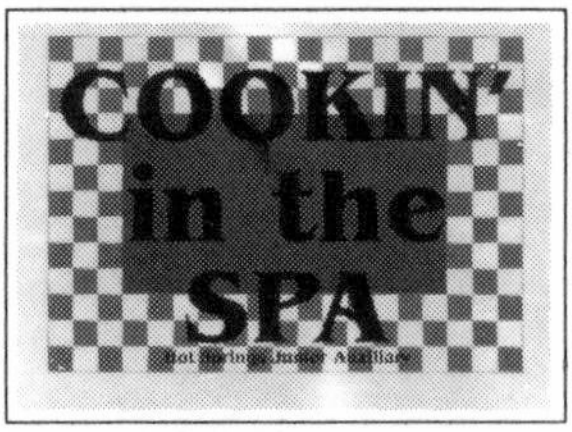

COOKIN' IN THE SPA

Hot Springs Junior Auxiliary
Hot Springs, AR

"A taste of Hot Springs"—with over 250 carefully tested recipes reflecting the heritage and culture of Hot Springs. The colorful cover is laminated for durability, while the cookbook itself is small, compact, ring bound, and has a cross-referenced index. Eight sections of easy to prepare recipes with clear, concise instructions. A welcome addition to any collector's bookshelf. Currently out of print.

COOKING FOR GOOD MEASURE

Hughes High School Mu Alpha Theta
Hughes, AR

Cooking For Good Measure, produced by a math honor society, contains recipes of parents and friends of the members. Containing 199 recipes on 77 pages, this spiral-bound cookbook with index has an assortment of salads, sauces, breads, main dishes, vegetables, desserts, etc., indicative of the cuisine of the East Arkansas Delta—where good cooks abound! Currently out of print.

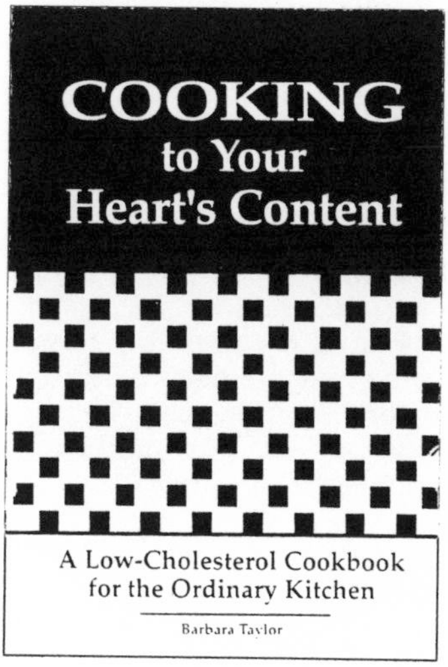

COOKING TO YOUR HEART'S CONTENT: A Low-Cholesterol Cookbook for the Ordinary Kitchen

The University of Arkansas Press
Fayetteville, AR

Offering complete meal plans and a week's menu as well as easy-to-follow discussions of handy techniques, *Cooking To Your Heart's Content* is essential to anyone preparing food for those on cholesterol-restricted diets. 121 pages, concealed wire-o binding. Currently out of print.

COOKING WITH MS. WATERMELON

by Donna Presley
P. O. Box 6677
Hope, AR 71801 870/777-6309

Cooking With Ms. Watermelon is a 52-page booklet cookbook. Every recipe in the cookbook contains watermelon in some form. There is everything from appetizers to desserts. Old favorites like watermelon pickles and preserves are included, along with cake, pies, and cobblers.

$ 5.00 Retail price
$ 1.25 Postage and handling

Make check payable to *Cooking With Ms. Watermelon*

CROSSETT COOK BOOK

Presidents' Council and Executive Board of Adopt-A-School
301 West 9th Avenue
Crossett, AR 71635 870/364-3112

The Crossett Cook Book is three-in-one, as it is a limited edition compilation of the 1931, 1947, and 1959 Crossett Cook Books printed in their entirety with tested recipes from Crossett housewives. Proceeds are used for educational purposes to benefit Crossett's national record-setting Adopt-A-School program. 254 pages.

$15.00 Retail price
$ 3.00 Postage and handling

Make check payable to Adopt-A-School Cookbook

THE DAIRY HOLLOW HOUSE COOKBOOK

by Crescent Dragonwagon
Cato and Martin Publishers
515 Spring Street
Eureka Springs, AR 72632 501/253-2726

"Dairy Hollow House, a small bed-and-breakfast country inn in a lovingly restored 1888 Ozark farmhouse, has been like sending out a party invitation to the world and then waiting to see who comes." And come they do, down a "lumpy bumpy dirt road" to some awfully good cooking. In 400 pages, the recipes are surrounded by delightful poems and charming stories.

$14.95 Retail price
$ 3.50 Postage and handling ($1.50 each add'l)
Make check payable to Dairy Hollow House

DIXIE COOKBOOK IV

First Presbyterian Church
116 North 12th Street
Fort Smith, AR 72901 501/783-8919

This fourth edition of the *Dixie Cookbook* of the First Presbyterian Church Women of Fort Smith contains tried and trusted recipes. These recipe gems will bring nostalgia to your tastebuds—good old-fashioned ideas for the real cooks of the South and West.

$10.00 Retail price includes postage and handling
Make check payable to First Presbyterian Church

DIXIE COOK BOOK V

First Presbyterian Church
116 North 12th Street
Fort Smith, AR 72901 501/783-8919

This fifth edition of the *Dixie Cookbook* of the Women of the Church of Fort Smith incorporates recipes from the 1920, 1929 and 1939 editions.

$12.00 Retail price includes postage and handling
Make check payable to First Presbyterian Church

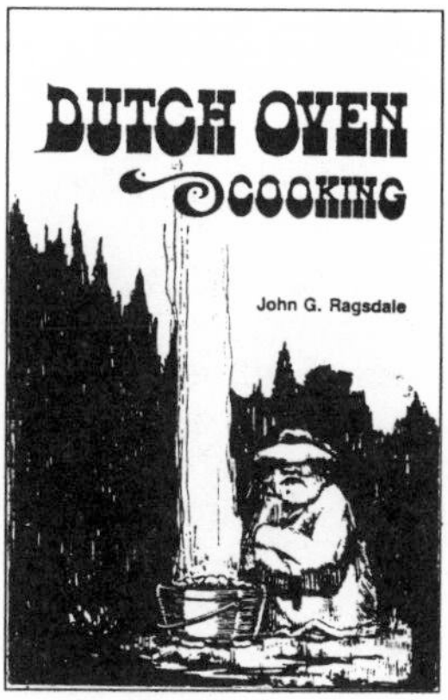

DUTCH OVEN COOKING

Camp Cookery
122 Neel
El Dorado, AR 71730 870-863-0880

When you want to prepare great meals in the historic Dutch oven, this book provides instructions for care of the oven, preparation of the campfire coals, cooking techniques and even cleanup after the meal. The book contains over 100 recipes including baked eggs, fish chowder, pot roast, biscuits, corn bread and cobblers.

$ 5.95 Retail price
$ 2.00 Postage and handling
Make check payable to Camp Cookery
ISBN 0-88415-224-3

EAT TO YOUR HEART'S CONTENT!

by Woody and Betty Armour
The HeartRock Cafe
Hot Springs, AR

At The HeartRock Cafe, healthful eating is fun eating! Low in fat, sodium, and cholesterol, and high in nutrition and enjoyment, here are over 70 delicious, easy to prepare recipes designed to keep your heart rocking. Spiral bound, laminated cover...and printed appropriately in "heart" red ink.

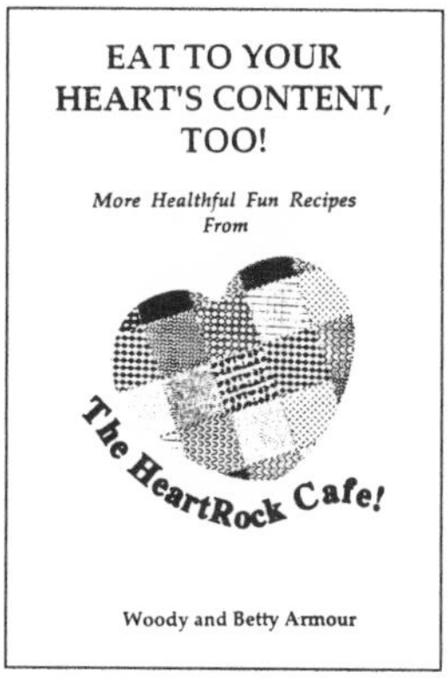

EAT TO YOUR HEART'S CONTENT, TOO!

by Woody and Betty Armour
The HeartRock Cafe
Hot Springs, AR

This new HeartRock cookbook is filled with recipes that offer more delicious and healthful dishes that are easy to make and fun to serve to family and friends. The nutritional information provided, as well as the informative articles, will help to educate and motivate you to a more healthful lifestyle.

EATING HEALTHY IN THE FAST LANE

by Cindy Arsaga and Ginny Masullo
Fayetteville, AR

Eating Healthy presents in a humorous format, recipes that can be prepared in 15-60 minutes. The recipes are low in fat, salt and contain no sugar. In these 85 pages of 56 recipes, the authors, both registered nurses, have included concise information on the healthy diet. Eat whole and healthy, spending less time in the kitchen! Currently out of print.

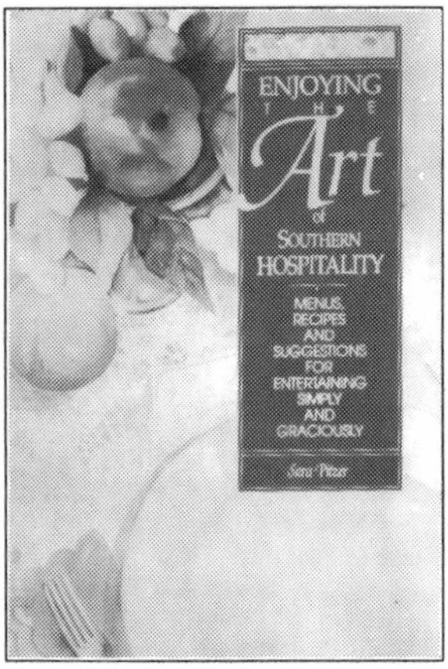

ENJOYING THE ART OF SOUTHERN HOSPITALITY

August House Publishers
Little Rock, AR

Sara Pitzer has updated many traditional Southern recipes to appeal to today's more health-conscious palates. Includes the history and tradition of entertaining in the South, in addition to scores of recipes, menus, and suggestions so you can perpetuate it today—even if you don't have the kitchen staff your grandmother always talked about. Currently out of print.

EVENING SHADE
Recipes from Burt Reynolds .....
and the Folks of Evening Shade

EVENING SHADE COOKBOOK

Evening Shade School Foundation
P. O. Box 36
Evening Shade, AR 72532 817-266-3590

Burt Reynolds, creator-producers Linda Bloodsworth Thomason and Harry Thomason, the "Evening Shade" cast and crew, and the residents of the real life Evening Shade, have joined forces to publish this cookbook. An FHA project, proceeds will be used to build a much-needed auditorium-gymnasium. 96 pages, ringbound. A good country cookbook with hometown recipes--and Burt Reynold's Beef Stew.

$ 5.00 Retail price
$ 2.00 Postage and handling

Make check payable to Evening Shade School Foundation
ISBN 0-9631000-0-9

THE FARMER'S DAUGHTERS

by Flora R. Sisemore, Martha R. Merritt
and Mary R. Mayfield
P. O. Box 243 — 870/946-3551
DeWitt, AR 72042-0243 — or 946-1891

Country recipes compiled by three sisters from three generations of good cooks. Most ingredients in every kitchen! 256 pages and 490 recipes. Spiral Bound, plastic cover, cross-referenced index. $1.00 from the sale of each book will be given to the National Multiple Sclerosis Society to honor one of the sisters.

$14.95 Retail price
$ 2.55 Postage and handling
Make check payable to S-M-L, Inc.

FAVORITE RECIPES FROM ASSOCIATED WOMEN FOR HARDING

Station A, Box 677
Searcy, AR 72143 — 501/279-4487

Favorite Recipes has 313 pages featuring 829 recipes in eleven different divisions, with sections on meal planning, nutrition, and practical hints for saving time and money. A special feature of the book is the International Section, which features recipes from 34 countries around the world.

$ 6.00 Retail price
$ 1.50 Postage and handling
Make check payable to Associated Women for Harding

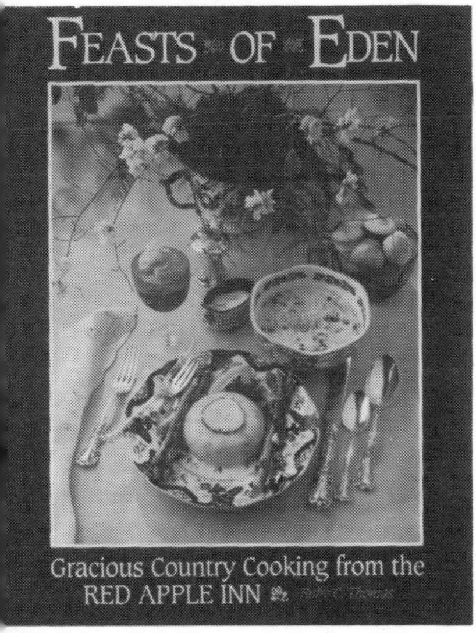

FEASTS OF EDEN

August House Publishers
Little Rock, AR

Gracious country cooking from the Red Apple Inn, which holds Mobil Travel Guide's coveted Four Star Award. Over 250 recipes and 50 menus are presented on an oversized, two-color page format and are accompanied by lovely, full-color photographs. Currently out of print.

A GREAT TASTE OF ARKANSAS

Southern Flavors, Inc.
P. O. Box 922
Pine Bluff, AR 71613 870-536-8221

More than 150 carefully chosen "best recipes" from Arkansas homes, premier industries, restaurants, and cafes! Included in the 4½ x 5½-inch cookbook are interesting facts and folklore about the state along with Arkansas festivals dates, and Arkansas "quotables." A delicious taste of what Arkansas cooks cook, and their families enjoy!

$ 6.95 Retail Price
$ 2.00 Postage and handling

Make check payable to A Great Taste of Arkansas
ISBN 0-9615252-0-7

A HERITAGE OF GOOD TASTES

Arkansas Post Museum State Park
5530 Highway 165 S
Gillett, AR 72055 870/548-2634

A Heritage of Good Tastes consists of 228 pages of favorite family recipes from Arkansas County Museum volunteers and friends.

$10.00 Retail price
$ 3.50 Postage and handling

Make check payable to Arkansas Post Museum State Park

HIGH COTTON COOKIN'

Marvell Academy Mothers' Association
P. O. Box 26
Marvell, AR 72366 870/829-2931

Here are 328 pages of great southern recipes. The pen & ink drawings of a slower-paced southern culture will delight you. The phrase "high cotton" means the best there is, that all is dandy. A "must have" for anyone who would like to "get away from it all" and find themselves walking in "high cotton!"

$12.95 Retail price
$ 3.00 Postage and handling

Make check payable to High Cotton Cookin'
ISBN 0-918544-14-9

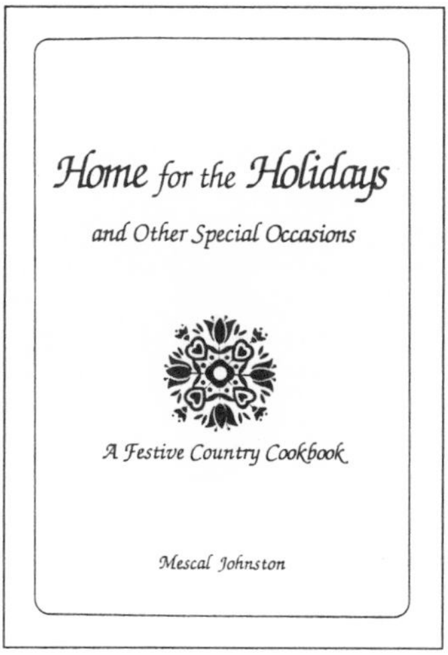

HOME FOR THE HOLIDAYS AND OTHER SPECIAL OCCASIONS: A Festive Country Cookbook

The University of Arkansas Press
Fayetteville, AR

Arranged by holiday seasons and presented within a menu framework, the nearly 500 recipes in *Home for the Holidays* are Mescal Johnston's "keepers" from over three decades' service with the Arkansas Cooperative Extension Service. 336 pages, 8-page color photo insert. Currently out of print.

IN GOOD TASTE

El Dorado Service League, Inc.
El Dorado, AR

Seven years of collecting, testing and editing have resulted in a cookbook that gives over 650 recipes in 440 pages, tasteful tips and many ideas for our readers. It will inspire gourmands as well as novices to create that "special" meal. The El Dorado Service League has worked for over 50 years to make life healthier and happier for the children of El Dorado. Currently out of print.

A KALEIDOSCOPE OF CREATIVE HEALTHY COOKING

Janet M. Boyce (R.N.)
9 Old Forge Court
Little Rock, AR 72207 501/225-8415

"Putting on the Ritz" and "Bone Tired After a Hard Day" are titles of two of the seven chapters. Original artwork and recipes feature herbs, spices, and suggestions for reducing fats, sugar and salt. "Menus," "Did You Know" and "Let's Set a Table" complete the Kaleidoscope of 184 recipes and 159 plus pages.

$12.95 Retail price
$ 2.00 Postage and handling
Make check payable to Janet M. Boyce

KIDS CUISINE: Healthy Recipes to Grow By

The Nancy Orr Family Center at Sparks Regional Medical Center
1311 South I Street, P. O. Box 17006
Fort Smith, AR 72917-7006 501/441-5445

Kids Cuisine: Healthy Recipes to Grow By features some 100 recipes, nutritional information on the recipes, and tips for healthful eating. The recipes were developed by hospital dietitians and taste-tested by the experts (the kids). All fun and easy to make, each recipe includes a list of ingredients, tools needed, and step-by-step directions for kids.

$10.00 Retail price
$ 2.00 Postage and handling

Make check payable to The Nancy Orr Family Center
ISBN 0-87197-287-5

NIBBLES COOKS CAJUN

Suzie Stephens
705 N. Sunset Drive
Fayetteville, AR 72703 479/527-6400

Family Cajun; Creole recipes. You need not live on the bayou to create the flavors of New Orleans.

$ 9.95 Retail price
$ 1.50 Postage and handling

Make check payable to Nibbles
ISBN 0-9610246-2-3

NIBBLES FA LA LA

Suzie Stephens
705 N. Sunset Drive
Fayetteville, AR 72703 479/527-6400

Traditional holiday cookbook. From hors d'oeuvres to roast turkey; eggnog to fudge favorites.

$ 9.95 Retail price
$ 1.50 Postage and handling

Make check payable to Nibbles
ISBN 0-9610246-1-5

NIBBLES OOO LA LA

Suzie Stephens
705 N. Sunset Drive
Fayetteville, AR 72703 479/527-6400

French cooking made so easy. A taste of France without the bother.

$ 9.95 Retail price
$ 1.50 Postage and handling

Make check payable to Nibbles

ISBN 0-9610246-3-1

PERFECTLY DELICIOUS

by Cornelia Pryor Lindsey and Elinor Pryor
Little Rock, AR

Perfectly Delicious was Susie Pryor's verbal stamp of approval on good food. Over 600 of her recipes are included plus her writings, family history, and photographs. Memories shared by her fourteen grandchildren and a brief summary of her life, 1900-1984, portray the character, talents, and accomplishments of this unusual lady. Good home-cooking served with loving hospitality! Currently out of print.

THE PINK LADY...IN THE KITCHEN

Medical Center of South Arkansas Auxiliary
700 West Grove 870/863-4681
El Dorado, AR 71730 or 864-3399

"The Pink Ladies" and "The Red Coats" are members of the National Organization of Hospital Auxiliaries. The aim of volunteer workers everywhere is to promote the welfare of their local hospital and its patients. All proceeds from the sale of this book will go toward the purchase of needed items for our Hospital.

$10.00 Retail price
$ 2.50 Postage and handling

Make check payable to Medical Center of South Arkansas Auxiliary

PRAIRIE HARVEST

St. Peter's Episcopal Churchwomen
P. O. Box 613
Hazen, AR 72064

Prairie Harvest contains over 700 recipes from appetizers to desserts. It features the "harvest" of the Grand Prairie of Arkansas— rice and ducks. "Our Prairie Harvest" section has over 100 recipes using rice in a variety of ways. A "guide to properly preparing game" prefaces a selection of wild game recipes. Hardback.

$15.00 Retail price
$ 2.75 Postage and handling

Make check payable to Prairie Harvest
ISBN 0939114-29-1

PULASKI HEIGHTS BAPTIST CHURCH COOKBOOK

Members and Friends of the Congregation
Little Rock, AR

Pulaski Heights Baptist Church Cookbook is the second cookbook published by members and friends of the congregation. This collection of favorite Arkansas and Southern recipes has 160 pages with almost 400 recipes. It includes family favorites, recipes for gourmet dining, and simple recipes that children can manage. Currently out of print.

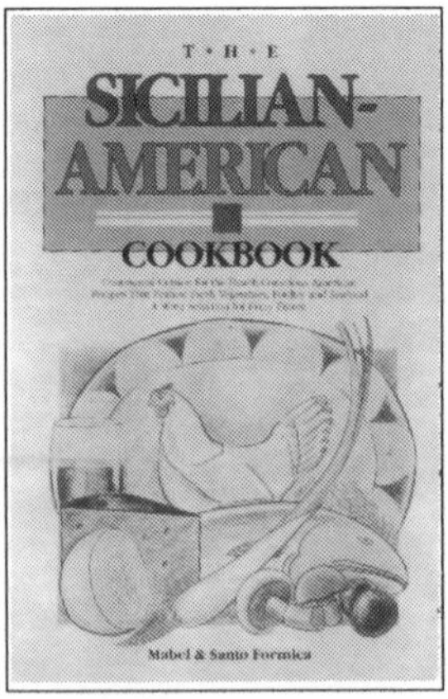

THE SICILIAN-AMERICAN COOKBOOK

August House Publishers
Little Rock, AR

Sicilians are a fiercely independent people, with a culture completely distinct from that of the mainland. Chefs Santo and Mabel Formica share a cuisine which combines the taste of Italian cooking with ingredients many health-conscious Americans are incorporating into their diets. Includes index, herb guide, and wine recommendations. Currently out of print.

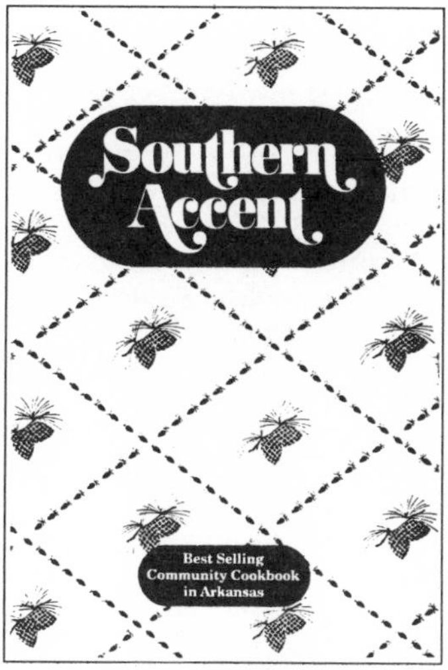

SOUTHERN ACCENT

Junior League of Pine Bluff
P. O. Box 1693
Pine Bluff, AR 71613 870/535-5027

This #1 selling community cookbook in the state of Arkansas exemplifies Southern cooking and hospitality at its finest. An original inductee to the Walter S. McIlhenny Cookbook Hall of Fame, *Southern Accent* entertains with a delightful menu section featuring lovely table setting ideas. Over 750 recipes ranging from appetizers to a wild-game section are included in 340 pages.

$16.95 Retail price
$ 2.50 Postage and handling

Make check payable to Southern Accent
ISBN 0-9607548-0-6

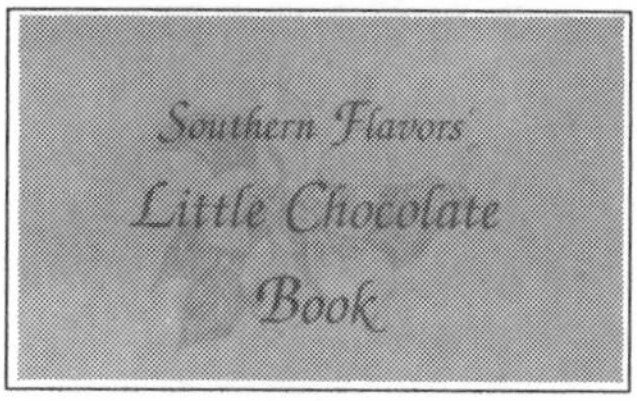

SOUTHERN FLAVORS' LITTLE CHOCOLATE BOOK

Southern Flavors, Inc.
P. O. Box 922
Pine Bluff, AR 71613 870-536-8221

The Little Chocolate Book's wonderful, kitchen-tested chocolate recipes, collected from some of the South's finest cooks, are guaranteed to totally satiate every chocolate lover's palate!! The book's format is unique--each page is a postcard with 1 or 2 recipes. Those buying the little book will either have a marvelous collection of chocolate recipes or 22 note cards to share with friends!!

$ 4.95 Retail price
$ 2.00 Postage and handling

Make check payable to Southern Flavors, Inc.
ISBN 0-9618137-4-1

SOUTHWEST COOKIN'

Southwest Hospital Auxiliary
Little Rock, AR

Our book is a spiral-bound, soft-cover cookbook with approximately 300 recipes. The cover and division pages feature original pen and ink sketches in four colors by a noted area artist. The general collection of favorite recipes was submitted by the staff and volunteers of Southwest Hospital. Currently out of print.

SUNDAY GO TO EATIN' COOK BOOK

by Nita Sappington
Decatur, AR

This cookbook is written in a "down-home" dialect with a southern country flavor. Along with 69 recipes, covering 119 pages, there are many stories and much simplistic cooking advice to the reader. This book makes an excellent choice for a beginning cook.

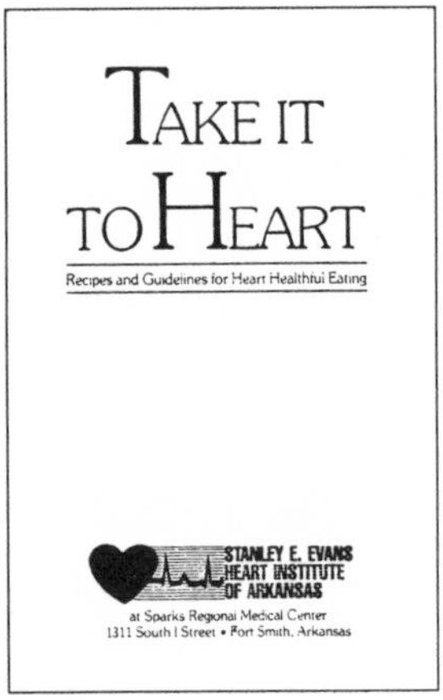

TAKE IT TO HEART: Recipes & Guidelines for Heart Healthy Eating

Stanley E. Evans Heart Institute of Arkansas
Sparks Regional Medical Center
1311 South I Street, P. O. Box 17006
Fort Smith, AR 72917-7006 501/441-5445

Good Housekeeping Magazine said, "Take Heart! Foods that are good for you can taste good, too. And the proof is between the 128 pages of *Take It to Heart*, a cookbook filled with more than 200 delicious recipes for healthy eating." Recipes list calorie count, fat and sodium contents.

$ 6.00 Retail price
$ 1.75 Postage and handling
Make check payable to Stanley Evans Heart Institute of Arkansas

THIRTY YEARS AT THE MANSION

August House Publishers
P. O. Box 3223
Little Rock, AR 72203-3223 800/284-8784

Liza Ashley, cook at the Arkansas Governor's Mansion for over 30 years, presents favorite recipes of and reminiscences about the state's last seven chief executives—Governors Cherry, Faubus, Rockefeller, Bumpers, Pryor, White, and Clinton. Over 200 photographs, some in full color, illustrate this collection of wonderful Southern recipes.

$24.95 hardcover; $16.95 paperback
$ 4.00 Postage and handling
Make check payable to August House Publishers
ISBN 0-935304-88-6 (HC); 0-87483-135-0 (PB)

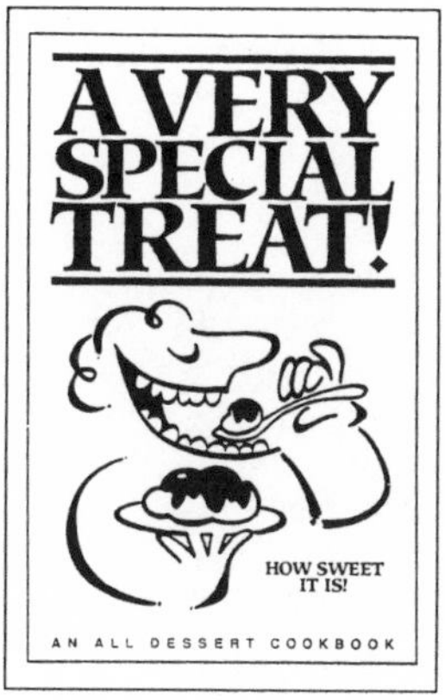

A VERY SPECIAL TREAT!

Arkansas Special Olympics
Little Rock, AR

Join in the spirit and taste the best desserts ever! Chocolate pies, sauces, cakes; unique snacks, and sweets make this book a must for any cook. Get your book now and discover just "How sweet it is!" Currently out of print.

VICTORIAN SAMPLER

Jim Spears
P. O. Bx 190
Eureka Springs, AR 72632 501/253-8374

Over 500 recipes in 195 pages from the personal collection of the authors, owners and operators of the Victorian Sampler Restaurant in Eureka Springs. Simple enough for the novice, yet exciting enough for the gourmet. Over 40,000 copies in print.

$10.95 Retail price
$ 3.00 Postage and handling
Make check payable to *Victorian Sampler*

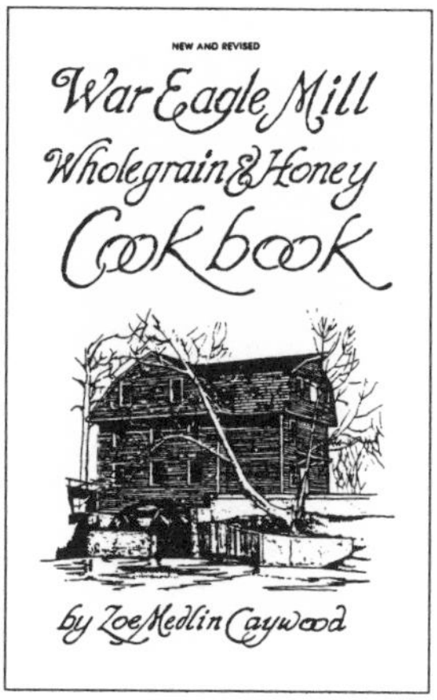

WAR EAGLE MILL WHOLEGRAIN AND HONEY COOKBOOK

by Zoe Medlin Caywood
War Eagle Mill
11045 War Eagle Road
Rogers, AR 72756 501/789-5343

A wholegrain cookbook featuring breads-muffins-waffles-appetizers-main dishes and desserts. Over 200 recipes in 120 pages. Build your meals around the delicious taste of nutritious fiber-filled grains. Try the simple "War Eagle Deep Dish" pies—country quiches made with a cornmeal crust with fillings like "Spinach & Cheese" or "Christmas Chicken." A household must.

$ 9.25 Retail price
$ 4.75 Postage and handling
Make check payable to War Eagle Mill
ISBN 0-9616521-1-X

The Wonderful World of Honey
A
SUGARLESS
COOKBOOK
*How Honey Helps You in Every Day Living
*Facts You Should Know About Nutrition
*The Miracle Healer
*Honey as a Beauty Food
*Honey as a Preservative
by Joe Parkhill

THE WONDERFUL WORLD OF HONEY: A Sugarless Cookbook

by Joe M. Parkhill
1241 Highway 62 W
Berryville, AR 72616 870/423-3131

Gathered from beekeepers and nutrition-minded people from all over the world, here are over 300 tested recipes cooking with honey...a "sugarless" cookbook! Included are health hints, beauty ideas, and facts you should know about honey and the history of honey.

$ 8.95 Retail price
$ 1.05 Postage and handling
Make check payable to Honey Inc.

ISBN 0-936744-01-4

Best of the Best State Cookbook Series

Best of the Best from
ALABAMA
288 pages, $16.95

Best of the Best from
ALASKA
288 pages, $16.95

Best of the Best from
ARIZONA
288 pages, $16.95

Best of the Best from
ARKANSAS
288 pages, $16.95

Best of the Best from
BIG SKY
Montana and Wyoming
288 pages, $16.95

Best of the Best from
CALIFORNIA
384 pages, $16.95

Best of the Best from
COLORADO
288 pages, $16.95

Best of the Best from
FLORIDA
288 pages, $16.95

Best of the Best from
GEORGIA
336 pages, $16.95

Best of the Best from the
GREAT PLAINS
North and South Dakota, Nebraska, and Kansas
288 pages, $16.95

Best of the Best from
HAWAI'I
288 pages, $16.95

Best of the Best from
IDAHO
288 pages, $16.95

Best of the Best from
ILLINOIS
288 pages, $16.95

Best of the Best from
INDIANA
288 pages, $16.95

Best of the Best from
IOWA
288 pages, $16.95

Best of the Best from
KENTUCKY
288 pages, $16.95

Best of the Best from
LOUISIANA
288 pages, $16.95

Best of the Best from
LOUISIANA II
288 pages, $16.95

Best of the Best from
MICHIGAN
288 pages, $16.95

Best of the Best from the
MID-ATLANTIC
Maryland, Delaware, New Jersey, and Washington, D.C.
288 pages, $16.95

Best of the Best from
MINNESOTA
288 pages, $16.95

Best of the Best from
MISSISSIPPI
288 pages, $16.95

Best of the Best from
MISSOURI
304 pages, $16.95

Best of the Best from
NEVADA
288 pages, $16.95

Best of the Best from
NEW ENGLAND
Rhode Island, Connecticut, Massachusetts, Vermont, New Hampshire, and Maine
368 pages, $16.95

Best of the Best from
NEW MEXICO
288 pages, $16.95

Best of the Best from
NEW YORK
288 pages, $16.95

Best of the Best from
NO. CAROLINA
288 pages, $16.95

Best of the Best from
OHIO
352 pages, $16.95

Best of the Best from
OKLAHOMA
288 pages, $16.95

Best of the Best from
OREGON
288 pages, $16.95

Best of the Best from
PENNSYLVANIA
320 pages, $16.95

Best of the Best from
SO. CAROLINA
288 pages, $16.95

Best of the Best from
TENNESSEE
288 pages, $16.95

Best of the Best from
TEXAS
352 pages, $16.95

Best of the Best from
TEXAS II
352 pages, $16.95

Best of the Best from
UTAH
288 pages, $16.95

Best of the Best from
VIRGINIA
320 pages, $16.95

Best of the Best from
WASHINGTON
288 pages, $16.95

Best of the Best from
WEST VIRGINIA
288 pages, $16.95

Best of the Best from
WISCONSIN
288 pages, $16.95

All cookbooks are 6x9 inches, ringbound, contain photographs, illustrations and index.

Special discount offers available! *(See previous page for details.)*

To order by credit card, call toll-free **1-800-343-1583** or visit our website at **www.quailridge.com.**
Use the form below to send check or money order.

Call 1-800-343-1583 or email info@quailridge.com to request a free catalog of all of our publications.

Order form

Use this form for sending check or money order to:
QUAIL RIDGE PRESS • P. O. Box 123 • Brandon, MS 39043

❑ Check enclosed

Charge to: ❑ Visa ❑ MC ❑ AmEx ❑ Disc

Card # ____________________

Expiration Date ____________________

Signature ____________________

Name ____________________

Address ____________________

City/State/Zip ____________________

Phone # ____________________

Email Address ____________________

Qty.	Title of Book (State) or Set	Total

Subtotal ______

7% Tax for MS residents ______

Postage ($4.00 any number of books) + 4.00

Total ______